In and out of the lim

Ann Matilda Dis

Her life and times

by

Margaret Christopoulos

Dear Eve,

This bk. was given to me in the History dp. Thought you might like to read about this (19ᵗ actress. I don't need the bk back.

Regards
Joyce (Lewsey)

Published by Helmos Publishing

Nottingham UK

Copyright © Margaret Christopoulos 2013

First edition April 2013

ISBN 978-0-9576295-0-9

Printed by Russell Press Nottingham

This book is dedicated to Bert, Katherine, Alex, Michael

and all the descendants of Ann Matilda

whoever and wherever they are.

CONTENTS

List of illustrations

Cover Illustration of Katherine Christopoulos. Design by Isaac Short.

The preface and acknowledgements

This biography started as a family history article in 2008. Ann Matilda emerged late in the family's excavations into the past, she popped up from church records found by dedicated family members in the 1990s – having effectively been absent from family folklore for nearly one and a half centuries. Bert and Peggy Hooper were the first for me to stir off the dust from the Ann Matilda records. Their energy and footwork in the pre IT days unearthed the beginnings of the story. Unbeknown and parallel to their searches was the fantastic research carried out by Roger and Bette Kearin, both in the UK and in Australia. A key to opening this door was provided by the information gleaned from the writings of Frederick Turner Elliott, Ann Matilda's great grandson. The Kearins' dedication to providing additional and fresh information continues in 2013. Likewise Carole Hooper's original research has been central to making Ann Matilda's story as interesting and evidence based as possible and continues to shed light on the misty 19th century narrative.

Lorna Cowan and Debra Smith have been well informed family historians whose work has revealed new and valuable data sources. In particular their work on genealogical sources has been excellent, helping to make sense of the messy information surrounding Ann Matilda, especially, but not exclusively, in the era pre 1837 when UK state records are often missing or confusing. My thanks too to the many family members, authors and researchers who have provided me with additional information related to Ann Matilda and her times: in particular Hilda Varley, Tony Bingham, Andrew Cunningham Clarke, Ray Farr, Arnold Myers & Eugenia Mitroulia, Deborah Rohr, Gilbert Cross of the Adelphi Theatre project, Ann Willis and many others.

Staff from specialist centres have been most helpful; including Nottinghamshire Archives, the Royal Academy of Music, the Herschel Museum in Bath, the Galpin Society, the Royal Archives at Windsor, the special Theatre collection at the University of Nottingham and the Southwark Local History Centre and Library and Archive centre (John Harvard Library). Particularly valuable has been the help from Anne Buchanan from the Bath Central Library, Phil Hocking from the Somerset Heritage Centre, Alan Shellard of the Grenadier Guards Archives, Donald Straughan of the Bath Georgian Newspaper project and Andrew Lamb from the Bate Collection at the University of Oxford.

The expert editing and advice from Katherine Christopoulos has been immensely valuable. The ongoing support and encouragement from Carole Hooper has been great. The additional editorial support from Francis Nugent, and Phil Broxholme has strengthened the script considerably and Nicki Moore and Alex Christopoulos have been invaluable for formatting help. Thanks to

Adrian Robins for the excellent photography, Julia Poulter for her illustration and Isaac Short for the cover design. Chris Christopoulos has been a magnificent production assistant. Bert Hooper remains a stalwart and has actively supported this project in many ways. Everyone involved in this biography has helped to fan the flames of my enthusiasm for Ann Matilda, whoever she was. The mistakes, omissions and interpretation remain my own.

Margaret Christopoulos, April 2013

Setting the scene: an introduction

The stage started to sparkle brightly during Ann Matilda's career. Limelight had arrived. The limelight effect was discovered in the 1820s by Goldsworthy Gurney. It was based on his work on the 'oxy-hydrogen' blowpipe. In 1825 Thomas Drummond saw a demonstration of the effect by Michael Faraday and realised that the light would be useful for surveying. The light is sometimes known as the Drummond light. Limelight was first used in public in the Royal Opera House in Covent Garden in 1837 and its use quickly spread to other theatres. Limelights were employed to highlight solo performers in the same manner as modern spotlights. In the 21st century theatre followspots are sometimes referred to as 'limes'. The generation of limelight was a complex operation involving the mixing of two bags filled with gases using pressure boards, with one operator responsible for generating one limelight. Limelight was rapidly replaced by electric lights in the late 19th Century.[1]

This is the life story of Ann Matilda Distin who spent most of her life out of the limelight. It is the story of a minor 19th century celebrity who peeps out of history during the reigns of four British monarchs, from George III to Victoria. Diaries, letters and personal effects she may have had, if so, they were lost long ago, making the search for Ann Matilda tough, and hunting for clues to her character an obstacle course. Starting her career on the Bath stage in the early years of the 1800s, she danced and acted in London in the following decade, then, following a disappearing act she emerged as Mrs Distin and toured the UK with the famed Distin band consisting of her husband, and four sons – described as the Beatles of the day.[2] She was behind the piano, but also behind the scenes, barely visible for much of her life.

Hers is a story of immense talent. Spotted early in the crowded competitive arena of the theatre, she remained a supporting player with much of her energy devoted to her complicated emotional life in the days when women had very few rights and opportunities.

Ann Matilda's story touches on the theatre, music, dancing, Bath, London, and European and UK wide tours, but most of the time she struggles to record her own voice; this must be imagined. She can only be understood through the more detailed stories told about the menfolk she was surrounded by at various times - her husbands, sons, brother, father and uncles. This is a life story in two parts. The first part is her life and times; the second, the endnotes, is a record of the traceable evidence around her life.

Loved, cherished and respected by many, Ann Matilda, as a stage performer, may have been loathed and looked down upon by others. Chameleon like, she peeps out from behind the curtain in the playbills and the theatre notices, whilst her personal life is often shrouded in mystery. Not much is absolutely certain about this vivacious, multi talented, energetic woman who walked the stages of several countries, performing to nobility, and the crowds of London, Liverpool and Bath. This biography attempts to unpick fact from fantasy, weaving her story into the context of the time. Making sense of Ann Matilda's life is like peeling an onion – it is difficult to reach the core, and there are tear jerking surprises. Like many women of her time she was airbrushed from history. Even her son, interviewed by the New York press about the heady days of family fame made no mention of his mother, or indeed his sister, his fellow performers.[3]

Ann Matilda's life reflects the society she lived in. Hers was a life squeezed between major tectonic forces in Europe, the French revolution starting in 1789 and the pan European revolutionary year of 1848.

Besides the erosive passage of time, two factors hamper a sparkling, clear view of the individual in England before 1850: the role of women and the lack of consistent records. For most of the time in England women took a backseat in society. They had precious few rights to property and no effective roles in most of civil life. When things went wrong on the domestic front men had the ultimate custody of children and the education systems, such as they were, were primarily designed for boys and men.

Through the upheavals of the agricultural and industrial revolutions, from the 17th to the 19th centuries, official record keeping was patchy until 1837 when new systems were heralded in. Thus records only open an official window on life events in the last decade of Ann Matilda's life. Many of the women living at this time are invisible to history, with their records often dusty, mysterious or non existent.

It is doubtful whether Ann Matilda appeared in the bright beam of limelight, she was in the background, in the shadows. When good records exist, as many do for Ann Matilda, they are open to interpretation and controversy, as discussed further in the Sources and Evidence section. She was a controversial woman. This is my best guess of her life story.

Where did it all start? Bath and Ann Matilda

'Bath's role in the life of the nation was never to be greater
or more flamboyant than it was between 1700 and 1790,
when the city was the premier resort of frivolity and
fashion.' (Davis and Bonsall) [4]

Pleasure and leisure, excitement, fashion and passion. Maybe the most
auspicious place for a budding dancer to be born in 1790 was Bath and Ann
Matilda was a child of Bath.[5] For some the cultural capital of Europe, Bath
offered everything an 18th century aristocrat or would-be member of gentility
could wish for in the field of entertainment. Besides the rich scene in music and
theatre, the city offered an exhilarating cocktail of other 18th century activities:
cockfighting, duelling, circuses, gambling and banquets.[6]

The city itself became magnificent in the reigns of the first three Hanoverian
Kings and for decades parts of the city were a substantial building site.[7] The
designs and work of architectural and engineering geniuses and entrepreneurs
developed Bath to be a place of pilgrimage for tourists and budding artists and
architects for centuries to follow. Giants of building design like Thomas
Baldwin (1750 – 1820)[8] and the elder and younger John Woods (1704 – 1754,
and 1728 – 82) possibly mingled in the Bath streets alongside Georgian
entrepreneurs like John Palmer (1742 – 1818). The latter was responsible for the
development of the early national postal system as well as being instrumental in
the establishment of the Orchard Street Theatre Bath, where later Ann Matilda
performed.

Royalty, aristocrats, politicians, writers and artists of all sorts thronged the
streets of 18th and 19th century Bath. Writers like Jane Austen, Oliver
Goldsmith, and later Charles Dickens, artist Thomas Gainsborough, poets,
playwrights, William Wordsworth, Richard Brinsley Sheriden and Walter
Savage Landor and actors David Garrick and Sarah Siddons visited and
sharpened their skills there among many more. Bath also attracted other
notables like Lord Nelson, Josiah Wedgwood and William Pitt.[9]

During the later 18th century Bath became an adjunct to London life,
strengthened by the Duke and Duchess of York's frequent presence in the city.
Their patronage of musical life ensured that musical entrepreneurism spread
seamlessly between the two cities. Eminent musicians like Handel, Haydn and
J.C. Bach who were based in London felt the compulsion to visit Bath on at
least one occasion, such was the importance of its role in English social life.[10]

If you wanted to make the bigtime in English music or theatre in later 18th century, sooner or later you would gravitate to Bath. It was the ultimate entertainment centre for a good half a century and was a magnet pulling talented musicians, actors, would be performers and pleasure seekers of all types. Leading musicians with a major impact on Bath's music scene included Thomas Linley (1733 – 1793), William Herschel (1738 -1822) and Venanzio Rauzzini (1746 – 1810).[11] It was into this maelstrom that Ann Matilda was born.

Ann Matilda's forbearers were typical examples of the mass cultural immigration to Bath during the 18th century. The population explosion, a ten-fold rise in inhabitants in the city during the 18th century, meant that visitors could no longer be vetted personally and by 1800 the new middle-class residents outnumbered the nobility and gentry.[12] Among the incomers were musicians, keen to make their names and fortunes in this explosion of culture and performing creativity. New churches, new and developing assembly rooms and the famous Pump Rooms beckoned to musicians from both home and abroad.

An example of a music immigrant was the famous astronomer, William Herschel, born in Hanover, who moved to London with his brother as street music players in 1757, and then arrived in Bath in 1772.[13] William played several musical instruments and composed some 24 symphonies in his lifetime. Whilst in Bath he became its Director of Public Concerts and of the Bath Orchestra. After discovering the planet Uranus, in 1781, in his back garden in Bath he left the City to become Astronomer Royal at half the annual salary (£200) he had earned as a musician.[14]

The Loders: Andrew and John, Ann Matilda's uncle and father

There were loads of Loders in Bath from 1780 to 1850. Untangling the twisted Loder thread is tough.[15] The nature of contemporary evidence about the family is not certain and opens up a myriad of possible interpretations and controversies.[16]

Two brothers, Andrew and John lived in Bath from the 1780s, settled and had families. Both were musicians , well known in Bath and beyond. Andrew (baptised in 1752) and John (baptised in 1757) were likely the sons of Andrew and Mary Loder of Stourton Caundle – a village some 49 miles from Bath. Possibly Andrew (senior) and his wife moved with their children, maybe eight of them, to Bath in the 1760s or 1770s to cash in on the immense opportunities in the burgeoning city. Maybe the two brothers just gravitated to Bath independent of their parents. Ann is connected to this line of Loders, and to John Loder in particular.[17]

From the view of the young Loder children born in Bath, like Ann Matilda, the bigger family was critical. There were trials and tribulations for both Andrew and John's families and careers from 1780 and it is very likely that both supported each other. Establishing a concert career in London for instance at the turn of the 18th- 19th century was tough because of the exposure to intense competition, high living expenses, the short winter season, lack of job security, illness and old age.[18] The Bath concert scene is likely to have been similar. The musician was dependent on the influence and support of his family as well as professional peers. Training was subject to apprenticeship or private tuition and this often required money and wider family support.[19]

John and Andrew were accomplished musicians. John was a violinist, violist, singer and actor.[20] A suggested first known performance was when a 'Master Loder' performed – possibly as a singer – at Covent Garden in London in 1774/5.[21] He was recorded as appearing in *Messiah* for the opening of a new organ at St James's Church in 1782 and he was noted as a performer in the 1780s in Bath and probably London.[22] In 1789 a Mr Loder appeared in the arrivals listed at Weymouth, recently popularised by the visit by George III. There was a regular summer coach there from Bath and John may even have taken his growing family of five children and his wife.[23]

However John was not a superstar. His name frequently appeared,

'in advertisements for music festivals in towns and cities surrounding Bath, yet rarely for those concerts in his home city. This is almost certainly because he was never regarded more highly than third among local violinists.'[24]

His brother Andrew, Ann Matilda's uncle, appears to have been both a musician and Bath businessman. He married well, to Jane Goodall in 1773; the wedding was noted in a London newspaper.[25] The couple's esteem was so great in Bath that the new Mrs Loder's arrival in Bath was noted in the local newspaper – a custom normally accorded to the nobility and gentry.[26] Andrew kept an interest in the theatre, his daughter Amy married the actor Thomas Cunningham in 1798 and she later performed on the Bath stage.[27] Doane's contemporary musical directory of 1794 lists Andrew as a bass singer, violinist, horn player, clarinetist, and violin cellist.[28] Andrew was important in the local Bath music scene, in 1799, Andrew offered the services of his son (probably another Andrew) as organist of St James's church.[29] When Andrew died in Bath, aged 55, in 1806, he was described, 'as eminent musician of this city and principal of the Pump Room Band.'[30] Ann Matilda's childhood was coloured by the influences of this gifted family.

1785 was a tricky year for the Loders in Bath. Although evidence is cloudy, either father or son Andrew was involved in the hostelry business.[31] There is reasonable circumstantial evidence that an Andrew was the landlord of the Lion and Lamb Coaching Inn in Bath and in 1785 a letting notice for his house and shop claimed a business of 'thirty years.' He was described as a brandy merchant.[32] If this property was Andrew junior's it was possibly inherited from his father. This urgent letting notice may have been precipitated by a severe illness in the family. One of the Loders was seriously ill at this time and a breakfast concert was arranged to provide funds to support him in the September.[33] It appears that this sale did not solve more deep seated financial problems and a few weeks later, father or son, Andrew Loder, 'Maltster and Dealer in Spirits' was declared bankrupt.[34] If this was Andrew (junior) it did not appear to blemish his reputation for long, 'this was a man who had had influence in many commercial aspects of the city and which, as a result, had gained him the respect of its citizens.'[35] This event may have given Ann Matilda and her siblings confidence that bad situations could be reversed and resolved.

Bathsheba Richards: Ann Matilda's mother

Ann Matilda's mother, Bathsheba is more of an enigmatic figure. Talented stage performer or musician she might have been – there is no indisputable track record. Records of achievements of women in the 18th century are particularly poor.[36] She was a Bristol girl, baptised there in 1763 as Bathsheba Wansey Richards,[37] although sometimes found in Parish records as 'Barbery.'[38] In all probability she was reasonably well educated for her time. Her younger brother, David, was a musician[39] and Bathsheba herself was able to write.[40] Her mother was born Mary Cantle [Cantel] and may remotely have been related to the musical Cantelo family.[41] Bathsheba most likely took her name from her maternal grandmother, Bersheba, possibly born around 1722.[42] Piecing together Bathsheba's early life is impossible. Like her husband John, she may have migrated with her family, including around five siblings, to Bath in the 1770s. This scenario is possible - both her mother and brother lived in Bath in the following decades. Bristol and Bath were closely connected by the then transport means and the flourishing Bath scene attracted talent from surrounding towns.

Music might have provided common ground for the couple. Whatever the attraction John and Bathsheba married in Bath in 1782.[43] If Bathsheba was baptised within 30 days of her birth – and there is no evidence on this – she would have been married at the age of 19 years, and likewise John 25 years. The chances were Bathsheba was pregnant at the time of the marriage. The birth of their first child, Mary Anne came seven months later on Christmas Eve 1782, the only one of their children's birth dates to be noted at the time.[44]

Whatever shaped Bathsheba's early life, she proved to be a resilient and long lived woman. Despite the vicissitudes that fate threw her way Bathsheba outlived two husbands and died in Bath in 1845,[45] at a recorded age of 86. She was hardier than her nine children, outliving at least two of them. None of her children with surviving records lived to beyond 58 years old.

John and Bathsheba Loder: the domestic situation, 1782 -1795

Effectively Bathsheba became a baby machine during the dozen years of their marriage. Mothering some nine children during these years, it is hard to know what her or the family's lifestyle was. Although musicians like Herschel could command an enormous income, it is likely that John's incomings were much more modest and possibly the family lived in a gentile 'hand-to-mouth' mode. As a second son, he probably had to make a living for his family without much – or any - financial support from his parents; there is no record of financial support from either set of families.[46] The bankruptcy of his father or brother in 1785 must also have been a blow on John's family's resources. That said John may have owned a shop which was either adjacent to or part of the family's home.[47]

The arrival of their first daughter Mary caused some kind of stir and made a press entry,

'26 Dec 1782 Births: On Tuesday morning last, the wife of
John Loder, musician in Bath, was delivered of a daughter,
whose great great grandmother, Mrs Cantel, is now living
in Bristol; and may say with propriety to her daughter,
"Rise daughter, and go to thy daughter, for thy daughter's
daughter has got a daughter."'[48]

This newspaper report was incorrect as the baby Mary's maternal, grandmother had been born Mary Cantel and unless there was much earlier inter marriage in the Cantel family this press report didn't make sense.[49]

Mary's birth was followed two years later by another child, Eliza in 1784.[50] Earlier that year Bathsheba's widowed mother married John Henrard and John Loder and Bathsheba are captured in the records as witnesses.[51] Whether or not John and Mary were able to offer help to Bathsheba's expanding family, is unknown, but a possibility.

Many of the parish records associated with the Loders show the family were located in a small geographical location. The churches of St Michael, St James and the Abbey were all close together located in central Bath, taking only a few minutes to walk from one to the other. It seems that many of the Loders lived around a similar area for much of this period.[52]

The third baptism was a bumper one. Three Loder children were baptised at the same occasion at Bath Abbey: John David, Harriet and Edward James.[53] All things are possible. They may have been triplets or a singleton with twins, although it would have been rare for triplets to survive at that time. From ages given for concerts of the young John David he may have been born in 1787.[54] It is likely he was the eldest of the threesome. Twins could have followed in the summer of 1788. Whatever the reality Bathsheba would have had her hands full with five young children and a husband away performing, earning a precarious living.

While John must have spent some time away from home playing in ensembles and similar, he must have had space for practising and learning his music. He also needed storage facilities for his instruments – or shared these with other musicians like his brother. As a professional musician his life would have been pressurised, keeping up his professional skills but also promoting himself to maintain the income level for himself and family. Bathsheba had been bought up in a family in which at least one brother had received musical training and it is likely that husband and wife started to plan early for the musical education of the children. That was certainly the case with John David who performed as a young child.[55]

Ann Matilda and her early years in Bath: 1790 – 1805

Ann Matilda – the nursery years, 1790 - 1795

Who would have guessed what the future had in store for Ann Matilda when they peeped over the cradle to look at the sixth Loder child? By the autumn of 1790, when Ann Matilda was baptised, Bathsheba was well on her way to be a well experienced mother. She was around 31 years old and the mother of six young children, with a husband who spent much of his time 'on the road', with a modest income, and no known financial assets. Looking at the arrival of her many children it seems likely that Bathsheba entered a cycle of breast feeding – pregnancy, probably nursing each child for several months before becoming pregnant again.

Her husband John continued to play at concerts – probably bringing in an adequate income. In 1794 he was a member of the New Musical Fund, performed violin and viola, and lived in Bath.[56] An idea of his income may be seen from what a German visitor noted of London life in 1790.

> 'It might be supposed that, in England, people in a musical line, if they are eminent in their profession, have the opportunity of acquiring some fortune, or at least a sufficient income to live upon, but the case is generally the reverse.'[57]

Bath offered plenty of musical opportunities and was in its zenith as a popular place for entertainment in 1790 when Ann Matilda was baptised and officially entered the scene, but the sands were beginning to shift. The French Revolution started a year earlier with the storming of the Bastille in July 1789 and the fast changing situation encouraged some French emigration to England and to cities like Bath.[58] French music had always been popular and teachers of dance and music with French names became fashionable.[59] The execution of the French king, Louis XVI in 1793, the declaration of war on Britain and the subsequent 'reign of terror' across the channel had its impact on the pleasure lovers of Bath.[60] The Bath local newspapers, the Herald and the Chronicle start to mention the news from France, concerts were given for the militia and some of the royal visitors to Bath were given additional military duties. Most importantly Frederick, the Duke of York – the second in line to the throne and frequent visitor to Bath - was awarded the title General in 1793.

In the UK the intellectual climate was changing. In 1790 Burke wrote his reflection on the French Revolution, and Thomas Paine produced 'The Rights of Man' in 1791. In the following year Mary Wollstoncraft composed the iconoclastic, 'Vindication on the Rights of Women' which questioned traditional views of the role of women.[61] The government and its members felt vulnerable to threats of revolution and in May 1794 the basic right of 'Habeas Corpus' was suspended.[62] The intellectual climate in which Ann Matilda was reared was very different to the culture which shaped her mother's childhood.

The baptism of Ann Matilda Loder

The first Ann Matilda mystery is her baptism. She was baptised on 20th October 1790 at St James Church Bath. Her record is out of date order by a couple of months, inserted at the bottom of a page in the Register. The record itself is unclear and dogged with controversy.[63] Bathsheba and John are recorded as her parents, but the name of 'John' is crossed through, either deliberately or mistakenly. If John believed he was not Ann Matilda's father, he did not make a fuss about it publicly and decades later Ann Matilda was noted as John David's sister. Two years later, like clockwork, he and Bathsheba were listed as parents for a seventh child, Jane Loder. Ann Matilda's baptism gives no absolute clue as to her birthdate. The balance of evidence gleaned to date suggests that Ann Matilda was born within the months of August, September and early October 1790. If the baptism followed some local customs her birth would have been in last week of September or first in October.

> 'The majority of children were baptised before their 30th day of age because parents believed not do so would mean they were not recognised by God as having a name as they entered Heaven, should they die in those first few days/weeks.'[64]

Whatever day she was born there was clearly some oddities about the records and possible controversy about her paternity at the time. This fact begs lots of unanswerable questions. There may have been confessions from Bathsheba. Enormous rows in the Loder household may have taken place when John did some calculations about the reckoned conception date. Bathsheba could have been lonely while John was on the road playing his fiddle in Weymouth, Bristol or wherever. The parish priest or clerk could have jumped to some conclusion or made a mistake. There was also the possible issue of the ailing baby Edward Loder. John and Bathsheba's second son, he died two months after her baptism.[65] Likely he was a toddler, two or three years old, and his poor health at the time of Ann Matilda's arrival may have been viewed as a 'curse'. It must have created unhappiness and tension. Deaths in early childhood were very common in English society and perhaps Bathsheba was an unusual mother with eight of her known children surviving into their teens.[66] However, from Ann Matilda's viewpoint it was not the best of times to arrive.

Where did the name 'Ann Matilda'come from?

Ann Matilda's name is another mystery buried by time. By the time the Loder parents had their fourth daughter favoured names and godparents may have been exhausted. Suspicion about her paternity may also have limited Bathsheba's options. Whoever were her appointed godparents, they, and Bathsheba did a great deal to encourage her training for the stage and perhaps her broader education. The name Ann Matilda may have come from a local woman, possibly midwife in the area, or from one of her – now unknown – godparents. Coincidence or not, there was another girl baptised Ann(a) Matilda in the same parish a few months before Ann Matilda Loder.[67]

Life with the Loders in the 1790s

The Loder household was a focus for music, perhaps a hothouse for the young children. Typical life for a musical family of the time is described as,

'social interaction would have extended beyond that of just playing together. It would have included living, sleeping, eating, drinking, arguing and relaxing together. Often concert preparation and rehearsal time would be conveniently set within the physical bounds of the household. This created a community which would have seen itself apart from others by the very nature of the working hours they kept.'[68]

As musicians the Loders had a life style that was distinct. Musicians were part of the Bath labour market and although the father's talents and authority were important, unusually, in the musical field, women could continue to work after marriage and their children were encouraged and often expected to work for the family. 'Father, wife and children would provide a multi-income stream into the family coffers.'[69]

Bathsheba maintained her role as mother effectively, her eighth and ninth children arriving in rapid succession, George, baptised in February 1794 and Frederick French baptised in October 1795.[70] Whether she had time between her pregnancies and child rearing times, she must have at least acquiesced in the educational plans for the children. She may have been a driving force, bearing in mind that her brother David was a musician. The three boys who survived childhood must have received musical education, two later became relatively well known musicians. Her daughters Mary and Ann Matilda were trained for the stage, probably from an early age, Ann Matilda having a significant training in dance. The Loder children based at home must have spent a lot of time practising, listening and being coached to perform, especially music.

In a parallel creative field, that of painting, the family background was likewise vitally important to career development, especially before the 19th century for women. To succeed as a female painter for instance, at that time, you needed to be related to better known male painters and therefore have gained access to vocational training through the family circle.[71] Ann Matilda fortunately had ready access to her family's skillbase and training opportunities.

As a musician John Loder, led a quasi itinerant existence. He played in Bath, London and Weymouth and likely elsewhere. For orchestral performers in general, the work was seasonal. A horn player, named Perry listed his employment in 1794 as Sadler's Wells Theatre, and the Edinburgh and Bath theatres, demonstrating the wide geographical hinterland musicians often had to serve in the 1790s.[72] The careers of orchestral instrumentalists were patchwork affairs, combining numerous forms of employment in a very busy environment. Covent Garden and Drury Lane gave performances five or six nights a week during the 35 week season of 200 nights with rehearsals in the day.[73] To compound the problems of living life on the move in the late 18th century, instrumentalists like John were not given the recognition or remuneration given to many singers, teachers and organists, 'the financial insecurities and the low social and professional status typify the persistently artisan identity of this group of musicians.'[74] So John's life was tough, involving lots of travelling over unsophisticated road systems, with a low to middle income and a large family to support.

Transport improved the lot of travelling professionals in the late seventeen hundreds. The introduction of the toll roads and improvements in the postal system in the late 18th century supported a frequency of coaches, reduced transit times and enhanced safety. Bristol and market towns in the neighbourhood of Bath could be reached in hours. County towns such Exeter, Salisbury and Gloucester could be reached within the day. No longer were just the main arteries from the heart of London providing the channels along which musicians travelled but the highways and byways could be included within the touring programme. An increasingly sophisticated system of support for the performance industries began to emerge. When soloists from the capital were booked, they needed the support of instrumentalists. So the web of interconnection grew with all the demands for promoters to ensure concerts were delivered to meet the expectations of their audiences.[75]

Where did the Loders live in Bath?

From 1784 John and Bathsheba lived in the network of streets in the heart of Bath around the Abbey and St James Church. Newspaper notices and the local rates books, for both the City and Parishes give some clues about where exactly John and Bathsheba lived. Street numbers at that time were not formalised or consistent, but from 1793 to 1799 the Loder family likely lived in Orchard Street, the same street as the Theatre.[76] John Loder may well have purchased this Orchard Street property in around 1792.[77] Part of their dwelling, at least some of that time, was used as a Drapers shop, probably managed by Mr Prynne. Mrs Loder advertised tickets for the benefit concert for her recently departed husband available from 5 Orchard Street, Bath.

Orchard Street and surrounding areas had become downmarket and possibly seedy around the 1790s so it was not a high status address, but it was convenient for the theatre.[78] People associated with the theatre, like Mr French, the stage designer, lived in the street in the 1790s.[79]

Orchard Street was poorly lit when the Loders lived there in the 1790s. Gas lighting as a form of public lighting came to Bath early in the 19th century. Street life was full of hazards from street sellers, beggars, pickpockets and prostitutes, as well as runaway horses and mucky pavements and streets.[80] In Ann Matilda's childhood this road was run down and had a regular change of residents.[81]

In 1781, Palmer persuaded the City Council to build a new coach road to Orchard Street from the newer and wealthier North part of the city, enabling carriages to drop off the well to do playgoers. He provided parking space for 50 carriages on a site adjacent to the theatre (on the right of the theatre as one looks at the building from the opposite side of the road). This carriage park was 12 feet below the level of the street and playgoers had to walk up stairs to enter the theatre. It appears that all the residential houses in Orchard Street in the 1790s were on the opposite side of the road from the theatre, the most likely position for a number 5 (or a number 3) Orchard Street was opposite the theatre and several houses to the left if you had your back to it.[82]

The death of John Loder

Tragedy struck the family in Autumn 1795 when, around Ann Matilda's fifth birthday, John Loder died. It had been a tough year. Bathsheba had become pregnant for the ninth time early in the year. The winter of 1794-5 was the worst for almost 50 years. It was so cold that the 'milk froze in the milkmaids' pails'.[83] January was the coldest month on record ever, with an average of -3.1 degrees Centigrade in the Midlands. The price of wheat soared and riots spread in places like Birmingham.[84] There were the inevitable food riots during the spring and summer in some towns.[85]

John died in Weymouth in September 1795. The cause of his death was unrecorded. Though only an ensemble player, his death was mentioned in the national press[86] and there were several notices in the Bath press.[87] It was not so easy for his widow; her ninth baby was probably born around the time of his death and she may have taken a pragmatic line by inviting the Orchard Street neighbour and theatrical character, Mr French, to become one of his godfathers – he was baptised 'Frederick French Loder'. Bathsheba was in a precarious situation financially and a benefit concert was organised to raise funds for her and the family. There was also a contemporary report of the actual event.[88]

> 'The Benefit Concert, at the Upper Rooms, for Mrs Loder and her family was well attended; but being in the large room but did not appear to numerous as "the Friends of the fatherless" could have wished. The Duke of York honoured the concert with his presence and his Royal Highness as well as every Musical Amateur was highly delighted with young Loder's Violin Concerto; he is to be numbered as one of those musical prodigees who have lately astonished the world with their excellence – not inferior to any of them in taste and in execution, perhaps, equalled. The greatest attention was paid to his performance and every pause he made was filled up by the most unbounded plaudits.
> Mr Richards, who we understand is the uncle to Master Loder made his first appearance in these rooms in a Concerto which was executed in the style which convinced the audience that he is an admirable scientific Performer to whom the care of that promising young genius may be happily entrusted'.[89]

Things were really tough for a widow like Bathsheba with a large, dependant family. She succeeded despite what must have been a challenging financial situation to educate well her three boys and probably found good opportunities for at least two of her daughters, although what all her children did is a mystery. Mary and John David were propelled into performing careers immediately after their father's untimely death. Bathsheba spent the following nine years as a widow.

Mary Loder: what happened to Ann Matilda's big sister, 1795 – 1798

After the death of her father, Mary was pushed directly into a career on the stage at the age of twelve and three quarters. She may have been in training earlier. Mary must have had some natural talent and she was surrounded by neighbours who worked for and in the theatre who would have helped her theatrical career. Mary found a place in the Bath Theatre Company, also known as the Company, for three seasons. She appeared in productions in both Bristol and Bath[90] and was shown performing the role of 'Edward' in 'Everyone has his Fault' at the Theatre Royal in 1797.[91] The play was radical and attacked by a London paper- the fact that it was written by a woman writer, Mrs Inchbald, in 1793 was regarded as subversive.[92] The part Mary played, at the age of 14, is a young boy and appeared in a scene described as 'vulgar' at the time.[93] Mary appeared alongside Mr Cunningham (who played, Mr Placid) who later married her cousin Amy, the daughter of her uncle, Andrew Loder.

John David Loder: what happened to Ann Matilda's older brother?

Certainly the premature death of John Loder speeded his son John David towards a performing career. John David must have received plenty of pressure as a child, not only to earn money but also to fill the footprints of his talented, deceased father. The newspaper report of the benefit concert for Bathsheba Loder in November 1795 is clear that John David was regarded as a highly talented child. But the benefit performance was not his debut, a year before his father's death the seven year old John David had played a solo written by James Brooks, the leader of the Bath Orchestra.[94]

Despite the early loss of his father, John David Loder was surrounded by family and professional friends who would assist his future career. He appeared in public life with several concerts in 1796 for the benefit of the Sunday Schools, attended by the Duke and Duchess of York, at the Bath Theatre and in Cheltenham, which 'afford universal satisfaction and entertainment to a crowded auditory.'[95] The following year he performed in a 'Choral Night' under the direction of Rauzzini in Bath. Weeks later he made his first appearance at the King's Theatre in London at a benefit concert for the New Musical Fund.[96] Given that the Duke of York was a patron of the fund, the royal influence may have secured this invitation which promoted John David Loder as 'an Orphan, aged nine years, under the protection of the Society.'[97] The band was led by a big name for the time, Wilhelm Cramer.'[98]

John David was taken under the wing of his maternal uncle either before or at his father's death. David Richards was his violin teacher. Later, in 1800, Uncle David advertised a 'Musical Academy' presumably having some musical talent himself.[99]

At the beginning of the 19th century a young Master Pinto was playing in Bath with his violin concertos. In 1800 he was joined by 'Master [John David] Loder' in a 'concertante' for two violins.[100] In 1800 Master Loder frequently appeared at the Bath Theatre playing between the two acts.[101] Child prodigies were often promoted in Bath at this time and, given the circumstances, it is easy to understand why John David was thrust into the centre stage. He was a source of income for his family and the close bonding of local musicians would have encouraged him to make full use of his talents'.[102]

Ann Matilda's education and training, 1795-1803

The if, what and hows of Ann Matilda's learning and development is largely circumstantial guesswork. What is clear is that she was prepared for a dancing and stage career. Her mother was literate, and the absence of a father figure from the age of five most likely resulted in her being taken under the wing by other men in her family's life, her Loder or Richards uncles. The family support could have taken many forms, payment for lessons, board and lodgings. At the age of five Ann Matilda may have been sufficiently talented or attractive to persuade relatives or friends to invest in her education and future. She was not of an age to offer any 'payback', like Mary or John David.

There was some education for girls in Bath at this time, however it is not clearly documented. Most of the institutional teaching was provided for boys. There was a Bluecoat school but there is no evidence it took girls in the 1790s. There was a network of small schools, based in houses which would typically take 12 to 15 pupils each. Some of these were for girls, called 'ladies academies.' A family might also employ a governess, and maybe also a music and dancing teacher. Bath was an attractive destination for French emigrees – frequently fro the minor nobility. These refugees were often escaping the French revolution and the consequent wars; many needed money. The French had a particular distinction for music and dancing and the reputation of French music teachers continued to be strong even during the Napoleonic wars. A French or supposedly French dancing teacher would provide a good training opportunity for a fatherless girl like Ann Matilda, if a relative or friend could contribute to the costs.[103]

Because Bath was an attractive social scene around 1800 there was a seasonal demand for dancing lessons from visitors. These teachers also sometimes looked for work throughout the year which could well have encompassed tutoring Bath residents and children. For a family like the Loders, whose daughter Mary was part of the Company, this was a source of expertise easily accessible for Ann Matilda and her bereaved mother.

In general in the late 18th century, secular singers and instrumentalists were trained by apprenticeship or private lessons.[104] The most common form of musical education was the private lesson – especially for children of musicians and particularly valuable for women. Quite often a child would work with a relative without charge.[105] This may have been the situation with Ann Matilda and some of the other Loder children.

Some press advertisements of the time illustrate the types of learning in Bath for girls. These illustrate the factors which may have influenced Ann Matilda's education and training in the years following her father's death.

' WANTED. A GOVERNESS, who can teach FRENCH and ITALIAN grammatically. – MUSIC enough to teach in the absence of a Master. She is expected to rise early, and will not have a maid to attend her. She is to sleep in the room with a Young Lady, and to eat with her when requested. The salary Sixty Guineas a year. – She will not visit with the Lady [of the house], as she is wanted to attend entirely to the education of two Young Ladies. A middle –aged person will be preferred, and of the Protestant Religion.'[106]

Another advert describes a new girl at the Misses Lee's establishment, around 1795. It describes, needlework, walking in the country, reading prayers, writing, arithmetic, music, drawing and dancing.[107] The Sunday Schools offered children a curriculum in 1789 of learning letters, spelling, reading and singing (Psalms).[108] Musical education in Bath for boys from middle or low income families was not a lot better than that for their female counterparts. It was limited to schooling, private lessons and apprenticeships.

John Loder's death must have focused Bathsheba's mind on the career prospects of her other children. It is likely that Ann Matilda demonstrated her abilities in music, dancing, singing and acting as a young child. If a young child had talents in these directions, the wider Loder family, Orchard Street neighbours and Bath society in general would have been receptive to supporting and developing them further. Either Bathsheba or Ann Matilda's carer – if she was farmed out or looked after by a godparent or family friend – might well have encouraged her skills in a field in which she could make a living like her older sister Mary. Ann Matilda may have made her debut on the stage at the Theatre Royal as a child dancer; other contemporaries, like Miss Decamp, the mother of Fanny Kemble started dancing on stage at the age of eight.[109] Another child performer, Clara Fisher, two decades younger than Ann Matilda, first started performing at the age of six.[110]

The Theatre Royal Bath in the 18th and 19th centuries

The theatre was integral to the life of the Loder family and key to Ann Matilda's blossoming career. Built in 1750, it was the most important theatre outside of London, especially for the period 1790-1805, before a new theatre was opened in Beaufort Square, after the sale of the Orchard Street theatre building.[111] The building was sold because its popularity had rendered it too small to cope with audience demand.

When the theatre was first opened in Orchard Street in 1750 it was located in the fashionable district of Bath.[112] However, as the streets and crescents of Northern Bath were designed and built in the 1770s the centre of social gravity moved in Bath and the area around the theatre began to deteriorate socially. The Company staff developed expertise and became moderately well known in the late eighteenth century.

'The last three decades of the century saw the company of some thirty salaried staff at the height of its reputation. While a permanent core of stalwarts gave solidarity, a regular transfusion of young stars – Siddons, Henderson, Wallis, Incledon and others brought freshness and excitement.'[113]

The plays and dances performed at the theatre were varied. Shakespeare – adapted in a Georgian way – was a 'perennial favourite.'[114] Hamlet was played almost every season and eight other Shakespeare plays appeared in more than 20 of the 31 seasons from 1770 to 1800. Modern comedies of manners, sentimental pieces, ballad opera, pantomime and in the 1790s German melodrama were all included in the catalogue. Sheridan's plays went down well with the audiences.[115] In the early 19th century melodramas, pantomimes and spectacles were very popular – scenery and special effects becoming important.[116]

Illustration I: Impression of the Bath Theatre Royal around 1800. Julia Poulter

Sarah Siddons was immensely popular in Bath and any child living in Orchard Street would have come under the spell of the actress and her return to Bath when crowds lined the streets for a glimpse of her in 1799 when Ann Matilda was eight years old.[117]

The musicians associated with the Theatre Royal were also outstanding for their times – including Cantelo, Brooks, Ashley and Herschel. The scene-designer Thomas French was considered amongst the best in the country – especially good for special effects and Gothic melodramas.[118]

'Mr [Thomas] French's scene of Mount Vesuvius, is universally spoken of as the best exhibition of painting that has ever been produced her; it is, we understand, an exact copy from the Moonlight View of the eruption that was taken on the spot by the celebrated Mr. Wright, of Derby.'[119]

A contemporary press report mentions, 'scenes and transparencies, machinery , mechanisms and expensive and elegantly appropriate dresses do infinite credit to the several persons by whom they were executed,' praising the younger French and his father.[120]

The audiences were mixed. A series of boxes offered the best views and comfort. Most of the audience would be standing, often with servants sent ahead to the theatre to reserve places. People would mill around during performances and poor performers would be given a rough ride.[121] The behaviour and composition of audiences changed in the 1790s because of the mobilisation of the militia for the Napoleonic wars. The first complaints about the rougher element of the audience came in the early 1790s. Members of the Royal family were supportive of the theatres in Bath and Bristol, for instance the Duke of York visited Bristol on 27th November 1795 to review the troops camped on the Downs and expressed a wish to visit the theatre which was especially opened on the occasion.[122]

The internal shape of Theatre Royal changed over the decades prior to 1800, with tiers of expensive boxes and a small orchestra area. The stage itself was, and in 2013 remains, hard and small. Ann Matilda never trod the boards - the stage is and was constructed of stone, not wood, it was also relatively shallow compared with 21st century theatres, making scenes with large casts and busy scenes particularly difficult.[123] There was a small area either side of the stage, the wings, in which actors could wait and there was a small staircase to the stage boxes – the one to the left of the stage (from the theatre entrance) still survives in the 21st century. Also surviving are the frames for the set scenes. The lighting was basic, candles and daylight as far as possible.[124] There was an important change to lighting in 1808 in Bristol, when there was substitution of Argand (oil) lamps for candles in part of the stage lighting. Early gas lighting was demonstrated in Bristol 1805, but these enhancements did not benefit Ann Matilda's performances in Bath and Bristol.

The Theatre was not cheap entertainment. The cost of a place for a Ballad-opera was seven shillings for the pit and four shillings for the gallery at Bristol in 1809, when a skilled workman's wage was little more than £1 a week.[125]

**The intertwined world:
everyone knew everyone else in entertainment in Bath**

Thirteen musician families living in Bath during the 18th century have been identified.[126] They were Ashe, Ashley, Biggs, Brooks, Cantelo, Fleming, Harington, Herschel, Linley, Loder, Richards, Rogers and Shaw. By the early 19th century there were others: the Windsors, the Philpots and the Giroux. James William Windsor was a cousin to the Philpot sisters, the elder being better known as Lucy Anderson, whom he taught the pianoforte.[127]Alicia Windsor, his wife, acted at the Bath theatre. They were both involved in the formation of the Bath Philharmonic Society. The Giroux were a family of dancers who came to Bath and settled there. Gabriel Giroux headed a family of the five daughters who worked at the Adelphi Theatre, London, with which Ann Matilda is later connected. Two daughters Louisa and Caroline established a dancing academy in Bath and later in Clifton, Bristol. [128]

Bathsheba's annus horribilis, 1798

Things probably started to go badly wrong for Bathsheba in 1797, for it was then that Ann Matilda's maternal grandmother died. Grandmother Mary must have lived nearby and the chances were that she had provided some practical and possible financial help to the fatherless Loders.[129]

It went from bad to worse a year later when the young, talented Mary Loder died in Bristol in September 1798. She was remembered in a poem by a friend that begun 'Ne'er shall I hear her sweetest harmony.'[130] Such a comment was not only a reflection on the quality of her singing but on how much she was valued during her short life.[131] She was three months short of her 16th birthday. Ann Matilda was eight years old and must have been aware of the tremendous respect her sister had gained in her short life. Mary's death may have given her a role model to aspire to. Perhaps at this time Bathsheba determined that Ann Matilda should follow in her sister's footsteps, one can only speculate that the older sisters Eliza and Harriet (if the latter had survived so far) were not considered suitable for the stage; possibly they had been cared for by friends or relations who encouraged a different future for them.

Potential financial and social ruin followed a week after Mary's death in September, when Bathsheba either went bankrupt or was closely associated with bankruptcy for her home.[132] A reasonable scenario is that John Loder had purchased the freehold of a property around 1792 with some of his earnings. When he died, this would have been passed to Bathsheba. She must have been in a desperate situation financially. Sale of the freehold of her home to a local business man, Mr Prynne, would have been a logical step, releasing some capital for her and the brood of young children. In 1798 Prynne was declared bankrupt leaving her in a precarious situation. Her reaction to this was to move in with a neighbour – Tebay – further down Orchard Street for at least a few months. Mr Tebay and other Tebays (Miss and Mesdames…Tebay) popped up regularly as members of the Theatre Royal Company in the early 1800s.[133]

What happened to Bathsheba and the brood of young Loder children for a few years after this date is speculation. The talented John David was well established on his pathway to professional musicianship and appeared in concerts and similar for the rest of his life.[134]

Ann Matilda goes public, 'this budding flower of histrionic art'

Ann Matilda was bubbling with talent and her widowed mother must have been keen to find sources of income that would support the younger three of her children and herself. In keeping with the times the boys would have had special attention to ensure they both carried on in the family musical traditions. Jane, the seventh child would have had to demonstrate especial talent in stageworthiness to provide a stage career for herself. Perhaps Jane, like her older sisters Eliza and Harriet was put in the care of family members who encouraged some more minimal musical heritage, their fate is largely unknown.[135] Opportunities for fatherless girls of low income artisan families were very limited.

So Ann Matilda was something special to be singled out for development. She may have been supported by the wider family, perhaps Andrew Loder or one of the Richards family – like her older brother John David. Bathsheba, having the theatre connections, and probable sympathy and respect of the theatre folk may well have tried out each of her daughters on the stage as child dancers when they were aged under 10. Perhaps only Mary and Ann Matilda passed muster.

In any case Ann Matilda, as Miss Loder, first entered the public domain as a pupil of Monsieur Mingaud, 'Professor of French Dancing in this City', in June 1803.[136] She was the same age, 12 and three quarters, as her sister Mary when she joined the company of the Theatre Royal. Ann Matilda performed in 'Le Grand Ballet des Cerceaux' composed by her teacher Monsieur Mingaud. He was to 'sustain the principal parts, with the assistance of Miss Loder, his pupil'. This ballet was sandwiched between a play, 'Lovers' Vows' and a Pastoral Opera, the 'Gentle Shepherd'. 'Lovers Vows' was of the 'Theatre Royal Drury Lane – for that night only'.

THEATRE-ROYAL, BATH.

FOR THE BENEFIT OF

Mr. SMITH, *Treasurer*,

AND

Mr. BARTLEY, *Box Book-keeper*

On THURSDAY next, JUNE 2, 1803,

THE FAVORITE COMEDY OF

LOVERS' VOWS.

Baron Wildenhaim Mr. EYRE.	Cottager	- -	Mr. CHARLTON.
Anhalt - - Mr. SEDLEY.	Landlord	- -	Mr. LANGDON.
Count Cassel Mr. CUNNINGHAM.	Farmer	- -	Mr. PARSONS.
Butler - Mr. LOVEGROVE.	Frederick	- -	Mr. G. BARTLEY,

OF THE THEATRE-ROYAL, DRURY-LANE, FOR THAT NIGHT ONLY.

Agatha Fribourg Mrs. JOHNSTONE.	Market Girl - Miss SUMMERS.
Cottager's Wife Mrs. DIDIER.	Amelia - - Mrs. EDWIN.

END OF THE COMEDY,

A NEW SONG, CALLED PADDY O'TRIGGER's TRIP TO BATH,

WRITTEN, and to be SUNG by Mr. DEW.

PRECEDING THE FARCE, FOR THE FIRST TIME,

WILL BE PERFORMED,

Le Grand Ballet des Cerceaux,

COMPOSED BY

MONSIEUR MINGAUD,

PROFESSOR of FRENCH DANCING in this CITY,

IN WHICH HE WILL SUSTAIN THE PRINCIPAL PARTS, WITH THE ASSISTANCE OF

MISS LODER, HIS PUPIL.

To which will be added, a Scots Pastoral Opera, called the

GENTLE SHEPHERD

Patie .... Mr. TAYLOR.	Sir William .... Mr. EGAN.
Roger .... Mr. TEBAY.	Madge .... Mrs. EGAN.
Claud .... Mr. BENNETT.	Mause .... Mrs. DIDIER.
Simon .... Mr. EVANS.	Jenny .... Mrs. TAYLOR.
Bauldy .... Mr. EDWIN.	Peggy .... Miss EVERY.

⁎ TICKETS to be had of Mr. SMITH, No. 29, St. James's-Street; of Mr. BARTLEY, No. 5, Orange-Court; of Mrs. GYE, Market-Place, and at the Theatre.

GYE, PRINTER.

ORDER

OF

THE BALLET

Des Cerceaux.

FIRST.

A Pastoral Dance, by a Group of Villagers.

SECOND.

The QUEEN's MINUET, by *Mr. Mingaud and Miss Loder.*

THIRD.

Gavotte from the Grand Serious Opera of Armida,

BY MISS LODER.

FOURTH.

Gavotte, from the famous Chinese Opera, De Panurge,

BY MONSIEUR MINGAUD.

FIFTH.

An Andante Movement from the Opera, Le Rosiere de Salancy,

By an appropriate Group of Villagers.

PAS SEUL OF THE SAME, by Miss LODER.

SIXTH.

A GRAND PAS SEUL,

From the much-admired Egyptian Opera, " The Caravan of Cairo,"

BY MONSIEUR MINGAUD.

SEVENTH.

ADAGIO, from the interesting Ballet of Telemachus,

REPRESENTED BY VILLAGERS.

EIGHTH.

Pas de Deux, by Monsieur Mingaud, and Miss Loder.

NINTH.

A GRAND

PASTORAL CONCLUSIVE MOVEMENT,

With Garlands, and fanciful rustic Decorations,

BY

MONSIEUR MINGAUD, Miss LODER and the CORPS DE BALLET.

GYE, PRINTER, MARKET-PLACE, BATH.

Illustrations II and III. These show two sides of a Playbill from the Theatre Royal, Bath, 1803 and illustrate what may be the first time Ann Matilda Loder performed for the public. These two images are from Bath in Time – Bath Central Library [Copyright Bath in Time].

A couple of months later, in 1803 a Miss Loder sang at a gala in Sydney Gardens in honour of the birthday of HRH Prince of Wales, his birthday was 12th August. Most likely this would have been Ann Matilda.[137]

The literary connections with Ann Matilda:
Elizabeth Inchbald and Jane Austen

The well known actress and playwright, Mrs Inchbald (1753 -1821) wrote two novels and 18 of her plays were published, mainly between 1783 and 1803. Some of her plays were considered scandalous by some at the time. Her plays were shown in Bath, and two were associated with the young Loder girls, Mary and Ann Matilda, 'Everyone has his fault' in 1797 and 'Lovers Vows' in 1803.

'Lovers' Vows' was a well known and controversial play written by Elizabeth Inchbald in 1798.[138] It deals with the story of a mother who had had an illegitimate son, with no birth certificate. It is not known whether Bathsheba or any of the Loder family were concerned about the disreputable overtones in these plays and the danger to these girls by being associated with such riskee publications. The plot was also quite close to the bone if there was any serious concern about Ann Matilda's paternity.

Bathsheba must have known about the dodgy plays her young daughters were linked with. She may not have cared and was perhaps too busy trying to make ends meet with the young family to pay attention to the content of their work. Alternatively, it is possible Bathsheba was part of a freethinking or fun loving group in Georgian society and wasn't concerned about the presumed nuances associated with the theatre. Perhaps she aware of the enormous discrepancies about moral attitudes and practices and could shrug off the pretences and hypocrisies. The mores of the turn of the 19th century were different from those two centuries later.

Jane Austen's Bath novels give a contemporary account of the city during Ann Matilda's childhood and youth. Jane stayed in the city several times and in 1801 the Revd George Austen retired to Bath with his wife, and their two daughters Jane and Cassandra.[139]

During the 1790s she wrote the first drafts of 'Sense and Sensibility', 'Pride and Prejudice', and 'Northanger Abbey' – the latter and 'Persuasion' have a very strong Bath link. These novels give vivid descriptions of the life there around 1800 and the familiar landmarks of the Pump Room, the Assembly rooms and the Theatre Royal are bought to life. In 'Northanger Abbey' Catherine watches the hero, Mr Tilney, in a box opposite and then 'making his way through the then thinning rows' at the end of the play.[140] Clearly Jane attended the Theatre and was familiar with the hubbub – she may well have critiqued the performances she saw with the family. It could well have been in Bath that she came across the play, 'Lovers' Vows' which became fundamental to her own novel, Mansfield Park.[141] This play was shown in Bath on six occasions while Jane Austen was known to be in Bath, 1801 - 1805 including the occasion in June 1803 when Miss Loder danced with her dance master Mingaud.[142] One could speculate that Jane Austen watched Ann Matilda's debut performance at the Theatre Royal, there is absolutely no evidence.

Ann Matilda joins the Company

Respect, relief, surprise? Looking at the 13 year old Ann Matilda from the boxes or the crowded 'pit' the Loder family had another member earning money, and possibly earning her own keep from the autumn 1803. Ann Matilda is listed as a member of the Company of the Theatre for the two seasons, 1803/4 and 1804/5.[143]

She joined the semi iterant life of the Company commuting back and forward from Bath to Bristol, her work pattern described as,

> 'as the calendar shows, after a short period of experiment the working pattern soon became stabilised – during September and October they played three nights in Bristol and Saturdays in Bath, with the exception of Race Week in Bath, Christmas and Easter, when a full week was played there. Then from November to May there would be three nights in Bath, with Mondays in Bristol. Benefits in Bath were taken in the spring and early summer; in Bristol in June and July. The long coaches or 'caterpillars' as they were called – in modern times 'mini-buses' – which Palmer had constructed, each carried twelve of the company and their luggage, a reasonably pleasant journey in summer, a tiring and occasionally dangerous one in winter.'[144]

During her 18 months as an active member of the Company it had over 50 members, 30 men, 9 women ('Mrs'), 11 girls or young women ('Miss') and two boys ('Master') in addition to a Treasurer, a Prompter and a Box Book-keeper in both Bath and Bristol.[145] Not all company members appeared in every performance, and additionally national actors would make guest appearances, like Stephen Kemble, a member of the renowned Kemble family.[146] So Ann Matilda was rubbing shoulders with the stars of the national stage from an early age. The playbills of the time also note the names of those who supported the performances, like the writers, musicians and the set designer Mr French.[147]

Ann Matilda had four types of role in her Company career: as part of a chorus, acting in a child's part, as a specialist dancer and as the star in Pantomime.[148] In the first category she pops up in choruses - as part of a chorus of nuns, as one of a group of three 'young women of the island.'

There is one example of Ann Matilda playing a child in a serious play: in April 1804 she plays Prince Arthur in Shakespeare's King John. She performed this in Bath[149] and almost certainly in Bristol where the press were impressed.

> 'Yesterday evening Shakespeare's celebrated Historical Play of Henry the Fourth was performed here, for the benefit of that laudable institution, the Bristol Infirmary. We cannot pass by unnoticed, the charming little girl who impersonated Prince John, and who so correctly impersonated Prince Arthur, on Monday last; and we trust that the Managers will foster, by the sunshine of their patronage, this budding flower of histrionic art.'[150]

Arthur was a powerful and significant part for the 13 year old Ann Matilda to be given. In Shakespeare's character design of Arthur he took a freedom in making Arthur younger than he really was, and used the character as a vehicle for childish innocence and wit. The Arthur of the play is a naive, gentle, natural-hearted, but eloquent boy, who pleads for nature's rights. Arthur is also threatened with the loss of his eyes. In Arthur's dying speech, 'O me! my uncle's spirit is in these stones,' the character intensified feelings against John. Some consider the part of Arthur as Shakespeare's most powerful one in that genre.[151] Handling this role successfully as a 13 year old was a considerable achievement for Ann Matilda.

Thirdly Ann Matilda was a star performer as a dancer on the Bath stage. [152] One playbill has her listed as the 'Genius of the Fountain of Oblivion' in Sadak and Kalasrade, followed by, 'in the course of the Pantomine a fancy dance by Miss Loder.'[153] Another day Ann Matilda is down to appear, 'In Act 1 a hornpipe, incidental to the piece, by Miss Loder, in the Character of a British Sailor,' in the play 'Wife of Two Husbands'. That same day as well as appearing as the

Fountain Genius again, she is billed yet again, 'in the course of the Pantomime, a fancy tambourine dance by Miss Loder.'[154]

For the Christmas season, in 1804, she appeared in several productions with Mr Ridgway, as a dancer, in the 'Hunter of the Alps'[155] followed rapidly by her star performance in 'Magic of Hope or Columbine Captive', as Columbine.[156] This was an almighty set of performances in early 1805, 'with entire new music, scenes, machinery and decorations.' The well known Mr French painted the scenes and Mr Sheldon had provided 'transparent portraits of the British Admirals.' No tickets were available 'under full price', so it was presumably immensely popular.[157]

Mr Ridgway directed a 'new ballet dance', called 'the Coat and Badge', in which he took the lead with Ann Matilda as Wilhelmina.[158] Ballet was not an art in its own right in provincial theatres in 1805[159] but the form was starting to develop. The Giroux family later established dancing academies in both Bath and Bristol. The final time record of Ann Matilda on the Bath stage is dancing with Mr Ridgway is 2nd March 1805.[160]

The reports of the Magic of Hope were particularly spectacular,

> 'The favourite comedy of The Blind Bargain was followed
> on Monday night by a new Pantomime called The Magic
> of Hope, which was received throughout by a fashionable
> company with great applause. The new Pantomime was
> afterwards repeated with increased effect; from the rising
> of the curtain to the close of the piece, the house was in
> one continued roar of laughter and applause; indeed neither
> pains nor expense seemed to have been spared to render
> this the most complete Harlequinade, ever exhibited on our
> stage: the beautiful scenery, surprising changes, in short
> the whole magic of the piece, with the matchless
> whimsicalities of Gomery's Clown, the nimble grace and
> agility of Ridgeway's Harlequin, and the simple elegance
> and beauty of Miss Loder's Columbine, will, we have no
> doubt, amply repay the Managers for the expense of
> getting it up.'[161]

and,

> 'The new Pantomime which followed is by far the best
> Harlequinade we have seen for many years. Gomery's
> Clown is inimitable; and the Harlequin and Colombine of

Ridgway and Miss Loder, are each excellent in their kind.'[162]

Ann Matilda was doing extremely well in the eyes of local newspaper critics. Her career was well launched she was recognised and appreciated. She was in the spotlight.

Reflections on Ann Matilda's stage career in Bath

During her short introduction to a theatrical career in her early teens Ann Matilda made her mark. She was chosen for a spectacularly difficult Shakespearean role and impressed the press with her performances. She danced, she acted and maybe sung. She was part of an important company and respected as part of the group. There was a benefit performance for her and fellow colleague, Mr Lovegrove, in May 1804, in the programme 'Clandestine Marriage' between 'the play & the farce a New ballet by Miss Loder & 4 young ladies', the benefit thanking 'their friends and the Public for the very liberal patronage they experienced.'[163] She and Mr Lovegrove must have shared a reasonable sum for the benefit night. Miss Wallis was the leading lady of the Company from 1791, until her departure to Covent Garden in 1794. At her Bristol benefit there were receipts of £163.[164] So the young teenager almost definitely paid her own way.

As an actress in the Company Ann Matilda was travelling frequently between Bath and Bristol in 1804, and in June, she was performing in Swansea.[165] The press echoed her appearances in Bath, Bristol and Swansea. The Bristol paper, The Mirror, on 17th July 1804, noted that Miss Loder was playing Fanny in the 'Lock and Key'.[166]

Things had changed on the domestic front in 1804. Her mother, Bathsheba, married John Richards in the summer 1804, in Bristol.[167] John was also an actor and musician and likely a relative of the enormous Richards family. Although her mother and step father later returned to Bath, effectively Ann Matilda, and possibly her siblings, were 'on their own'. Ann Matilda had some kind of base, possibly rented rooms, near to the theatre from where she handled tickets for her benefit performance.[168] Life may have quietened in the theatre resting season in Bath in the summer/autumn 1804, but by the end of the year Ann Matilda was moved to the centre stage for the Pantomime season.

Romance on the candlelit stage

On the stone stage the Harlequin and Columbine couple, Thomas Edmund Ridgway and Ann Matilda fell rapidly in love, if we are to believe the press reports, during a brief three or four month courtship.[169] Thomas was from London and performing on the London stage before he came to Bath.[170] He was about 24 years old, when he joined the 'Company'. It was likely a career move, he arrived in fashionable Bath to play the lead role, Harlequin, for the season.

For at least some of the season he lived in the parish of Bradford on Avon, some eight miles away from Bath. Why an actor would live in Bradford and commute to Bath is puzzling. The journey was and is a hilly one and likely to take about an hour on horseback. Although there was usually a daily wagon from Bradford to Bath it would not have been possible to use the wagon as a commuting vehicle for the theatre.[171] The parish of Bradford was large and it is possible that Thomas lodged in a village or hamlet nearer to Bath than the small town itself. The months Thomas was acting in Bath and Bristol were winter and the eight mile journey would have been hazardous as well as time consuming. One strong theory about Thomas and his time in the Bath area is that he had been invited there by friends or contacts from London who had a holiday residence in Bradford and he was offered some kind of base there. He may have taken in pupils there. He definitely would have spent some time staying in Bristol as part of the travelling 'Company.'[172]

Ann Matilda and Thomas marry: the real Clandestine marriage?

Ann Matilda and Thomas married at the Holy Trinity Church Bradford on Avon, by banns, on Monday, the 11th March, 1805.[173] This was only a week after Ann Matilda's last known stage appearance in Bath. The local newspapers rang out with the news.[174] One put it poetically,

> 'Miss Loder, the promising young dancer and Columbine
> of our Theatre, preferring the pas de deux to the pas seul,
> has tript off to the Altar of Hymen, with Mr Ridgway, the
> Harlequin - "Motley's your only wear."'[175]

This announcement unleashes a number of tricky questions. The parish record is quite clear, both sign their names. Thomas is recorded, as living locally, 'of this parish'. Why the wedding was held in Bradford and not in Ann Matilda's home town of Bath is not known. Weddings would normally be held in the bride's parish. There is no evidence of the signature of Bathsheba, the parent, giving consent to the marriage of the bride who was under 21 years old. Another serious issue is the question of why they married in Lent. These are three great imponderables, a possible explanation being that Thomas was offered some interesting work back in the capital and wanted to leave Bath quickly with his new, attractive bride. She might, have suspected she was pregnant, he might have been pursued by debts, the person who performed the marriage ceremony, J.D. Nicklin, the curate, may have been an easy going man of the church. In the early 1800s the local vicar had an enormous amount of local discretion and records of parental permission were not universal in Wiltshire in the early 1800s.[176]

Whatever the locals thought the marriage was an excellent proposition for Ann Matilda. She had struck theatrical gold. Thomas was regarded as a good catch and Ann Matilda was released from the trap of having to work in the socially questionable career of acting. There were two similar contemporary press reports.

> 'We understand that Mr Ridgway, who lately married Miss Loder of our Theatre, is possessed of a handsome property, independent of his profession, and has still further expectations at the death of a near relation; and that it is his intention to withdraw Mrs R. entirely from the stage. We rejoice to hear, that one, who we have always heard spoken of as a deserving young woman, is likely to be so eligibly settled.'[177]

and,

> 'We understand that Mr Ridgway, who lately married Miss Loder, of our theatre, is possessed of a handsome property independent of his profession; and that he means to withdraw his bride from the stage. It is gratifying to the friends of this deserving young woman, to find that she has a prospect of being so happily settled'.[178]

A playbill, announces their departure from Bath,

> 'The Public are respectfully informed, that the pantomime cannot be performed after this Evening, Mr. Ridgeway being obliged to attend his Engagement in London at Easter; and Mrs. Ridgeway retiring from the Stage.'[179]

Everyone appears to have rejoiced in the fine marriage Ann Matilda had made. She had socially arrived. She was to retire from the stage.

Reflections on another marriage

Attempting to fill the vacuum in Bathsheba's life path between her sorrowful move from Orchard Street in 1799 and her marriage in July 1804 to the moderately famous actor John Richards is speculative. As a widow, in 1799, without known funds Bathsheba would have had in her care the three youngest children (aged from four to seven) as well as some responsibility for the older ones. John David was probably earning enough for his keep in some apprenticeship or similar arrangement with his uncle. When the life of Bathsheba's second husband, John Richards, is examined possible clues emerge about what may have happened to Bathsheba. John was a relatively well known actor, known by his stage name of Richardson. The fact that his surname was Richards would indicate that he may have been related to Bathsheba, although there is no evidence for this.

John's first performance in Bath was in 1790, and he appears to have spent much of his time in the 1790s working in Covent Garden. He also spent time performing in Norwich and Manchester – where he acted for much of the eight years prior to 1805. From 1805 to 1809 he performed for the Bath and Bristol Company. Most interesting is the appearance in Manchester. An actress with him is a Mrs Richardson in December 1803 and June 1804. It is not known when his first wife died but the appearance of a Mrs Richardson on stage alongside him a month before his marriage to Bathsheba, in July 1804, would make it a reasonable possibility that he and Bathsheba lived together as man and wife for at least a few months, before their marriage. It also opens the door for Bathsheba to have been a performer in her own right. The stage could have offered her an independent income stream in the dark days of 1799, when she could have off loaded her offspring on willing friends, godparents and relatives and/or possibly have paid for their training and education in some kind of residential situation.

Returning to the mystery of Ann Matilda's baptism record, John Richards is at least a candidate for the paternity of Ann Matilda. He may also have contributed a useful contact list for Ann Matilda in her later life, one source notes his occupation as 'Band Leader' and 'Captain of the 43rd Foot'. There is conflicting evidence about his possible date of death, indeed, there may have been more than one John Richards in Bath.[180]

Another possible scenario which emerges about Bathsheba is that she had more or less abandoned her children and it was possible that the young Ann Matilda could feel justified in getting married without parental involvement, feeling herself, an orphan. Bathsheba didn't cut herself from the Loder family though. Later she appears as a witness at the second marriage of her son George Loder.[181]

Looking back at Ann Matilda's childhood

Her childhood was short, truncated by the early death of John Loder. Whether or not he was her parent was immaterial, his death made things considerably more difficult for the five year old girl who was part of his establishment. Ann Matilda was different. A possible scenario emerges in which the girl was recognised as attractive and talented from early on; singing, dancing mimicking, laughing and entertaining could have made her recognised as a young girl. These types of skills could have received the backing of friends and relatives prepared to invest in her future as a star pupil of Monsieur Mingaud at the age of twelve and three quarters.

Her childhood had been immersed in the stories and rumours of cultural misdemeanours, both through the theatre and from the street gossip of the local stars, like Elizabeth Linley and Sarah Siddons. She knew all about children with shadey birth records, illegal marriages and the immorality, fun and risk associated with the theatre.

Once on the Bath stage, she shone. Talents often associated with this type of actress would include being able to learn lines, cues, interpreting complex rules, doing what she was told, and super communication skills. She would have needed to be mature beyond her years and extraordinarily confident. She adapted and fitted into the life of the Company and was singled out for a principal role, Columbine. She was mentioned in despatches, she was in the 'limelight.'

Ann Matilda: the London Ridgway years 1805 – 1815

'Composed Upon Westminster Bridge September 3, 1802[182]

By William Wordsworth

Earth has not anything to show more fair:
Dull would he be of soul who could pass by
A sight so touching in its majesty:
This City now doth, like a garment, wear
The beauty of the morning; silent, bare,
Ships, towers, domes, theatres, and temples lie
Open unto the fields, and to the sky;
All bright and glittering in the smokeless air.
Never did sun more beautifully steep
In his first splendour, valley, rock, or hill;
Ne'er saw I, never felt, a calm so deep!
The river glideth at his own sweet will:
Dear God! the very houses seem asleep;
And all that mighty heart is lying still!'

The newly weds, Ann Matilda and Thomas, would likely have taken the daily coach service to London. It wasn't an easy ride. By 1800 a journey to London could be completed within the day, along bumpy roads following the Thames Valley.[183] The happy couple must have travelled in sufficient time for Thomas to take up his Easter commitment. Ann Matilda would have packed up as much as she had, her stage costumes would have been an essential part of her trade if it had been envisaged she would continue on the stage. Perhaps the groom persuaded her to quit the theatre, or forbidden her from future work on the stage, as the Bath press reports suggested. However she wasn't leaving behind Bath for ever: throughout her life she kept a close relationship with her brother John David who lived there for many years and she later performed there.

Going to London was an excellent career move for a prospective actress, so Ann Matilda may have wanted to pursue opportunities London had to offer, with or without her husband's support. She had dabbled in singing and dancing. During the century to 1850 most branches of musical careers were closed to women, but female singers were well known to the public and respected, acting was not a respectable career for women.

'For most of the century actresses were assumed to be sexually disreputable and of the lowest moral level.[184]

Ann Matilda may have been star struck with her new husband; the couple may have been deeply smitten and in love. One way or another she had little to lose. She may have missed the camaraderie of the Bath Theatre Company and the companionship of her family in the large capital city. She could have felt abandoned by her mother. Her brother John David was around 18 years old in 1805 and continually on the move to further his career. It is possible that her other siblings were 'farmed out', being educated or working, so London and Thomas offered her a new beginning in all senses. Her choice of husband was good. He had made his mark at Bath and seemed to be in demand in London. He was a gentleman there was no need for her to work in a disreputable stage job any more.

Introducing Thomas Edmund Ridgway

Thomas joined the cast of people surrounding Ann Matilda. Like most of the other members his background is murky. Ridgway was a relatively common name in London at that time. He was about 25 years old when he married Ann Matilda and had a strong association with Southwark.[185]

It is quite likely that from the age of 16 or less he was performing on the London stage. A Ridgway appeared at the Haymarket in 1792.[186] 'Ridgway', quite likely Thomas, acted and danced in the spectacles at the Royal Circus from the summer of 1802 or earlier.[187] There are many performances at the Royal Circus that a Ridgway played in, most of which appear to suit his subsequent career development as a Harlequin and dance master. [188] Seven of these are listed in present day records, including – being a participant in 'new and appropriate Combats' in 'The Black Forest' or 'The Natural Child' from June through to mid-November 1803 at the Royal Circus. So having cut his teeth in spectacles in London he may have been offered some 'leading' roles as a member of the Bath Theatre Company in the summer of 1804, hence his journey down to Bath and Bradford-on-Avon.

Thomas' pedigree is not known for certain. His father, another Thomas lived locally in Southwark. Either his father or another Thomas Ridgway also is recorded in the Southwark records for 1760, 1768 and 1774-7. In the records of the latter the Thomas in question is noted as poor. There is no Thomas recorded as a Southwark ratepayer for the decade 1881 – 1891 – the first years of the Thomas (senior) marriage to Mary, Thomas Edmunds' mother.[189]

The Royal Circus, later the Surrey Theatre, a short history

'And burnt the Royal Circus in a hurry:
'Twas called the Circus then, but now the Surrey.'[190]

The theatre, where Thomas likely made his first entrances was based in the Blackfriars Road, South of the river Thames. The road started at Blackfriars Bridge and was straight, and about two-thirds of a mile in length. It crossed St Georges Fields. Near the bridge on the West side was a series of buildings, including the Magdalen Hospital, and beyond it the Surrey Theatre. The early history of this theatre, appears to show the difficulties which the minor theatres experienced against the patented monopoly of Drury Lane and Covent Garden. The building was first opened under the title of the 'Royal Circus and Equestrian Philharmonic Academy,' in 1782 by the composer and song writer, Charles Dibdin, aided by Charles Hughes, an equestrian performer. It was originally designed for the display of equestrian and dramatic entertainments on a plan similar to the performances at Astley's, an older circus establishment, which was located in the area around the Westminster Bridge.[191]

Thomas had close links with the Dibdins especially Charles the Younger. The Dibdins, father Charles (1745 – 1814), and his two illegitimate sons, Charles (known often as Charles the Younger, 1767 – 1833) and Thomas (1771 – 1841) had a major influence on the English theatre in the late 18th and early 19th centuries. They were authors, managers and sometime performers in the London theatre scene. The writings of Charles the Younger are particularly interesting to the story of Ann Matilda as he wrote about Thomas Ridgway in 1830.[192] Besides being an actor manager Charles was a prolific author, producing and composing numerous plays and 'near five thousand' songs.[193]

The entertainments at the Royal Circus were at first performed by children, developing into a quasi circus cum nursery for actors – it may have been that Thomas was one of these. The theatre in the 1780s, having been opened without a licence, was closed by order of the Surrey magistrates. This caused a disturbance, and the Riot Act was read on stage. A licence was obtained, and the theatre re-opened followed by differences among the proprietors which seriously threatened its success.

The Circus was destroyed by fire in August, 1805; it was rebuilt and re-opened at Easter, 1806. In 1809 Elliston took up the lease. He introduced several of Shakespeare's plays, and tried to raise the character of the house to enlarge the privileges of his licence. Up to then dialogue was not permitted except if accompanied by music throughout. In 1810 there was petition to the House of Commons to enable the Theatre to show,

> 'all such entertainments of music and action as are commonly called pantomimes and ballets, together with operatic or musical pieces, accompanied with dialogue.'

The petition was rejected, on the ground that it would,

> 'go far to alter the whole principle upon which theatrical entertainments are at present regulated within the metropolis and twenty miles round.' [194]

Tom Dibdin, in 1816, offered his services as stage-manager under Elliston, the Circus was extensively altered and re-opened as 'The Surrey,' which he managed until 1822. After 1822 the theatre had a chequered existence, and focused on sensational melodramas. Later, Thomas and Ann Matilda's son, Tom, was a bridegroom in a performance of Don Giovanni (alternatively 'A Spectacle on Horseback') in 1826.[195] The Lord Chamberlain did not have censorship powers over St George's Field giving the Theatre managers a little more freedom that on the North side of the Thames.[196]

Thomas and his developing career

Thomas appears to have filled his professional diary reasonably well. There had been a hint at connections to property or at least an inheritance in the wedding announcements in the newspapers in Bath and Bristol 1805, but these are not apparent from the London records of the time. It is likely the happy couple stayed with his mother, Mary Ridgway, from their arrival in London that Easter, 1805. Mary had a close connection to 17, Tower Street in the parish of St George the Martyr and the adjoining parish of St Marys Newington, St Georges Field where Thomas and his expanding family lived over the next decade or more.[197] It is not known where Thomas' 'handsome property' talked about in Bath was, and if it existed.

Thomas' pressing London engagement mentioned in the Bath and Bristol press at the time of the announcement of his and Ann Matilda's marriage was likely to be the one in which he performed at the Royal Amphitheatre, Astleys in April 1805.[198] In August 1805 the Circus was burnt down. 1805 to 1815 was a decade of turbulence for the London theatres and many of the performers, like Thomas, had to duck and dive between theatres and venues. It is likely that he took up his performance work at more than one theatre for a season. He appears fleetingly in newspapers, playbills and other literature of the time. During the quarter century after his arrival back in London he appears to have worked at Sadlers Wells, Covent Garden, Drury Lane and the Surrey (also known as the Royal Circus). He also appeared in the Circus in Liverpool. The same job descriptions follow him wherever his name occurs in records: harlequin, choreographer and dancer.[199]

The state of the London Theatres around 1805 to 1810

Not only did the Royal Circus burn down in 1805, but this was followed by a similar fate for Covent Garden in 1808[200] and Drury Lane in 1809.[201] The Astley amphitheatre was a rather different type of building, and this had burnt down in 1803.[202]

Many of the Theatres were built of wood and highly flammable materials and in the days before electrical and gas lighting the stages were lit primarily by large numbers of candles. In any circumstances where props and theatrical dresses were flounced around the candles a major fire was often the consequence. A contemporary print, encapsulates the fear of fire in theatres. While Thomas was part of the Charles Dibdin company, at the Sadlers Wells Theatre in 1807, some 18 people died in the stampede following a mistaken fire 'alarm'. The print shows audience members throwing themselves out of boxes and upper circles in the chaos.[203]

> 'the house was lighted by glass chandeliers in front of each circle – 270 was candles was the nightly supply; 300 patent lamps lighted the stage and the scenery.'[204]

Limelight came late and was not necessarily safe either. A consequence of the hiatus of theatre destruction and rebuilding cycle in the early 1800s meant there was a dislocation of leading actors and supporting theatrical personnel, some London players would choose to make tours of the provinces, whilst others would move rapidly to London. Egerton, for instance moved from Bath to London in 1808.[205]

The London theatre: the contemporary movers and shakers

Thomas Dibdin records in his own theatrical biography seven London theatres in 1824; the Drury Lane, Covent Garden, Haymarket, Lyceum, Surrey, the Coburg, and the Adelphi. The book also contains 100 names of leading actors and actresses of the time, of whom 37 were female. Names like Madame Vestris and Grimaldi, the famous clown Thomas worked with, are included, but not the Ridgways. Thomas Dibdin didn't regard Thomas as a 'principal.'[206]

On the home front: Ann Matilda's primary role, 1805 to 1807?

Living in St Georges Fields, not far from the Surrey Theatre, Ann Matilda followed in her mother's footsteps. During the decade after she and Thomas came to London as a married couple at Easter 1805 she gave birth to six children. If she had expected a life as a respectable Mrs Ridgway she had been in for a rude awakening.

She was thrust upon the London stage first just a couple of months after their arrival in Southwark, when in July and September she made her London debut.[207] Possibly Thomas was a man of weaselly words –he may have boasted in Bath that he was a man of substance, shortly to come into a fortune, and that Ann Matilda would never need to work. This did not happen. She was propelled onto the Royal Amphitheatre stage - seemingly into productions in which Thomas also performed - whether she needed to earn her keep, or whether she jumped at the opportunity to keep on the stage. Either way she was initially type cast, she danced her famous hornpipe and played the part of Columbine to London audiences at the Royal Circus (also known as Astleys, later Davis') by the time she was 15 in September 1805. She had also appeared there for several days in July. She performed in a benefit production for her new husband amongst others, for the benefit of Mr Robert La Toise, Mr Gourid and Mr Ridgway. Mrs Ridgway played a principal character….and 'for this night only will dance a hornpipe in the character of a British sailor.' Mr Ridgway was Harlequin Albion.[208]

The following year, in 1806, saw Thomas occupied on stage at the Astleys Royal Amphitheatre, where he was working, among others, with the three young Giroux sisters.[209] This particular year must have been a tragic one for Ann Matilda and Thomas, their first child, Thomas Joseph was buried. Poignantly the burial date is close to that given in a newspaper announcing another stage performance by both Ann Matilda and Thomas.[210] In the dearth of information about Thomas Joseph, a probable scenario is that baby was stillborn or lived a very brief life, likely unbaptised, he was probably buried within a couple of days of his premature death. At this time tradition was that only men attended funerals, so Thomas may have come fresh from his first son's funeral to act his Harlequin part on stage.

The Ridgway home area: Southwark

Thomas had bought his young bride to one of the less sought after areas of the capital. The town of Southwark was the largest town in the county of Surrey at the time and for many years had a dubious reputation for bawdiness, prostitution, the theatre and was known as the 'Borough'. It was unhealthy, noisy, crowded, and distinctive from other parts of London. It contained courts, prisons, factories, hospitals, shops, inns and wharves. The inhabitants ranged from the medical experts, inn keepers and wharf owners, to the shop keepers and small business owners, to the prison staff vagrants and other unfortunate residents. A number of eminent doctors made their names at Guys Hospital including Richard Bright and in 1799 it was the first hospital to appoint a dental surgeon. Nearby St Thomas' hospital was also important.[211]

Nearly all the residents rented their homes from private landlords in the Borough at this time. For many, there were shared facilities and an intermittent water supply. Few buildings survive from 1805 in today. However the prestigious Trinity estate survives somewhat intact in 2013 – this includes Harper Road which had later connections to Thomas Ridgway.[212]

The Borough was one of the most unhealthy areas to live and adult death rates, infant mortality and infant life expectancy were among the poorest in London. In 1857, in St George's parish, a few decades after Ann Matilda lived there, the number of people per acre was 184 compared to the London average of 30. Schools were mainly based on the churches and in 1808 the Newcomen Charity built its own school in the area though there is no evidence as to how Ann Matilda and Thomas educated their children. The prison buildings undoubtedly added to the grim surroundings: Marshalsea Prison moved to close to St George the Martyr's church in 1811, this was the prison in which Charles Dickens' father spent time in 1824. Despite the threatening surroundings communications were good for the time. There was a Post Office in Borough High Street in the early 19th century and the railway movement became important in the 1840s with frenetic building of lines and stations from 1839 to 1844.[213]

The street in which the Ridgways lived, Tower Street, had a mixed history. It is a turning off the Westminster Bridge Road. A plan of St George's Fields of the 1760s shows the land which later became Tower Street as owned by Rev Thomas Clarke. Another map, of 1807 illustrated the proposed new layout of the area – certainly shortly after Ann Matilda arrived in Southwark there was extensive redevelopment and much of the former cultivated land was consumed by housing.[214] In 1813 James Smith wrote.

'Saint George's fields are fields no more;

The trowel supersedes the plough
Swamps, huge and inundate of yore,
Are changed to civic villas now.' [215]

Ann Matilda and teenage motherhood

Her production of children was similar to Bathsheba's, roughly a new baby
every couple of years. Between times, in the early days, she was doubling up as
a performer at the Adelphi Theatre. The early death of Thomas Joseph was
likely to have been difficult for her, a teenager in a big city with the new
Ridgway family. Four other sons followed,[216] Thomas Frederick Ridgway born
in September 1807 and George Norman Ridgway born in November 1808. Both
these older two were baptised at St Marys, Newington, giving the presumed
address as Kennington Park Road. The three later Ridgway children were listed
at arriving at 17 Tower Street and baptised at St George the Martyr,
Southwark.[217] Both churches are near to each other, it is possible that Ann
Matilda and Thomas lived locally in Kennington Park Road in St Georges
Fields before moving to Tower Street – probably coinciding with a move of the
older Mary Ridgway who appeared to start paying the rates on that property in
1811.[218] Ann Matilda's subsequent three Ridgway children were: John Henry
Ridgway born in August 1811, the only daughter, Marian Ridgway arrived in
July 1813[219] and the final Ridgway child Charles, in July 1815. Being a mother
was no joke in the 19th century, many women would die in childbirth, and
surviving mothers would typically witness the deaths of many of their children.
Women had few rights and almost no right to property or keeping their children
if their marriage failed.

The atmosphere at the Ridgway home in Tower Street may well have been very
similar to that of the house where the young Loders were raised before John
Loder's death; there was a discreet theatre culture with rehearsals, learning
songs and lines, music, costumes and storage issues. There may well have been
a piano and other musical instruments. There may have been servants. Mary
Ridgway may have been helping out or managing professional and or domestic
activities. There is no illuminating evidence.

Focus of Thomas' career 1805 to 1813: Harlequin, Pantomimist, Dancer

Thomas' career would have had priority. Much of Thomas' time was devoted to
work at Sadlers Wells Theatre, under the management of the younger Charles
Dibdin. Thomas appears to have had a positive long term business relationship
with Charles Dibdin the Younger, who described Thomas, 'who was in his
grade of performing, taking skill and versatility of talent together, unrivalled'.[220]
Thomas appeared in Sadlers Wells' productions managed by Charles for seven

years from 1806 to 1813, 'we engaged too, Mr. Ridgway, the Harlequin and Pantominist and Dancer, who continued with me for seven years.' [221]

Thomas didn't work exclusively for Charles Dibdin, he performed as ever as a Harlequin at the Astleys in 1806, performing with the Giroux sisters whom Ann Matilda later must have had contact with at the Sans Pareil Theatre.[222] His apparently favoured role, Harlequin, was immensely popular at the time. There were many different types of Harlequin. The Harlequin role was a precursor of both the 20th Century roles in Pantomime and opportunities for a male dancer. In one Harlequin role, Harlequin Asmodeus, in 1810, Grimaldi, the famous clown, made the vegetable man that may have contributed to the Frankenstein story.[223]

After a break of around seven years Thomas worked again closely with Charles as a member of his management team in the 1820s. In parallel he was also part of the dance corps during some parts of the seasons at Covent Garden from 1807 to 1810.[224] Besides developing his career as a dancer, Thomas also had a try at direction, whilst in Bath in 1805 he had directed a 'new Ballet dance called The Coat and Badge' in which he and his wife-to-be took parts[225] and he devised a dance in 1807.[226] The Percival Collection at the British Library gives a little colour to Thomas' early career at Sadlers Wells. It gives notices of Ridgway as a harlequin and choreographer from 1807 to 1809 at Sadlers Wells; as a dancer in a benefit performance on 3 November 1807; introducing Hastings, his pupil, and devising a dance at some other date in 1807; dancing as Jongbongee in Charles Dibdin's 'The White Witch and Slave', Harlequin in Dibdin's pantomime Thirty Thousand in 1808, and as Harlequin in Dibdin's pantomime Fashion's Fools in 1809.

Under Charles' management of Sadlers Wells at this time Thomas appears often in supporting roles. Charles wrote that he, 'engaged for the next season,' (1809-10), the supporting players included, 'Ridgway to be with Grimaldi' in the Aqua Drama, 'The Wild Man'.[227] One of his performances with Grimaldi was captured by the press on Friday 26 July 1811 when mention was made of a new comic pantomime at the Aquatic Theatre, Sadler's Wells in which a new comic dance was performed by Mr Ridgway in 'Hearts of Oak'. Mr Ridgway played Harlequin Selim and Grimaldi was one of the other performers.[228]

Thomas' close relationship with the Sadler's Wells 'Company' came to end in 1813. Charles records that, for the season 1813 in the new pantomime,

> 'Mr Ridgway played the Harlequin with us for the last time, as at the close of the season he left us, for the Amphitheatre, Westminster Bridge.'[229] [This would have been the 'Astleys' Amphitheatre]

This last performance may have been around the Summer 1813, when the Times newspaper noted on Tuesday 6th July 1813 that the Harlequin was played by Mr. Ridgway at Sadler's Wells [230] A week earlier Thomas had performed in a play written by Charles, The Brachman; or Oriental Harlequin.[231] Later in November 1813 Thomas was off to Liverpool as the pantomimic Joey.[232]

Ann Matilda develops her act on the London stage

While Thomas was pursuing his dancing career in 1807, and the family appeared to be settled in St Georges Fields something did not add up to the picture painted so positively in the Bath and Bristol press in early 1805. Perhaps his career was not living up to his anticipated earnings, or maybe Ann Matilda was frustrated being at home with the growing family and possible in laws. Ann Matilda may have been in demand as a performer. Either or both of them might have got into debt. Whatever the reason it appears that Ann Matilda was not sitting at home like a lady, she was working actively on the London stage, from 1805 for several years. More famous celebrities than Thomas were near the financial breadline, Grimaldi was often close to bankruptcy despite a high income, earning £625 in benefits in 1812.[233]

The kind of stage Ann Matilda stepped on was a specialised one. Her appearances in plays with him were of the rowdy, extravaganza type in which there were lots of devices to attract and amaze the audiences. Some were influenced by the Prince Regent's taste for things Chinese, others involved horses and other animals on stage. Chunee, the largest Indian elephant ever seen in England had been introduced around 1812 and had to be coerced into 'performing' by tots of rum.[234] Thomas' acts were usually in the more 'rough and ready' type of performance, than serious melodrama.

After Ann Matilda's forays into the London stage with her husband at Astleys in 1805 and 1806 she started to perform in plays without him. Whatever the reason for the intensification of her stage career Ann Matilda was a regular performer at the Sans Pareil Theatre (later named the Adelphi Theatre) from 1807 to 1810.[235] During this time she must have invested a formidable amount of energy into her stage performances while also working through pregnancy and motherhood of a growing number of babies. She was 17 years old in 1807.

In June 1808, before embarking on what seems like a long innings at the Sans Pareil, she appeared at the Theatre Royal Covent Garden; she is mentioned a couple of times, once, for the benefit of the four misses Adams, Mrs Ridgway was Ivy, in allegoric ballet called the Oak and the Ivy.[236]

Ann Matilda, as Mrs. Thomas E. Ridgway, performed in the Sans Pareil 1808 summer and the 1808/9 season, both as Columbine; it appears that she also appeared in this role in 1807. Ann Matilda's performances and roles played have a familiar ring, she took roles similar to the ones she played in Bath. Her performances are recorded as Columbine (48 times) in Mother White Cap (3 Apr 1809 - 27 May 1809); principal characters (34) in Rozelli and Rosa (1 May 1809 - 10 Jun 1809); Two Little Savoyards (40 times) in Two Little Savoyards (24 Apr 1809 - 10 Jun 1809); Hornpipe in character of British sailor: (06 Jul 1809).[237]

Likewise Ann Matilda was in demand as a performer for the Sans Pareil during the Spring and Summer, 1810, the summer season. The list is significant and an exhausting schedule: principal characters (15 performances) in 'All Alive in Greenwich' (23 Apr 1810 - 9 May 1810); Statue Columbine (6) in 'Fiery Cauldron' (25 Jun 1810 - 30 Jun 1810); Fortune (45) in 'Fortune's Gift' (28 May 1810 - 15 Aug 1810); Mary Ann (12) in 'Intrigue' (11 Jun 1810 - 30 Jun 1810); Fanny Maythorn (18) in 'Jack Grapplehard' (27 Aug 1810 - 15 Sep 1810); Susan (30) in 'Little Aaron' (7 May 1810 - 16 Jun 1810); principal characters (12) in 'Love in a Village' (23 Apr 1810 - 5 May 1810); Malvina (45) in 'Oscar and Malvina or the Hall of Fingal' (26 Jul 1810 - 15 Sep 1810).

In this hiatus of activity, for these seasons, Ann Matilda was amazingly busy. She played both principal and supporting roles. She either excelled at, or was type cast in her previous role of Columbine, but also continued her expertise as a dancer – specifically a Hornpipe in the role of a British sailor. Not much is known today about the works she performed in at the Sans Pareil, some were romances, some with lewd titles like 'Jack Grapplehard,' probably aptly named.

A reckoning of Ann Matilda's performances from April 1809 to September 1810 at the Sans Pareil, show that she appears in at least 12 plays, and is recorded as playing a total of 306 times. For the final three weeks of recorded appearances to mid September 1810 she was appearing in two plays simultaneously. Not bad for a nineteen year old girl from the provinces. This period of theatrical activity for Ann Matilda coincides with a convenient break in her known pregnancies: George Norman had arrived in November 1808 and it is likely she became pregnant with her third son, John Henry, around December 1810.

Ann Matilda and Thomas most likely lived in the Kennington Park Road, Newington Parish of Southwark from 1805 to 1811. Convenient as that area was for the Surrey (Royal Circus) Theatre where later Thomas performed, it wasn't quite so handy for the Sans Pareil Theatre in the Strand. It might have been hard for an actress to commute frequently for multiple performances from St Georges Fields to the Strand.

ENTRANCE *IN THE* STRAND.

London *Published d⁸Oct¹ʳ₁₈₁₆ by* Robert Wilkinson r⁹ Fenchurch Str.

Illustration IV The Sans Pareil Theatre c1806-1819 [later Adelphi Theatre]

(Copyright © 1988, 1992, 2012 by Alfred L. Nelson, Gilbert B. Cross, Joseph Donohue.)

It might have been hard for an actress to commute frequently for multiple performances from St Georges Fields to the Strand. She, or the family, may have had another base near to the Strand during the busy seasons, from which she may have performed more than once in a day. The contemporary Grimaldi performed three times in one night in 1815, laying on cabs from the Surrey Theatre, across the River Thames to Sadlers Wells to Covent Garden. On this occasion, John Fawcett, the step father in law of John David Loder, withheld Grimaldi's salary for not seeking leave to perform at another theatre.[238]

The Sans Pareil Theatre, later known as the Adelphi

The Sans Pareil, 'without compare', was a theatre developed by a feisty woman, Jane Scott, a performer and author, with the support of her father, John Scott. [239] Jane (1770 – 1839) was a contemporary of Ann Matilda and may have sought out talented actresses for her theatre.

> 'This house is worthy of its names, since all theatres in London it can claim to be the prettiest....His [Mr Scott] success is almost wholly to be attributed to the versatile talents of his daughter.' [240]

A press notice of the time states, 15 November 1807,'a new theatre, the Sans Pariel was opened on Saturday night. It is under the direction of Monsieur Giroux.'[241] It appears that Ann Matilda was involved from early on in this unusual theatre.

The Sans Pareil, in common,

> 'with all other theatres of their time, operated on a repertory system, under which a number of plays and other pieces were performed--normally several on any given night--in alternation with one another, over the weeks and months of the season. As a result, the bill changed from night to night, reflecting a managerial policy in which variety and its attraction for paying customers took precedence. When some piece or other proved to be sufficiently popular, however, it was likely to be repeated on succeeding nights; if not every night, then frequently, for as long as it remained in favor with audiences. Achieving a long run was the hope of every management, even though additional pieces were kept in readiness--and often mounted even while a long or moderate run was in process. In a repertory theatre, success in the form of repeated performance occurred within the context of constant novelty, which itself spelled success of another kind.'[242]

Along with her father John, Jane was a theatre manager, performer and playwright.

Ann Matilda and Thomas on stage together in Liverpool

In 1812, Ann Matilda's year off from childbirth, she and Thomas performed in Liverpool, at the Olympic Circus. Thomas had a creative streak and he is noted as a composer, 'new dance composed by Mr Ridgway called the Miser.' He also wrote a new ballad. [243]

Both Thomas and Ann Matilda continued to make excursions to Liverpool in 1813 and 1814 and performed at the Olympic there. Ann Matilda was on stage in January 1813, in the early months of pregnancy and the resulting press notice offers a possibility that the five year old Tom Ridgway was also a performer. On one of the occasions Ann Matilda sang a Ballad, and in another the press report records,

> 'Ridgway went through the part of Selim with spirit and discrimination, but his complexion was too light for a swarthy son of the East…There is a sweet and plaintive expression in Mrs Ridgway's countenance which gave much interest to the subordinate character which she personated'. [244]

Thomas Ridgway's career continues, 1813 – 1819

Although Thomas appears to have been respected by Charles Dibdin the Younger his career lingered in the shadows in both the circus and the theatre. He left Sadlers Wells for the Amphitheatre Royal (Astleys) and seems to have been invited back for a short production at the Surrey by Thomas Dibdin or someone working in the Surrey. His appearance at the Surrey again suggests he went for supporting roles. In November 1816 a playbill for the Surrey advertises from Friday next 'Silver Swan or the Wizards Dream' in which 'Miss Taylor and Mr Ridgway late of the Theatre Royal Covent Garden and Amphitheatre Royal will make their first appearance. [245]

A second playbill/poster of 1816 notes that he plays Rudiger, a German Knight November/December 1816. [246] Subsequent surviving playbills of the following year show another actor playing Rudiger, Thomas had disappeared from the Surrey.

Thomas is recorded in the Times newspaper, [247] performing at the Royal Circus and Surrey Theatre and dancing the pas seul 'by Mr Ridgway,' on 8 July 1818. Interestingly there is a 'Ridgway' noted as having performed a 'Hornpipe in Fetters', as a dancer in the last days of the management of the Sans Pareil with

John Scott. As no title is given for this Ridgway, it could have been Thomas Edmund or perhaps one of the older Ridgway boys, Thomas Frederick, who would have been around eleven years old in 1819, or nine year old George. This was on the 1 April 1819, on the 3 April Mr Smollett made the closing statement for that episode in the theatre's life. The Theatre reopened as the Adelphi. Ann Matilda was long gone from the Ridgway establishment.

Thomas never seemed to have made the centre stage, either in acting nor direction nor dancing. It is not clear that he was the leading harlequin either. Perhaps he was dwarfed by the stars like Grimaldi or maybe he preferred to specialise in a mixture of roles involving dance and humour as a supporting player. He appears to have been busy with lots of engagements, and would probably been sufficiently well paid to support his family. If he had come into inherited property it would have helped. When he died in 1829 he left, £100 which was moderately significant for that time.[248] He definitely wasn't poverty stricken.

Women who shook the stage: The petticoat revolution

Things were sluggishly changing on the stage in the early 18th century. The first real revolution for women and the stage had taken place when Charles II was on the throne. Changes in Restoration theatre permitted women to take female roles on the stage for the first time for many years. Actresses like Nell Gwynn in the 1600s had broken the male/female stage divide. A century later many women earned a living in the theatre alongside their male counterparts. It was not a respectable career though, and acting for women continued to be regarded as akin to prostitution until late into the 19th century.

One well known actress could be regarded typical of her late 18th century peers in some ways, Dora Jordan 'became a symbol of the strength a stage career could confer on a woman, and a warning of its dangers: independence, yes, and professional satisfaction, but also the risk of degradation.'[249]

Bit by bit the societal mold cracked. In the couple of decades around 1800 able and challenging women became prominent in and around the stage. With the parallel development and widespread distribution of newspapers, word got around about these actresses. There were many women who contributed to the stage revolution, easing the careers of their daughters and grand daughters in the late 19th century and beyond. These thespian pioneers of the 18th century conveniently provided excellent role models for budding stage performers like Ann Matilda. Several women, contemporary with Ann Matilda, made their mark in this quiet revolution. In the last two decades of the 18th century and the early

1800s there was a blossoming of female stage talent. They were in the news, their public performances were celebrated and criticised, and their private lives were picked apart in the press for everyone to see and digest.

Both in Bath and London Ann Matilda learned her trade from some of these women; how to survive in a world dominated by men and how to keep within the bounds of respectability yet achieve the family and professional life she wanted. She herself was part of this advancing change. The issues tackled by these pioneering ladies included the power imbalance between women and men, and the development of a new moral climate around the theatre. None of this happened quickly. There are some common threads with some of these women and Ann Matilda: starting on the stage as girls, relationship difficulties and broken marriages, and having several professional identities – acting, dancing, music, singing, writing. She may even have met and performed with some of them, as part of the petticoat revolution. Many women, contemporary with Ann Matilda, shook the stage and influenced young performers like her. Some of them were Francis Abington, Elizabeth Inchbald, Elizabeth Linley, Sarah Siddons, Dora Jordan, Mary Wells, Elizabeth Billington, Maria Theresa Kemble, Jane Scott, Maria Foote and Madame Vestris (Appendix 1).

The winds of change for Ann Matilda: 1815

1815 proved an eventful year in so many ways. Not only were the balances of international power changing, as the British won the day at Waterloo in June, banishing Bonaparte to the wilds of St Helena, but on a local level, for the Ridgways, lives were being reconstructed. The mother-in-law and rate payer, Mary, died in April. Perhaps her death initiated a series of events that we can only speculate on.[250] A couple years after the arrival of her daughter, Marian, in 1813, Ann Matilda again is 'captured' in the limelight, Ann Matilda – or just possibly another Mrs Ridgway, appears on stage again, on Tuesday 6th June 1815 – there is a advert proclaiming her performance as Joan, the wife of the cobbler in the Royal Circus - 'Henry VIII and the Cobler.'[251] At this time she would have been around seven months pregnant with her final Ridgway child, Charles, who arrived in August.

The two younger Ridgway children were baptised in the summer and Thomas continued his itinerant career going from theatre to theatre, and perhaps from town to town in search of the roles as a Harlequin. While he managed to be in demand for supporting roles, it must have become apparent at this time, aged around 35, that his most active dancing days were over. To put it bluntly, there must have been a realisation that he was past his sell by date for lead dancing parts.

On the positive side Mary may have left some kind of financial legacy and Thomas was certainly known as a 'Gentleman.'[252] Mary's death may also have 'released' both Thomas and Ann Matilda from keeping up the pretence of a happy family. Thomas may have started to develop relationships with other women or perhaps men. Certainly Ann Matilda's eye started to wander. She was 25 years old.

What were the Loders doing from 1805 to 1815?

Ann Matilda's brother John David married Rosamund, 'Rose' Mills in 1808.[253] She was the same age as him, and also came from a theatrical background. Her father died when she was very young, her mother remarried the comedian John Fawcett and Rose probably spent her early years brought up in his household, Rose's mother died when she was a child. John in effect brought her up. He was a leading actor in London in the 1790s and around 1800 became interested in pantomime, where he wrote, and worked with Charles Dibdin at the Haymarket Theatre. His and Charles' plays, like the 'Enchanted Island', were performed there in the years when Thomas Ridgway was acting there in the three or four years before he married Ann Matilda. As John David was often travelling from Bath to London in the period 1800 to 1808 he would have been familiar with his sister's family – a possible connection and introduction to his future wife.[254]

> 'From 1799 to 1836 he played in the Orchestra at the Theatre Royal [Bath], most of the time as leader. From about 1812 his annual benefit night there became a considerable occasion, with visiting celebrities from London.'[255]

John David had regular employment leading the Bath Theatre and the subscription concerts in the winter months, from 1812 when he was in was in his mid twenties.[256] In the summer John David led the grand galas in Sydney Gardens.[257] John David was a busy man, whether he could and did support Ann Matilda in the next stage of her life is unknown.

Ann Matilda's disappearance: the start of the missing years, 1815

Ann Matilda's last formal appearance as a Ridgway family member was at her daughter's baptism on 9th August, 1815 at St George The Martyr, Southwark, London. The baptism is rather odd seen from a 21st century viewpoint. The youngest son, Charles, was baptised (at the age of two weeks) the previous week, on the 4th August. The best explanation is that the baptism of the only daughter, by then aged two years, warranted an extra special occasion. The role of godparents was especially important in the 19th century. It was likely that many children would lose their parents at an early age and the role of godfather was a serious one – and godparents were expected to come along to the baptism ready to pick up the pieces if necessary. Ann Matilda and Thomas had had four surviving sons and may have been running out of appropriate godparents for the boys, perhaps the daughter was considered special – Marian would have had two godmothers and one godfather. It is possible that one or more of these were from the Loder family in Bath, John David being a strong candidate as godfather.[258] Ann Matilda's last recorded stage appearance as a Ridgway followed a few weeks after these baptisms, on 27 September she appeared at the Astleys amphitheatre as 'and Jenny' in a production of 'Blindmans Bluff.'[259]

Speculation: why did Ann Matilda walk out on the Ridgway family?

Ann Matilda left the Ridgway household, that is certain. Whether she was pushed or attracted out and when this was is unknown. Unless and until spectacular evidence is found one can only presume that there were various possibilities. Ann Matilda must have been desperate and/or strong willed to leave the Ridgway home in Tower Street. She had no inherited money or property, and she had no legal rights to any of the Ridgway resources or property. She had no rights to care for or make decisions for the children.[260] If she 'walked out' on Thomas she could have been destitute and reliant on others to make her way. Her next long term partner, about whom there will be more later, John Distin, was not a wealthy man, nor from a wealthy background.

There are a number of possible theories concerning Thomas and Ann Matilda's separation, there is no evidence to support any one of these. On the Thomas-the-rogue set of theories, Ann Matilda may have been mistreated by Thomas, physically, emotionally. He could have used the occasion of his mother Mary's death to start having affairs, perhaps bringing back partners to Tower Street, displacing or threatening his young wife. At a more moderate level he had failed to make the centre stage, it is possible he had had pretences to grandeur – the inheritance he was shortly to come into when he married in Bath, in 1805, his description as a 'gentleman' may have disguised an actor supreme who had more limited resources and was bound in the end to let people down.

Ann Matilda's couple of years on the stage from 1808 at the Sans Pareil, and then her continuing one-off experiences on stage may have demonstrated that the family urgently needed money. Perhaps Thomas was wanton in his behaviour, and his lifestyle could not be accommodated on his middling income as a second rate clown or dancemaster. In 2013 there has been no additional evidence of Ann Matilda's career as an actress after 1815, but it is possible she contributed in other ways to the family coffers – she may have given piano lessons or coached actors. Possibly career wise she was more passionate about her piano playing than being drafted onto the stage to bring in some more money. Looking into her future, she focused definitely on performing music. Perhaps this was her real passion.

On the other side of the separation coin, Ann Matilda may have met the young John Distin and the pair fell deeply in love. She must have had considerable attractions, she was a talented actress and only 26 years old in late 1815. Distin and other potential suitors would have known that she was the mother of five children with no great wealth.

When a woman married in the early 19th century, everything became her husband's, her wages or her own property. She could not incur her own debts nor sign contracts. In practice some of these rules were loosened.[261]

She may have planned an escape from Thomas and squirrelled away her own earnings. She may have had friends, and even networks including Loder relatives who could have helped her as she made her exit from Tower Street. Care of the five Ridgway children is a moot point. Although all the power was in the hands of the father, practice had ameliorated the law informally to recognise mother's rights by 1815. The later Custody of Children Act in 1839 was no use to Ann Matilda.[262] Certainly, if the recent role model of Dora Jordan was followed, women would have had some informal access and care rights for children under seven years old. This would definitely have included John, Marian and Charles Ridgway. This opens the possibility that Ann Matilda took another household and looked after the younger three children, although this seems unlikely as she would move herself to Plymouth in the next year or two. It was more traditional for actors and actresses to put their children into the care of a family or informal boarding school. Certainly this is what happened to Ann Matilda's grandson George a couple of decades later and also to Ann Matilda's later daughter Louisa. So maybe one or two of the Ridgway children were boarded out.

Thomas and Ann Matilda may well have sought a 'third way' to separate. They were in the theatre. Lots of their fellow theatrical friends would have multiple or serial partners. London was especially cosmopolitan, with famous people like Dora Jordan and the future William IV who provided iconoclastic role models, demonstrating effective ways to break society's 'rules'.

Au revoir to the Sans Pareil

The freethinking theatre in which Ann Matilda had performed for two or three busy years closed on 3 April 1819. An advertisement stated: 'persons having any demands on this concern are desired to send in their accounts with all convenient speed, that the same may be discharged.' The Sans Pareil closed its doors for the last time before reopening under new management as the Adelphi Theatre.[263] Ann Matilda had left it eight or nine years earlier.

On 18 October 1819, the theatre reopened under its present name, which was adopted from the Adelphi Buildings opposite.[264] Ann Matilda had flown. She had quit Southwark and London theatreland at least two years before.

A speculative view on Ann Matilda's adolescence and early adulthood

One of the many plausible theories about Ann Matilda in this decade, 1805 – 1815, is that it started, for her, with an unpleasant shock. She was duped by her new husband. If she had been persuaded by the promises that she would never need to work again, she was let down and back on the stage in weeks after her arrival in London. The streets of Southwark were not the most salubrious and she was under the management of an elderly mother in law. Her new in laws had included a recent pauper. Her first child, born when she was just 16, tragically died. She was drafted onto the stage in roles to support her husband who never quite lived up to his pretensions. A magical episode began in 1807, when she was talent spotted by the new management of the Sans Pareil Theatre and she joined the 'Company' there for three years taking on principal and supporting roles.

Why this phase of successful acting abruptly came to an end is uncertain; her acting may have been wanting, her intensive regime of child birth and rearing may have created serious problems, or Thomas stepped in to limit her professional advances. After this Ann Matilda retired again to play supporting roles, mainly with her husband in Liverpool and London.

Something snapped in the Ridgway household following the death of Mary, the mother in law. Ann Matilda was unhappy with the new situation, and so possibly was Thomas. It released them both. Neither of them appeared on the stage in Liverpool in the early 1816, as they had in the previous couple of years. There may have been some passionate scenes in Tower Street as their relationship deteriorated. In the spring 1816 the Grenadier Guards and their band triumphantly returned to London and it was time for a new romance to be born.

Matilda: change of direction, change of name. The early Distin years 1816 – 1829

A magnetic attraction? A social pariah?

While nothing is absolutely certain in the Ann Matilda story, it seems very likely that she became, for the rest of both their lives, the only partner to the talented young musician John Distin. It is certain that he and Ann Matilda moved in similar circles. Her step father, John Richards, was described as a bandsman, her brother John David was fast becoming a well known musician in Bath and often performed in London. Two of the children of her younger brother George (George and Kate Loder) were later to spend considerable time in London and were well connected to the musical world. John Distin may also have had connections to Bath; it was not far from his early career in Devon. Through now unknown networks someone like John Distin may have been offered piano lessons by Ann Matilda, or met each other in a multitude of situations. One way or another they met and a relationship commenced.

> 'John was a handsome man, as he stood on the concert platform.'[265]

He must have been dazzled by Ann Matilda's talents and skills. She had five young children, was almost four years older than him, with no known assets. She must have been amazingly attractive to him. When and how she joined John is unknown, so too is how she called herself. She may have been called 'Matilda' since childhood, but from snippets of information available it would seem she wanted to be known as Matilda from the start of her relationship with John, this possible 'rebranding' of herself might have covered her Ridgway links, but it is a matter for conjecture.[266]

The mores of the time

There was a moral shift in society in the 18th and 19th centuries. In the century from the early 1700s the age at marriage dropped, the bastardy rate rose from 2% to 5% and the percentage of pregnant brides increased from 15% to 33%. These changes contributed to the expanded population of Great Britain from five million in 1701 to eight and a half millions in 1801. Religion played a big part in peoples' lives although different Christian groups had different views on the rights of women. The Church lost its legislative powers over sexual matters in the mid 18th century and slowly the moral climate had changed.[267]

Escape from Tower Street to Plymouth

Ann Matilda appeared, as Mrs Ridgway, with her husband at the Astley's amphitheatre in September 1815. The first of the Distin boys, George Frederick, was born at the latest in April 1818 in the Plymouth area.[268] It was on her escape to Plymouth for the forthcoming birth that she may have changed her name to 'Matilda Distin',[269] presenting a new image to the world. Whether she talked of her first marriage as a disaster area, of herself as a wronged woman, or whether she simply airbrushed the Ridgways out of the life she presented to others it is unknown. She may have acted the 'widowed lady.' It is more probable is that she braved it out, either portraying herself as the wronged woman or a party to a mutually agreed separation.

She was back in London for the birth of the next Distin son, Henry on 22 July 1819.[270] Here, she would have been moderately well known, staying within walking distance of the Astley's Amphitheatre where Thomas performed at that period of time. She probably started to settle into her new life as 'wife' of a Grenadier Guards bandsman, and they probably lived in accommodation related to the band. The next Distin son, William, arrived in regular succession, probably around the summer of 1821, born in 'Middlesex.'[271]

An interesting 13 years? Matilda morphs into a musician, pianist and composer

This was an exhilarating, exciting and challenging period for Matilda and John Distin. It is also part of her 'missing years' episode, from the age of 26 to 38. In all likelihood Matilda left Thomas in 1816. She was an actress and presumably could keep up whatever appearances were required. Besides her appearance as the mother of their fourth son Theodore, in 1823 there is only one trace of her in these dozen years. There is no evidence of her appearing on the stage as an actress from the autumn 1815. Much of her energy was devoted to her maternal role – mothering the four Distin boys, and possibly other young Distins who may have been born from 1824 to 1830.[272] It seems likely that she was a significant player in helping her partner John to build and shape his career. She was also reshaping her own career. Naturally a performer, bought up in a family of musicians, she would have been encouraged to learn to play the piano from an early age. As the mistress of a Royal bandsman she would have watched the antics of the Duke of Clarence and understood the fate of his abandoned long term mistress and actress – Dora Jordan. Dora died about the time Matilda had moved away with John. During this time Matilda was in the wings and her life can only be surmised by looking at what her 'partner' John did.

Socially she was in a vulnerable situation, she was an unmarried mother of four boys who later became talented musicians. They would have been groomed and trained in the music business from an early age. The family lived with the Royal Band entourage, for part of this period, sometimes in Windsor, sometimes in Brighton. They were presented as husband and wife, she called herself Mrs Distin. As a previous actress on the London and Bath stage there was a strong possibility that she would be recognised. Her legal husband, Thomas Ridgway must have known about their arrangements, he might well have known where they lived in Westminster and Middlesex from 1819 to 1821. Thomas was busy working nearby and he started introducing their Ridgway sons to the stage during this time.

In response to the widespread scandals, including the dubious role of the sons of George III, there was an active attempt to legislate on adultery. The planned legislation was 'blown apart' in 1811 when Prince George took the regency when his father, George III, entered the final debilitating period of illness. This left a legislative vacuum on matrimonial issues for decades, making it hard for those in unorthodox relationships like John and Matilda.[273]

Distin the rising star: his early years and the South Devon Militia band[274]

John Henry Distin was born in January 1794 in the small rural community of Plympton St Mary.[275] Not much is known about his parents, John Distin[276] and Susannah Tucker[277] who had married there – his mother was illiterate, signing the register with a cross.[278] He had an older brother Thomas, and maybe other siblings.[279] It is likely that young John spent his early years in the Plympton parish, a little way outside Plymouth. [280] He was talent spotted as a boy, according to his son, at the age of 11. This would have been around 1805, perhaps at the same time as his future bride, Ann Matilda married Thomas Ridgway.

> 'at 11 years of age, he in company with his brother two
> years younger, appeared in public in a flute duet at a
> concert given by the Band of the South Devon Militia, and
> not only achieved great popular success, but so impressed
> the band-master of that regiment that he obtained their
> enlistment as band boys under his instruction.'[281]

The South Devon Militia band was an official reserve army made up of conscripts and volunteers.

> ' The band of the South Devon Militia probably had a
> corps of drums, a fife group or a corps of bugles, which

was used for military parades, but whatever the make-up of the band, John Distin was given a bugle, a keyed bugle and a trumpet to play. The difference in the technique required to play a bugle and a trumpet is not great, except that the register required for the trumpet is often much higher and therefore much more difficult. However, at the age of fourteen John was invited to play the trumpet part in a performance of Handel's Dettingen Te Deum at a grand musical festival in Exeter in 1812 and was rewarded with a fee of £10.. ... The trumpet which John played was a slide trumpet; this was the instrument in common use in Britain at that time. Its usual spring-loaded slide and set of crooks was capable of full chromaticism but was a very difficult instrument to master.

The South Devon Militia Regiment spent most of 1812 and 1813 in the north Midlands and an advertisement in the Sheffield Mercury shows that John Distin was engaged to play principal trumpet in the Sheffield Festival Orchestra while he was stationed in the area....... Unfortunately, in November 1812 the South Devon Militia band, of which John Distin was a member, was the cause of a fatal accident. 'As Mr. Kirkby and his son returned home from chapel in his gig, the horse took fright at the noise of the drums which were beating for the evening parade of the South Devon Militia.' The horse bolted and Mr. Kirkby was subsequently killed and his son injured.'[282]

As a military musician from an early age, John Distin became familiar with professional freelance musical engagements and got to know about the broader musical life. He must have realised that he had developed expertise which was in demand and that such expertise could open career opportunities for him.

The South Devon Militia regiment returned to Plymouth in December 1813 and was demobilized in August 1814. By now unknown means John Distin came to London and enlisted in the renowned Grenadiers Guards' band. This was an important appointment to a prestigious position in an outfit that was considered the best in the country, at that time. This band was significant because of the strong influence professional military bands had on the developing amateur brass bands. According to the Musical Times of 1907, 'British military music seems to have had its origins in the Grenadier Guards.'[283]

John Distin and the Grenadier Guards

King Charles II laid the foundations of the Grenadier Guards band when he commissioned 12 hautbois (early oboe) players to the First Regiment of Foot Guards in 1685.[284] The Regiment became known as the Grenadier Guards after their victory on the battle field at Waterloo.

The Grenadier Guards band is symbolic of London and British history. It has been present at all the major royal occasions: births, coronations, weddings and funerals. Over its three centuries long history the band has travelled abroad frequently. One visit included Paris in 1815 after the Battle of Waterloo. John Distin went as part of this trip.

John had enlisted in the band of the 1st Regiment of Foot Guards (which later became the Grenadier Guards) in Plymouth on 5th November 1814, at the age of 20.[285] John was 5ft 8 inches tall on enlistment and he served until 5th November 1821.[286] During his employment with the Guards he was, at the age of sixteen, a solo keyed bugle player.[287]

> 'The band of the 1st Guards, at that time, was quite small by today's standards with between twelve and nineteen musicians with an instrumentation of a mixture of wind and brass instruments but, like most bands during this period, the choice of instruments was left to the preference of the players or the personal choice of the conductor who was in this case, Mr. James Blaney. 1814 was the beginning of changes in the makeup and character of bands in this country and abroad which was brought about by the rapid development of instrument design and manufacture.'[288]

The band sailed from Brighton to Dieppe on the 10 September following the Battle of Waterloo in the summer of 1815, and John was part of the band. It joined the service battalions in the Bois de Boulogne, and performed there. John was known as a virtuoso performer on the keyed bugle and he attracted the attention of the Grand Duke Constantine of Russia, and a Parisian instrument maker, who copied the instrument and from this the family of musical instruments known as the Opheleide was invented and developed.[289] The Opheleide was significant because it provided the brass family of instruments with its first adequate chromatic bass instrument.

It was an exciting time to be a bandsman, and their march towards Brighton to travel to Paris was recorded in the papers,

'Yesterday afternoon a few minutes before five o'clock,
Mr. HUNTER, the Kings messenger, arrived in Downing
Street with dispatches, from Paris. The Band of the 1st
Regiment of Foot Guards received orders yesterday
morning, to hold themselves in readiness to march
themselves for foreign service'.[290]

It was a time of immense patriotism and a contemporary diarist in Paris says,

'To-day we went to Colonel West's to hear the Band of the
1st Regiment. It is a remarkably fine one and we heard it to
the greatest advantage, the pieces of music being well
chosen, and the day fine. On our standing while the
National hymn was playing, great astonishment seemed
excited among some French ladies who were present; poor
creatures, they cannot comprehend the feeling that
pervades every British heart on hearing "God Save The
King."'[291]

The Duke of Kent had encouraged keyed bugles in most British bands by the
time of the occupation of Paris in 1815.[292] These bugles were louder than
conventional models. Bands that had keyed bugles were thought to be, by
contemporary commentators, to have provided psychological advantages to the
British in their victory at Waterloo. The bands of the 1st Grenadier Guards, the
Coldstream Guards and the Scots Fusilier Guards spent almost half a year in
Paris after Waterloo, all three had good keyed buglers in their ensembles.
Sergeant James Blaney, the Irish bandmaster of the Grenadier Guards, was a
friend of Halliday who was the inventor of the keyed bugle. Henry G. Farmer
documented an account of the growing popularity of the keyed bugle in Europe
as a result of a parade given after the Battle of Waterloo; this may have been the
occasion recorded by Colquitt in September 1815.[293] At a review at which the
Grand Duke Constantine of Russia and other Allied dignitaries were present, the
band of the Grenadier Guards and its star keyed bugle virtuoso, John Distin,
attracted attention.

Henry Distin, John and Matilda's second son recalled this story eighty years
later. Henry backs up Farmer's version of the incident. Henry's account
describes the details of the purchase of the keyed bugles by the Grand Duke, a
transaction in which a black Janisary musician participated.[294]

John was on the payroll of the Grenadier Guards, and there were 35 band
members. They were each paid £1.12s 6d for four months a year and £1.6s for

the other months. The cost of a new keyed Bugle was £10.10s – a significant expense. [295]

> 'The most important figure in the development of keyed bugles was John Distin, of the famous family of touring musicians, and 'solo keyed bugle' player with the bands of the Grenadier Guards. In 1817 he developed, in conjunction with a French instrument maker, a family of keyed bugles in various sizes.' [296]

In 1816 John Distin was an attractive proposition

Fresh from his French trip John returned with the Grenadier Guards band around spring 1816. He must have been regarded as a potential good match for any girl in search of a partner. He had made his mark in the band, and mingled with international aristocrats; he also moved in similar circles to Matilda. Two family networks may have facilitated the introduction of John to Matilda sometime in 1816 or earlier. These networks were critical for professional success in the music industry. John David Loder may have been a catalyst, he was busy in the London and Bath music worlds. A second family connection that could have facilitated a meeting between John and Matilda was that of the Bath born Lucy Philpot.[297] Lucy was seven years younger than Matilda and came from a similar musical world in Bath. As a highly talented pianist she came to London in 1818 and married the well known violinist, George Anderson in 1820. George was a member of the Kings band during the reign of George IV and later. Lucy was to be later pianist to both Queen Adelaide and Queen Victoria. Lucy later tutored Kate Loder, Matilda's niece, who achieved fame as a pianist in the 1840s. George Anderson and John Distin must have worked together in the Kings band, and probably known each other before the Regency ended in 1820.

What was Matilda doing as a bandsman's wife?

It is hard to know how Matilda spent her time as a military mistress. She devoted some time to her role of continual mother, producing two sons, George and Henry within the four years or so of John's second half of Guardsman band service. She may have focused on perfecting her own musical skills, particularly playing and even taking on pupils for the piano. There remains a possibility that she coached her own children, both Ridgways and Distins. Teaching music provided a good career opportunity for women – especially for those wanting their daughters to have lessons, there appeared to have been heightened competition for pupils in the 1820s and 30s.[298] It is unlikely that the Grenadier Guards women lived in the communal barracks, although it is possible.

Up to the time of the start of the French revolution there were no barracks for most soldiers, but with the threat of war and invasion there was a major barrack building programme in England from 1792. The barracks were not pleasant places for a recently married couple, married soldiers were permitted to install their families in the corner of a dormitory room on a couple of beds, with a makeshift curtain giving a minimal of protection from other soldiers.[299] Given that their second son, Henry John was born in 1819, in 'Pimlico' it is likely that the couple had digs in the Pimlico area and that John walked the short distance from Pimlico to the Headquarters of the Guards in 1819.[300]

The state of the nation from 1815

There had been a sea change in the nation during Matilda's girlhood and early adult life. The UK population more than doubled from 9 millions in 1800 to 20 millions in 1825 and the march towards industrialisation and urbanisation accelerated – developing the cities of Manchester, Birmingham, Leeds, Sheffield and others. Newspapers mushroomed in the 1820s with papers like the Manchester Guardian and the Scotsman read by the literate and disenfranchised.

The end of the wars with France, in 1815, saw a big shift in society in the UK. There were 200,000 disbanded soldiers and a recession in the following years. In 1819 there was the famous Peterloo Massacre in Manchester, and a year later, in 1820, there was the Cato Street plot which had aimed to assassinate cabinet ministers. George IV was a particularly disliked king and his estranged wife, Caroline was popular. On the occasion of his lavish coronation, on 19 July, 1821, he had to hire thugs to prevent Queen Caroline from entering the coronation. This was an occasion when John Distin would have performed as a Guardsman for the new King, and inevitably would have needed to take a pro-monarchy stand at these types of occasions.

The early 1820s must have been a particularly challenging time for Matilda, as there was an enormous public groundswell of support for the wronged Queen Caroline, and if the fellow Grenadier Guardsmen and their friends had known that Matilda and John had an unconventional relationship, it could have put the spotlight on the couple and their illegitimate Distin children. The Distins were based around Middlesex and Westminster in 1820 – not far from the Ridgways – so a likely conclusion is that Thomas Ridgway knew where they were but chose not make a public fuss about Matilda leaving him.[301]

John Distin joins the King's band

John Distin left the Grenadier Guards' band to become a member of King
George IV's Household band, formerly known as The Prince Regent's band
which was stationed at Windsor. This would have been after his release from the
Grenadiers in November 1821. He and Matilda joined the broader company
there and had two or possibly three toddlers, under five years old with them at
that time. John had contributed to the development of the Royal Kent Bugle,
having received a special invitation from the Duke of Kent himself, and became
a member of the King's private band as trumpet-player and solo bugle-player.[302]
This was a position he held, enjoying the especial favour of the King, until the
monarch's death in 1830. The bandmaster and Master of the King's Music was
William Shield from 1817 to 1829 and from 1829 to 1834 was Christian
Kramer. Kramer was also responsible for the recruitment of musicians and was
often sent abroad to scout for good players. Kramer was a much respected
musician.[303] The master of music in the Royal household was entirely
responsible for selecting and managing the musicians of the Kings band.[304]

'King George IV, who was very musical himself, took a
personal interest in his musicians and on one occasion
enquired after Distin's absence from a performance, which
was brought about by a sore lip.[305] John Distin was
regarded as the best keyed-bugler of his day, and as a slide
trumpeter he was also thought to be without rival.'

'Mr. Distin .. is utterly without rival in his mastery over
the trumpet, perhaps the most intractable of all
instruments. In his hands it is made subservient to every
intonation; from the passage which starts the hearer like an
electric shock, to the softest cadence. His execution is
wonderful- brilliant energetic and thrilling; and anon,
delicate, and smooth, and finished too, by, unquestionably,
the most perfect shake we ever heard. His finest
performance is, perhaps, his celebrated solo, the voice part
of "The Soldier Tired". No one who witnessed it, and
possesses the smallest appreciation of what real excellence
is, can easily forget the effect produced. It is a
performance full of true genius, and we were glad to see it
acknowledged by the audience last week at the concerts
given in the Athenaeum –room, in this town.'[306]

There is a discrepancy. Not only was Matilda absent from the eye of history, but John doesn't appear in the limited records of the Royal household. He is not named as a bandsman in the Royal household records of 1823 and 1830.[307] The explanation was that George IV, the ever extravagant and music loving monarch had his own 'private' band as well as making use of the Royal household band.[308] This developed from his private Prince's band and was separate from the King's household band which was administered by the Lord Chamberlain; the latter having some members appointed for favours. The private band had no sinecures.[309]

Christian Kramer was the bandmaster of the private band, which had 42 players at some times, with a preponderance of German players and a large number of instrumentalists who played brass instruments. Unfortunately there is no complete list of the private band members.[310] John played the English slide trumpet and the keyed bugle.[311] All the band's players were personally known to George when he was Prince – and presumably later when he was King. They wore elaborate uniforms covered with gold lace and the trumpets and drums were of solid silver. The Prince's band practised daily from 11 until 1 in the morning when the Regent was away, but when the court was in Brighton they played from 9 until 11 in the evening and were given supper and a pint of wine. Rossini spent three days with George IV at Brighton in December 1823 and the band played some of his music arranged by Kramer.[312] The private band was said to have cost between £6000 and £7000 per annum.[313]

Perfecting the piano playing

Matilda's early life must have included some musical training, an element of which was usually getting familiar with the piano; boys tended to learn the violin, girls the piano. The piano started life in around 1700 and developed six octaves by 1810, and seven octaves by 1820. During the prolonged period of peace in Britain after 1815 the economy prospered and the middle class grew. One of the first domestic sign of this new middle class was the piano. Trapped around the rules and rituals of the King's private band, it is likely that Matilda would have ready access to pianos, and that perfecting her next 'craft' would be an excellent way to pass the time.

In the early part of the 19th century songs were published with piano accompaniment. Charles Dibdin the elder introduced it at Covent Garden in 1767, and Drury Lane had an official pianist in 1770. However the piano did not replace the harpsichord in the King's band until the early 1800s. There was a great variety of pianos in the 1830s (grands, squares, upright grands, upright squares, cabinet pianos, table pianos, giraffe pianos, lyre pianos), but Robert

Wornum's cottage piano became most popular and his designs developed from 1811 to the 1830s and 1840s.The grand piano continued to be the first choice for the concert platform; the upright was considered a domestic instrument. Pianos though were luxury goods:

> 'Wornum's cottage pianos sold for between 42 and 75 guineas in 1838, while a Broadwood's price list of 1840 puts the cost from 44 to 80 guineas (their grands cost 90-125 guineas, and their squares 38—85 guineas)... These prices have to be measured against average middle-class incomes of £100-500 a year.'[314]

Illustration V. A piano from around 1840, similar to ones Matilda may have played. From the Baines Collection, University of Oxford.

Matilda the composer

During this phase Matilda lived at Windsor, alongside other staff and their families in service of the King, George IV. She wrote and published several melodies for the piano or harpsichord.[315] She had these published privately and dedicated them to Lady Coyningham – who was the quasi live in mistress of the king for the period.[316] Perhaps a driven person, Matilda may have focused much of her time on perfecting her piano playing, and possibly was able to offer lessons to others around her, including her Distin boys in the 1820s. Her publication and its dedication would be an ideal opportunity of making herself known and appreciated in the Windsor court.

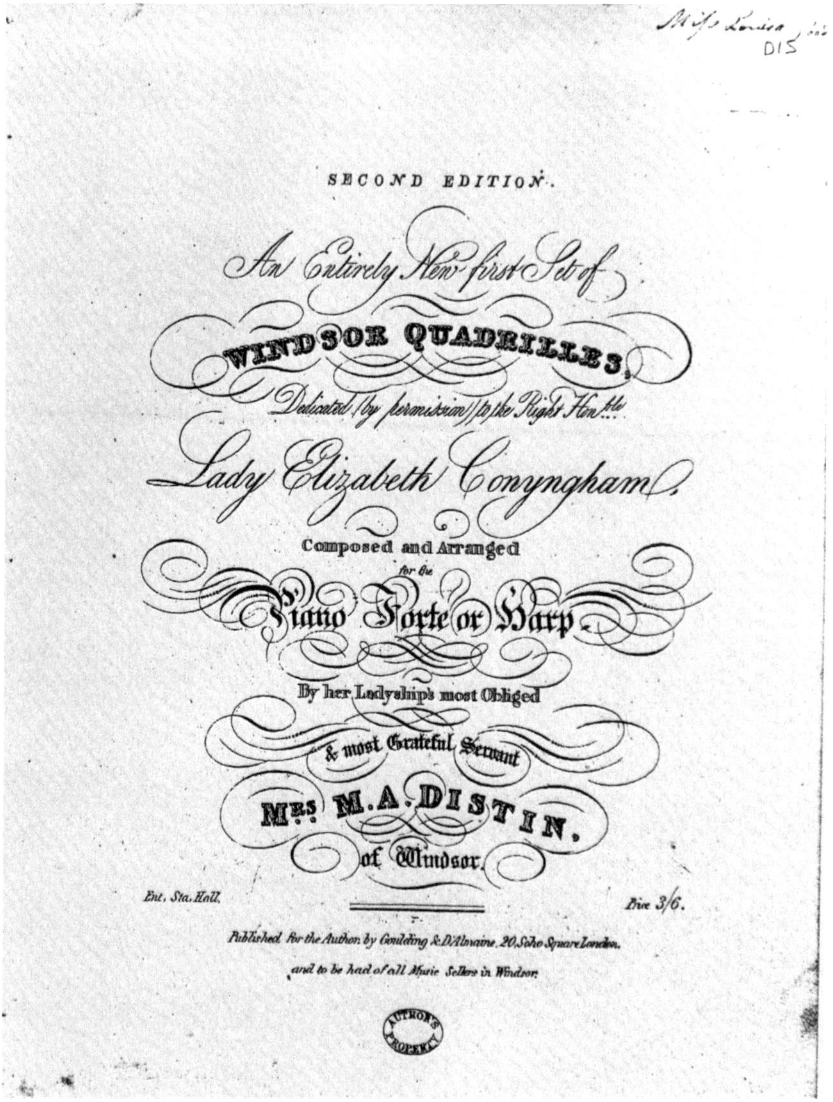

Illustration VI. Mrs M.A. Distin, National Library of Australia, Bib ID 1426588 "An entirely new first set of Windsor quadrilles, dedicated by permission to the Right Hon'ble Lady Elizabeth Conyngham".

The Kings band

Life in the King's band must have had considerable kudos. Positions would have been sort after and the band members would have had considerable respect from the musical fraternity. The King was known for his appreciation of the arts, and music in particular, although he was the centre of fierce and comic criticism for many things, including his weight and his mistresses. At George's coronation, for instance,[317] 19th July, 1821, it was the hottest day of the year and he arrived at Westminster Abbey 30 minutes late, a female witness said,

> 'anyone seeing this disgusting figure, with a wig the curls
> of which hung down his back, and quite bending beneath
> the weight of his roles and his sixty years would have been
> quite sick'.[318]

In the early 1820s George would demonstrate his enthusiasm for music, and after dinner the entire company would retire to the music room where the King would often sing to his guests accompanied by his resident orchestra, the Kings band. 'With over seventy musicians this was as large as any modern symphony orchestra.'[319]

Over time, the King's ill health was exacerbated by his increasing weight. He continued most evenings after dinner to entertain guests in the music room. As late as 1828 his voice remained strong, and he would join the musicians in singing. George had some paranoia about the dangers of the London crowds, and whilst he spent much of the first half of his reign in Brighton he found a mysterious prophecy had been written on a downstairs window and from then there was a decision to move from Brighton to Windsor – this move took place in 1826.[320]

When George was in the Royal Lodge at Windsor the band was stationed in the conservatory of the Lodge. John and Matilda's youngest son, Theodore, was born during the nine year period John was in the King's band. Theodore was born in Brighton in 1823 and John recorded his occupation as a Royal Bandsman for the occasion.[321] Their third son, William may have been born during John's last few months in the Guards or early in his Royal band career.

From Windsor, George liked to make excursions to an Island in Virginia Water, he and his mistress Lady Coyningham would be rowed, and alongside them was a larger boat with the King's musicians on board to entertain the guests.[322] In the later years of his reign, 1826 to 29, he continued to enjoy these trips and as the

Royal party arrived at the landing stage the band would strike up 'God save the King'.

What happened to the Ridgways in the 1820s?

The deserted Thomas kept a busy life. He maintained a close relationship with Charles Dibdin and appears to have become a member of a Dibdin management team in the 1820s. He continued to perform on stage, sometimes with, sometimes without his sons, Thomas, George and John who were around 13, 11 and 9 years old in 1820. The three older Ridgway boys began to develop their careers in the same style as their father during the 1820s. Charles the youngest Ridgway was five. Thomas performed at the Davis (Astleys) Amphitheatre, the Surrey Theatre and maybe elsewhere. He was appreciated for what he did. It is almost certainly Thomas who appears 'in the greatest collection of pantomimical talent ever assembled on a single stage.'[323]

It is hard to know whether Matilda had any personal contact with Thomas. Her children knew how to contact her as they must have done when he died in February 1829. She married John Distin within six weeks of Thomas' death, she appeared to want everything to be above board.

Some of what Thomas got up to is recorded by Charles Dibdin (the Younger). Charles managed the Davis Ampitheatre early in this decade, which had changed its name from 'Astleys' Amphitheatre. Charles wrote of the Davis Amphitheatre in the season 1822 to 1823,

'a young debutante, named [Miss] Louis (a pupil of Ridgway's)' with 'strong natural genius, and great versatility of talent, proved essential service to me.'[324]

Thomas' performance was captured in the press in October 1822 –' Davis's Royal Amphiteatre, Westminster-bridge - masters Ridgway a comic pas de trois; new melodrama 'The parricide''. Ridgway is included among principal characters.'[325] Charles was often writing new plays and he wrote that he had written a Melodrama, and continued,

'My Stage Manager and Mr. Ridgway, brought me, on the said Thursday morning, a paper of that day which contained a very short paragraph, merely intimating that a Melodrama, in which Diligence was robbed, was attracting **tout le monde** at Paris.'[326]

Preparing for Christmas that season Charles Dibdin recorded, 'Ridgway was my Harlequin and Miss Louis my Columbine.'[327] The previous season, Thomas had played alongside the famous clown, Grimaldi, for the benefit of Mr. T. Dibdin, at the Surrey Theatre, March 26, 1822. Grimaldi played his old part of Squire Bugle, in 'Mother Goose,' Ridgway again being the Harlequin.[328]

Thomas appears to have been a reliable substitute, understudy and someone who sourced new materials. After the 1822-3 season Charles Dibdin established himself at the Surrey Theatre and noted that Thomas was one of his minor stars, 'I had many minor theatrical Stars….Ridgway'.[329] Thomas filled in parts when needed. In June 1825 Charles bought in another new piece from Paris, 'Jocko.' A series of actors failed to keep going in one of the main parts in this play; one dislocating his ankle, and then 'Mr. Ridgway also played it for a night or two.'[330] Thomas supported a well known and up and coming acrobatic actor, known as Gooffe [or Gouffe]. 'Mr Ridgway practised chimpanzee, also took place of his substitute.'[331]Thomas also seems to have taken the initiative and possibly wrote or sourced plays,

'Mr. Ridgway bought a one-act piece, called Juan Fernandez, or the island ape. This was for the purpose of exhibiting Gouffe. The story of the piece was from that of Alexander Solkirk; from which it is said, Defoe took his idea of Robinson Crusoe.'[332] However this did not last long as 'Gouffe was re-engaged, and, as he had really worn out Mr. Ridgway's Ballet Pantomime, the Island Ape.'[333]

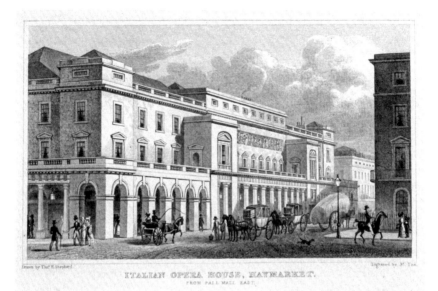

Illustration VII. The Haymarket Theatre London in the mid 1820s

In 1825 father and two elder sons were performing together at the Surrey Theatre, Tom, junior would have been 19, George, around 18 years old.[334] Charles also writes about Thomas' general skills and those of his sons,

> 'We engaged ...Miss Louis (our Fanny Kemble)...with Mr.Ridgway, our Ballet Master, Principal Dancer, Melodramatist, Harlequin etc. and his two elder sons, who possessed both talent and popularity.'[335]

At the time of Charles' own benefit night, in September 1826, near the end of the summer season of '156 nights', a benefit night, partly for Thomas, was arranged, 'On the evening following my Benefit another Novelty was produced for the Benefit of our Treasurer and Mr Ridgway.'[336]

In 1828, on the occasion of Grimaldi's farewell Benefit, Mr. Ridgway and his two sons also lent their assistance. The Ridgways were an esteemed pantomimic family. Tom Ridgway was a most excellent clown in the days of Madame Vestris's direction of Covent Garden, and he survived to help Mr. Phelps at Sadler's Wells during a season or two.[337]

The Ridgways continued to perform at the Adelphi just as their mother had done a few years earlier. Either John Ridgway or Thomas F. Ridgway performed in the seasons 1827/8 and 1828/9.[338] Charles Dibdin, writing in 1830 of Thomas Ridgway, notes,

'He also died lately and there are three of his sons now upon the stage, who possess much merit, and promise to follow the steps of their father.'[339] These sons that Dibdin describes were Thomas Frederick [Tom], aged 22, George, aged 21, and John 19.

Thomas, like his wife Matilda linked up with another partner, he married Elizabeth Mihill on 15 September 1828.[340] His bride was 16 years old. He died four or five months later, so it may have been that Elizabeth was regarded as a nurse. They married at a familiar place, St Mary Newington where the first two Ridgway boys were baptised. The letters of administration related to his estate note that he was from Harper House, Harper Street. This is very close to Tower Street [in the 21st century named Morley Road] where the family had lived earlier.[341]

Matilda in the shadows

Not much can be gleaned about Matilda's character from this shadey period in her life. Essentially she went to ground while John was a Grenadier Guardsman and member of the Royal band. What does seem evident is that she didn't appear again as an actress under a familiar name, Loder, Ridgway or Distin. Initially it appears she shunned the public eye in London to go to Plymouth for the birth of the first Distin son, George. However she returned to live in London, and possibly face the music, from 1819. The apparently missing baptismal records for the first three Distin sons may indicate that those records were hidden or disguised in some way. These three boys were born while John was a Grenadier Guardsman.[342]

Another almost certainty was that John and his new mistress were short of money. His meagre Guards salary was insufficient for a lavish lifestyle and a growing family. The need for money perhaps with a passion for music may have encouraged Matilda to look for income generating opportunities for herself and to start publishing her own musical compositions. It is possible to detect an entrepreneurial streak in Matilda with her dedication of the work to Lady Coyningham in this dark period of Matilda's life. Otherwise her developing personality is conjecture.

Matilda: the Distin years and fame 1829-1848

A marriage

Matilda formally broke her ties with the Ridgways soon after his death and had rejected any link to Thomas Ridgway's estate.[343] Barely had Thomas gone cold in his grave then Matilda and John married, by license,[344] in London on 17th March 1829. They were living in the then fashionable area in the capital. The church where they were married, St George's, was close to Hanover Square, Westminster, Middlesex.

1829 - 31: years of ups and downs

1829 to 1831were years of transition, not only for the country, but for Matilda and her family. The early 1830s were years of monumental change in the UK. There was a new monarch – the oldest one to take the British throne at 64 years old, and the political temperature was changing fast. In his short reign there were mammoth social and legal changes. There had been a series of poor harvests in the early 1830s and in response the New Poor Law was introduced in 1834 – the same year as the famous Tolpuddle Martyrs set up their friendly society. The Factories Act had been passed the previous year, 1833. The Great Reform Act was passed in 1832 after significant Parliamentary revolts, and the iconoclastic Slavery Abolition Act was passed in 1833.[345]

For the Distin family 1829 had started reasonably well. The death of Thomas Ridgway in February had enabled the Distins to marry and achieve respectability. Two of the younger Ridgway children were left in limbo whereas the elder Ridgways had made it onto the stage in the same style as their father by the time of their father's death. Matilda's only daughter, Marian, was sixteen at that time, and needed a home. She may have spent some of her childhood with relatives in Bath. Whether her early teenage years were spent in Bath or London she was almost definitely trained for the stage and had learnt to play the piano by 1829, these skills would equip her later for a career as a piano teacher and actress.[346]

Circumstantial evidence suggests that Matilda helped out Marian in the early 1830s, so Thomas' death may well have resulted in some urgent matchmaking to ensure the young Marian had a suitable husband. Thomas Elliott offered a reasonably good marriage prospect. He was from a business family with resources in Bristol.[347] Marian married Thomas in Bath in December, with Matilda's brother John David as a witness.[348] A year or so later Marian and Thomas' relationship may have been under strain and Marian supported their new family by taking an acting job, or jobs in Edinburgh for some time in the early 1830s. Her first son, Frederick was born in Edinburgh in 1833.[349]

The early career of the Ridgway 'baby', Charles, was associated with making clothes. He was 14 years old when his father died and by then must have been apprenticed – most likely to a theatrical tailor.[350] Whether or not he had any involvement with his mother at this time he was, like his elder brothers, in the same geographical and performance world as she was. The Ridgway boys could still have been a source of anxiety, fraction or support for Matilda and her new family. It was also around this time, in 1832,[351] that her second Ridgway son, George (Norman) died at the age of 23 of consumption in Glasgow.[352]

There was another death in the family. Early in 1829, Matilda's younger brother, talented flautist and pianist, died in Bath.[353] He may have been ill for some time, as in 1827 the Bath Journal announced,

> 'Mr G LODER most respectfully informs the Nobility,
> Gentry, Flute Amateurs; and his Friends, that his health
> being re-established since his return from the Continent, he
> continues to give lessons on the above named Instrument,
> and the Piano Forte; and will be happy to perform on the
> flute at Concerts and Musical Parties as usual.'[354]

George's oldest son, George, later to become a moderately famous musician, was 13 at the time of his father's death, and it was at this time he was apprenticed to his aunt, Frances, wife of Andrew Loder junior.[355]

A year after John and Matilda's wedding the prestigious job with the King's band ended, with the death of George IV in June 1830 and the inevitable clean sweep made by the incoming monarch and his entourage.[356] When George died the band members were dismissed and John Distin was made redundant. John took a leadership role to argue for a better deal for himself and the displaced bandsmen.

The bandsmen were asked to return their uniforms which were heavily coated with gold lace and had cost seventy five guineas each. John led the dispute, 'through the instrumentality of John Distin the Lord Chamberlain withdrew the demands for the coats.'[357] John promptly sold his uniform for twenty five guineas. John's leadership role was a success and his own career prospects did not appear to suffer from the stance he had taken. He continued later to play for royalty, he played a major part in the coronations of two monarchs including William IV's in 1831.[358]

John's redundancy from the King's band left the Distins without the steady and reasonable income of the Royal band. It may have necessitated a relatively quick move to central London. Matilda and John must have had a base in London in March 1829 for their wedding and it is likely that they kept up this foothold for some time. While John was busy job and contract hunting in 1830 and 1831, Matilda fell pregnant, probably for the final time, and gave birth to her second daughter, Louisa Rose, in December 1831.[359] The family base was in Gillingham Street, near Hanover Square, where Louisa was born at this time.

Matilda's brother, John David, was encountering difficulties. He had developed a career that involved performing regularly in both Bath and London. In the patchwork of activities in this career path there must have been a lot of travel and stress. In 1815 he became an associate of the Philharmonic Society (later the Royal Philharmonic Society), two years after its foundation; he performed in several prestigious concerts each year in the Hanoverian Music Rooms, near to the St George's church where the Distins married. In 1822 he had suffered from a mental breakdown and his doctor suggested rest in Exeter. In a letter that year he wrote about his ailment, 'which has materially increased of late.'[360] In 1830 he was still based in Bath but performing throughout the British Isles. He was criticised for being out of his depth in London.

'But Loder had yet to make the full transition from the provincial to the metropolitan and acceptance by the media. In 1830 the Examiner had described him as impatient and apt to set the wrong tempo. It continued. "We once heard him play the very deuce with a symphony of HAYDN'S at the Philharmonic Concerts. Mr LODER may take a hint from King James's recommendation to the Members of Parliament to retire to their country seats, because like ships in a river, they then become objects of admiration; whereas in London, they were like ships in the sea, which diminished to insignificance. Mr LODER is a first rate in Bath."' [361]

After the Kings band: Mr and Mrs Distin from 1830

It seems that John Distin found work easily in London after his Royal band work was over. He was 37 years old in 1830, Matilda 40, neither in their prime for the times. Initially he found work as an orchestral player in London.[362] His career may have been given a boost by Matilda and the Loders in April 1832. He appeared then in Bath at Widcombe Newchurch. A Bath musician, Viner welcomed him and wrote a harp obbligato for the occasion.[363] One of the other places he found work was the Adelphi theatre – suggesting that Matilda was helping him find work by reigniting the memories of venues where she had performed in her teens. Three Distins performed at the Adelphi on the 7th August 1832, one on the Trumpet and two 'masters' on the French Horn.[364]This was John and two of the boys, possibly George and Henry, the older two.

Bandmaster to the Marquis of Breadalbane

John went to Scotland for several years, from around 1831 as bandmaster and trumpeter in service of the Marquis of Breadalbane. The latter's vast seat was Taymouth Castle where John Distin presumably lived and worked with Matilda and his family.[365]

The Marquis of Breadalbane was a 'new creation' in 1831. The first Marquis was John Campbell and he died in 1834 when his son took over.[366] The second Marquis, another John Campbell, had a very active national political career and had served as an MP in the 1820s in Devon. It could well have been that John Distin and the Campbells' paths had crossed in the previous decades and when the Royal band was disbanded in 1830 the first Marquis was keen to step in and employ the Distins. Other 'noble' families at the time would typically employ their own band. Long term living in the castle would probably be a mixed blessing. Today, it stands on a remote and stunning location in the Scottish Highlands, the nearest town being Perth, 36 miles away. It is 80 miles from both Glasgow and Edinburgh.[367]

The Breadalbane estate gave John Distin a steady income and a base he could launch off from. As he was approaching 40 in 1834 he had to maintain an income for his wife, four sons and baby daughter. Although he had the Breadalbane job he may have spent some time travelling back and forth from London to Scotland. Some of the Distin children may have been left in London for some of the time. George certainly was old enough to start an apprenticeship. John, 'put his eldest son, George, upon trial to the jeweler's trade.'[368] John was in London for the Adelphi performance in 1832. The middle two boys, Henry and William, were given some training in the Royal Academy of Music in 1834.[369] They were both initially horn players and would have been aged 15 and 13 in 1834.

The times when John Distin was under contract to the Marquis were times when he and the family zig zagged across the United Kingdom. John and parts of his family played on the stages in Edinburgh and Aberdeen. In 1834, for instance he was in Aberdeen, and was reported as giving a 'wonderful fantasia' on the trumpet at a sold out concert. 'Numbers went away unable to gain admittance.'[370]

Theodore and the baby Louisa, may have been left in care for schooling and training in London or travelled with John and Matilda to Scotland. The journey to Taymouth in the 1830s from Scottish cities would have been substantial, and although the Marquis must have travelled to and from London for the appropriate seasons, it would not have been a journey to take young children too often. The role for Matilda is open, she may have spent time with husband and children, she may have coached them, she may have spent time playing the piano. As with other women of the time there were the usual domestic and craft occupations. Perhaps the Distins were preparing themselves for a relaunch and considering ways to start on the next stage of their family 'career.' It is possible that Matilda kept in contact with at least some of her Ridgway children and may have given Marian's acting career a 'leg-up' by enabling her to get on the stage in Edinburgh. Maybe it is more than coincidental that George Ridgway's last days were spent in Glasgow, perhaps his mother offered to support his care for his final consumptive months. There is no evidence either way.

The Distin band is born and starts to develop in Taymouth

Although John was in service to Breadalbane estate for several years,[371] he wasn't in Taymouth all that time. Things started to change in 1835.

John started feeling aggrieved about his financial and professional situation and wrote to Sir Andrew Barnard, one of the Patrons of the Royal Academy of Music (RAM) asking him to use his influence about this strained financial situation. John also revealed that he left London under a cloud. He complained that the cost of living in Scotland was excessively costly for his large family and overall sounds indignant, and deceived.[372] The catalyst seemed to be impending debt. Matilda and John had sent their sons Henry and William to study for six months at the Royal Academy of Music and with John's annual salary of only £100 and a high cost of living in Scotland, they could not repay their debts.

Whatever ripples this letter caused, it resulted in a change of the arrangements and from 1835 John started to appear in concerts, both in Scotland and elsewhere. He actively started taking up offers to pay at other venues, especially when the Marquis was not around in the season, usually the summer months.

The Scotsman of 11 July 1835 mentioned The Distins, the private band of King George the Fourth, playing at the Adelphi [in Edinburgh]. The following year a paper of the 16 April 1836 announced a forthcoming concert for 'the nobility and gentry of Edinburgh' in Hopestoun on April 21.'[373]

A dress rehearsal for the Distin band 1836

After complaining about his impoverished financial situation John and family appeared on the stage in Edinburgh several times in April. He also made a trip to the continent. Matilda's name is not given in the press and it is possible she stayed behind the scenes either in Edinburgh, Taymouth or just was not reported by the press. Newspaper records note that John appeared with his four sons, giving an address in the city. One newspaper report states the Distins' philanthropic endeavours: Mr Distin was 'suddenly and severely indisposed' therefore the concert postponed until Saturday 30th. The article refers to the 'generous and feeling sympathy he lately shewed the suffering whalers in Aberdeen, by devoting the entire proceeds of a night's benefit to relieve them'. Most interesting is the suggestion that John was leaving shortly for Europe and this was to be his last appearance in Edinburgh – 'being on the eve of visiting the continent in his professional capacity.'[374]

An overview of the Distins: travelling musicians from 1837 to 1844

> 'The Distin family (John, the father, and his four sons, George, Henry John, William Alfred and Theodore) were one of the most successful instrumental ensembles in the history of Britain. Their performances as a brass quintet, and later quartet, became legendary.'[375]

And,

> 'by 1837 John Distin had abandoned Service life and with his sons, and wife as a pianist, had embarked on the remarkable series of concert tours which were to take them all over Europe and to America during the next eighteen years.' [376]

The Distin performance band was a quintet which originally consisted of a slide trumpet, three hand horns and a trombone. Instruments were played by John himself, and his four sons, George, Henry, William Alfred, and Theodore. For some time, the instrumentation was a slide trumpet, a cornet, two hand horns, and a slide trombone.[377] John himself played star performances and one of the early special events that he played at, as the principal trumpeter, was the coronation of Queen Victoria [1838].[378]

After quitting the secure but impoverished base in Scotland the Distins started to branch out in a big way. The Illustrated London News 1844 mentions the group's recent performances at M. Julien's concerts. It recorded that the Distins had performed some 700 concerts in Scotland, Ireland and England.[379] This equates to around 70 concerts a year from 1835 to 1844. Ticket prices for concerts varied and ranged from five shillings to one guinea.[380] During the first seven years (1837 -1843) they successfully toured Britain Matilda usually accompanied the quintet on the piano. Very often local artists, mainly vocalists, participated in their concerts. Later, a couple of members of the extended family, particularly 'A.T.Loder', and Kate Loder appeared in the family's concerts.[381]

At some time they set themselves up with a base in London, maybe returning to one they had kept in reserve, possibly with Loder relatives or others. Alternatively they simply had a business use address. From Gillingham Street in 1832,[382] the Distins used the address of 30, St James Square in London in 1836.[383] At some stage in the early 1840s they lived at 3, Duke Street, Manchester Square – from where John wrote another letter and publicised the band.[384]

From the mid to late 1840s the Distin family lived, or was based at, 31, Cranbourn Street, London.[385] A new cut through road, 'proposing a new street from Coventry Street to Long Acre' was constructed about 1840[386] and Cranbourn Street is given as the Distin address from the late 1840s.[387] The Times mentions a Distin 'repository' at 31, Cranbourn Street, Leicester Square, and also the address is given for the No. 1 of Distin's journal, 2s 6d.[388]

On the road

Travelling around with large musical instruments and a group of teenage boys was no joke at that time. Travel was a key issue to a band. The ability to move around had been critical to the moderate success that the older Loder brothers had in the late 18th century, with regular travel from Bath, Bristol, London and other towns like Weymouth and Swansea. Matilda had gone through the Bath to Bristol commuting stage herself as a young teenager. In Jane Austen's times early in the 19th century travel was 'time consuming, costly and uncomfortable' and around ninety percent of the population never travelled far from where they were born.[389]

In general the early years of the 19th century saw the start of a transport revolution on the roads. Canals were constructed and developed from the late 18th century, railroads from the 1830s. The Liverpool to Manchester rail line opened in 1830 and the following decade, the 1840s, was known as one of railway mania.[390] Roads and the vehicles were improved during the decades of Matilda's lifetime. The newspapers of the time were full of adverts for the opportunities for the mobile to move, travelling was expensive, substantially more than a theatre ticket in London, and it was also uncomfortable and hazardous. Travelling with four young boys, possibly a toddler or baby, and with large and expensive musical instruments was time consuming and challenging.

> 'THE CHEAPEST TRAVELLING TO LONDON AND NO FEES. Is by the NEW STAGE COACH COMPANY'S BRISTOL, BATH AND LONDON elegant light Post Day Coach, carrying four Inside, leaves the CASTLE AND BALL, every morning at a ¼ before 8 o'clock and arrives at Hatchett's Hotel, Piccadilly, in the evening at ½ past Eight o'clock ……. Route – Chippenham, Calne, Marlborough, & Reading. FARES – Inside……£1.16s. Outside ….18s. Allowance of LUGGAGE to each passenger, Inside 50lbs, Outside 30lbs. Dine at the King's Head, Thatcham, at 2s.6d per Head. ALSO THE NEW COMPANY'S NIGHT COACH TO LONDON. Route – the same as Day coach – every afternoon at 3 o'Clock…….' [391]

In 1841, in Scotland, Matilda's brother, John David Loder was involved in a carriage accident, having experienced an earlier accident in 1813. The press report described the scene,

> 'proceeding from Glasgow in a carriage to Edinburgh, where he was to lead at the Grand Musical Festival, The Vehicle, we understand, was upset, the driver thrown from his seat and killed on the spot by the fall of some heavy luggage on his head … Mr Loder escaped with only some slight bruises, but was greatly shocked by the dreadful accident.' This description demonstrates the risks and dangers involved in travelling around the country at this time. [392]

The Distin band is launched in 1837 and Matilda is part of it

John kept in contact with his aristocratic boss for many years after he departed the castle in Taymouth. The first steps for the early band were cautious, it was a family affair, and it initially made a small tour around the North of Scotland, from June to September they played in Aberdeen, Banff, Elgin, Inverness and Glasgow. [393]

The contemporary accounts eulogise about the family and their performances. The fact that these were reported in the national publication, 'Musical World', would have guaranteed the band future bookings and current kudos. Two reports describe the early days of the band in Scotland.

'Our old friend Distin the trumpeter, has been giving concerts with his two clever boys, who were, when we heard them some time ago, extraordinary horn players for their years, which could scarcely exceed nine and ten. Distin himself is a very fine player of the trumpet; in tone and execution only second to Harper.'.... 'speaks in terms of great admiration of the perfect unity of the three performers on their several instruments ... His little daughter of five years of age, it seems, also gives much promise of future excellence as a singer, her pronunciation being remarkably distinct. They are certainly a clever family.'[394]

It was noted that the father was one of George IV's wind band.

'We perceive by the Inverness Courier that Mr. Distin, with his wife, four sons, and infant daughter, have been making a very successful professional tour through Banff, Elgin, Forres, and Inverness.' The article continues that although the little boys had been 'remarkably clever performers' when [the writer] had heard them, they must have now 'attained a rare proficiency' if the report in the Inverness Courier is to be believed. It claimed that what 'the first musician of the North' had said on the occasion that was, 'taking into consideration the sort of instruments here used, this performance is certainly the greatest musical treat I ever witnessed.'[395]

The enthusiasm shown in these early days was tremendous. The press reports emphasised the family inclusiveness and the immense talent of two of the boys; reports also confirm that the boys had performed earlier in Edinburgh or thereabouts. The five year old Louisa also made her debut which was applauded in the press. Their repertoire and type of instrument was also regarded as something novel. More usual concerts were given by musicians playing stringed instruments and the piano, like the more conventional concerts directed by Matilda's brother John David. The music the Distins played in those early days included pieces from the classics, like Handel's 'Water pieces' and exerts from the opera 'Norma'.[396] John Distin was a musician of the moment and he was leading a performance of music from 'Norma' which had been released only five years earlier in Italy.

The Distins then moved to Liverpool and Birmingham. In Birmingham John suffered from an accident and was out of action for a couple of months.[397] The family then continued towards Bath. An accident at the start of the band's first 'tour' would have had negative effects on the family finances and may have hastened their tour towards places in which they had contacts.

Reading the records of the first days of the Distin band, it is striking that there is an emphasis on the inclusive family, Matilda played the piano. As the pianist, it could have been a very difficult task – to coordinate the musical and personal antics of four teenage boys, and to keep pace with her ambitious and strong minded husband. She may also have been their coach and tutor. It would seem likely that she would be the prime tutor for the five year old Louisa who made such an impact on the stage in those early days. Somehow all these family egos needed to be successfully managed. John had been in doubtful financial position in 1835, with debts, and unless he had made a lot of money in the intermittent concerts in 1836, the family would not have had much money to spare on their launch in 1837. They probably had sufficient money to employ temporary help with washing and mending clothes, but the cost of travelling and staying at local hostelries would have been significant.

A second issue which emerges from the press reports of those first – and subsequent – concerts is the planning and management required for such a venture. Performances were advertised, venues located and enthusiastically reported. Maybe in those early days the family stage managed themselves, choosing areas they knew or had friends and relatives locally who helped them. Later word got around from individuals and the news media of the time. Arguably they knew how to manage the media of the time. As time went by and their fame spread they may have employed agents.

After completing their stint in Scotland the Distins moved to other familiar territory, to Bath. The family played enmasse at the Bath Assembly Rooms in November 1837, with Matilda at the piano. Bath as an early venue for the band made a lot of sense, there were family and friends there and Matilda knew the city. It may have been her brother John David who fixed the venues and promoted the band, he had a significant role in the music world in Bath at the time. Certainly the press report the band received was loaded with superlatives and could have been well written by an enthusiastic personal friend or relative.[398]

It may have been that back in home territory, in Bath, that Matilda and John decided that the inside of a carriage and constantly changing inns were not the best environments for young Louisa and her education. By the age of nine, Louisa was resident with a married couple who were teachers in Bath.[399]

In December 1837 there were family reunions and two examples of the new Distin band working with Matilda's relatives. It would appear that Matilda's brother John David Loder had a hand in the management of the Distin concert.[400] Finally, just before Christmas, Matilda's Ridgway daughter joined the vocalists supporting the Distin band in Bristol.[401]

Matilda the pianist 1838 - 1841

From the time that John quit Breadalbane in 1837, Matilda took publicly to the piano stool. Her name appears often in the newspapers, from 1837 to 1843.[402] After the Distins' energetic year in which Victoria came to the throne, the next few years were frenetically busy for the Distins. No sooner than the family had finished playing at the Bristol Assembly Rooms in late December than they emerged in mid January 1838 in London where they performed for eight months and were mentioned in the press 21 times. Matilda accompanied the band while they performed at high status venues like Drury Lane and the Theatre Royal Haymarket, and also at the smaller specialist places like the Argyle Rooms. They performed frequently with another family, the Rainers, in their first 'band' years as well as being on the bill with numerous other artists.[403]

The Distin Family.

Illustration VIII. The Distin Family, date unknown, with permission from the Royal Academy of Music. As the youngest member of the Band has no moustache, it would appear to predate the later Band print with Matilda, perhaps around 1840 when Theodore was 17 years old

The music the Distins played in 1838 is eclectic; a mixture of folk songs and arrangements of popular classical music. They played music from composers such as Mozart, Rossini, Bellini and Weber which had been arranged for brass instruments. During these six months the band made a short outing to Oxford, where Matilda played the accompaniment in March, and travelled to Bristol in May.[404]

Illustration IX The Rainer Family. C.1830. From the Keffer Collection, Special Collections Center, University of Pennsylvania

In September Matilda and her family were playing in Manchester, and, despite the general generous acclaim about their work it was not unanimous, their performance the following month in Leeds is criticised,

> '...they have not been well patronized. They are a deserving and meritorious family, but are apparently doomed to be unfortunate. We could wish "The light of other days", which is so ably executed by young Distin on the French Horn, would shine on them. The Strauss, when in London, completely put out their light, and caused them to try the provinces for support. We hope in other towns they will be more successful.'[405]

For the remaining months of 1838 the band played to audiences in the blooming new industrial towns of Yorkshire, including Bradford, Leeds, Pontefract and Halifax. Besides the frequent advertisements alerting the Yorkshire public of their imminent arrivals, there was one report which singled out Matilda, 'The Distins are a clever family, but especially Mrs. And Mr. H. Distin. The trumpet solos of the father, and the French-horn performances of his talented sons, were loudly applauded.' But the music 'sounded dead' on account of the performers being on the same level as the audience.[406]

The Distins were on the move the following year in 1839, and after an appearance in Aberdeen in January they spent the next nine months in Ireland with around 30 press reports covering their movements. For most of this time there were based and performed in Dublin, but they also visited other towns like Cork, Kilkenny and Killarney. They made a trip to Tralee in Scotland in September. It was probably in Ireland that the family established their repertoire. The performances would commence with a comic piece, followed by a Grand Concert perhaps including the classical adaptations, like Bellini's Norma.[407] Singers would then perform – accompanied by Henry on the French Horn. More group singing would be accompanied by John Distin on the trumpet, and then perhaps a soloist would sing. Next slot would be a melody composed by Distin played by William and Henry on the French Horns. Scottish music would round off part 1, and presuming an interval, part 2 would commence with John Distin playing 'The Soldier Tired'. This latter seems to be John's speciality, as he played it often in the following years. Other pieces would follow and the Distin entertainment would finish with 'God Save the Queen.' The whole evening would close with a pantomime which may well have included the ghosts from Matilda's past, Harlequin and Columbine.[408]

In late October the Distins left Ireland and sailed to England for a performance in York, only to return to Belfast for a couple of performances before returning to England to an audience in Carlisle in mid December. As ever Matilda 'presides' at the Piano Forte.[409]

The Distins' fourth year on the road, 1840, started with three months in Scotland and Northern England. They zigzagged across the country, moving between Glasgow, Carlisle, Newcastle upon Tyne and York, travelling further South to Hull in April. The family's travels must have echoed the same story as musicians and performers across the centuries, resting for a few nights in boarding houses or inns before moving on, travelling with most of their belongings and clothes needed – including warm winter clothes for the whole family. The travelling Distins party included the youngest two boys, Theodore and William, who were still teenagers. Also part of the load, the carriage 'train', would be the pricey instruments and the spare parts. Much of the time would have to be devoted to practising. To optimise their necessary rehearsal they would have required sufficient roomspace. Thus they may have had to choose between difficult options; expensive and roomy accommodation, the hire of suitable practice venues, or perhaps in these early days they focused on performing in towns where they had friends and relatives. It is doubtful whether they moved a piano. Matilda probably used whichever piano was available in the venue. She may have travelled with a small harp or similar small instrument. Her nephew, George Loder helped move a piano down a 'nearly perpendicular' mountain pass in California a decade later, in the 1850s.

'I had to provide him with ropes and blocks, had the piano securely packed I [in]an iron bound case, with rope-beckets or handles at the sides and ends, and sent two men with him to assist. We then started in a large open carriage or rather wagon, accompanied to Park's Bar, the first mining camp upon our route.'[410]

After a month in Doncaster and Hull, the family moved to Hereford and Worcester in May. The local press noting,

'...mother, Mrs.Distin, who ably presides at the piano forte, and to perform quintettes and sextettes, in a style of excellence and novelty, quite charming to the audience – the position of the parents, indeed a proud one.'[411]

Boyed on by the good reviews the Distins moved around for the next couple of months to Birmingham, London and Cheltenham, resurfacing in Ludlow in September. Looking though the press reports over the years, the family may have taken a break in August some years. For the remaining months of 1840 the Distins performed on Matilda's home territory in Swansea, Bristol, Falmouth, and Exeter. In November it was recognised that she was good, but not in the front line,

'... which Mrs. Distin — a sister of Mr. Loder — displayed great care and judgment. We cheer- fully accord our thanks to the Lady who rendered a sub- ordinate, but all important part in concerted harmony, so efficient an auxiliary to the general effect ...' [412]

A report from Christmas Eve notes how sweetly she plays the piano.[413] The short Christmas to New year period, 1840-1, was quickly followed by more performances in the south west commencing early January in Taunton. This was the start of a spectacularly busy year for the band. Various towns in Devon and Dorset provided the venues for the Distins late winter and early spring concerts in 1841: Weymouth, Sherbourne, Exeter and Plymouth all give advertising space in their publications to the group. Travelling back and forth between these venues would have been slow, uncomfortable, expensive and brought the family close together for long periods of time. Because the press reports and advertisements can only record the family's whereabouts spasmodically it is not certain how much time Matilda and her family had in any one place, or whether there was ever a possibility of being alone. From April to May the family performed in Salisbury, Winchester and Bath. In June they were in lodgings in Portsmouth.

By 1841 they had an established regime of travel and the family are captured in the 1841 census in Portsmouth, with John listed as a Professor of Music.[414] He stayed with Matilda in the High Street along with Henry and William and a maid, while George and Theodore stayed further along the road. This continued to be their pattern of life for several years. The main instruments on which they performed were the bugle, trumpet, trombone, and French horns. From the concert announcements it appears that at times they attempted to introduce some novelties, such as the "Tenor Horn", the "Tenor Cor", the "clavicor" and other instruments with which the general public was not very familiar at the time. Distin's walking-stick cornetto (usually played by Henry) was frequently used and it often made the press reports. It was claimed that it was invented by a family member.[415] Henry appeared to be a performer par excellence, often making the newspapers, with the other brothers mentioned less often.[416]

Matilda: a lady of great sweetness and taste

Matilda herself was mentioned in the newspapers occasionally,

'..Piano Forte. Mrs. Distin (sister to Mr. Loder. of Bath) presides at the Piano-Forte, and her execution is marked by great sweetness and taste, and she Inherits the talents that have so identified her maiden name.'[417]

The band continued, in 1841, to play at venues in Berkshire, Southampton, Reading and Salisbury, in June and July. Their tour finishes, perhaps for their summer break, on 7th August in Reading. The Reading paper acknowledges her role, sounding rather patronising in the language of the time.

'the Piano Forte accompaniments of Mrs. Distin, are admirable ; with an ease, rapidity and accuracy worthy of the performances of the other artistes.'[418]

During this break the family had a base in Maidstone, Kent – perhaps a seaside holiday opportunity. Here John wrote to his former sponsor, Lord Breadalbane updating him and giving him a forwarding address for September in Brighton.[419] Maybe John regarded Lord Breadalbane as a kind of benevolent godfather, and possibly wrote to him often. The family cannot have rested long at Western Road, Brighton because after a performance in Rye the family played in Chelmsford and Ipswich in October and November. John seemed always a man ready to organise things. The multitude of staff that exist in the 21st century to plan, produce and promote concerts were either non existent or thin on the ground in the 1840s. John wrote a letter to the local magistrates in Chelmsford asking them for the use of a county room for a concert.[420]

There followed another rapid deviation from what appeared to be a sound geographically planned tour. The group appeared in Hampshire in late November following a performance in Ipswich 10 days earlier. Two weeks later, in December, they were noted as performing at a benefit concert for the Sick, Poor and District Visiting Society in Norwich. The local papers of Christmas Eve show that the Distins were performing in Wisbech and Kings Lynn on those pre Christmas days.

Around the United Kingdom 1842-3, Matilda continues at the piano

1842 heralded concerts in Lincolnshire in January and February. In March and April they were making their music in Derby and Derbyshire towns, like Buxton and Chesterfield. From June they moved back to Worcester, Hereford and Monmouth playing in August. From there the six family members travelled through Wales, performing in September and October in Aberystwyth and Carnarvon. The family were enroute for a performance in December in Cork, and settled again in Dublin for another performance over Christmas and New year.

The early months of 1843 were spent in Ireland – in Limerick, Dublin, Londonderry and Belfast where they left in late April and moved to Glasgow in May where they were greeted by superlative press comments and in May they played at the Scottish Musard Concerts. Matilda was noted as playing a Grand Pianoforte 'made by Joseph Kirkman & Sons, London' in May 1843.[421] The band moved to Perth the following month and they played in Kelso at the beginning of August. That month they were busy in Newcastle and journeyed Southwards in September to perform at Durham, Harrogate, Leeds, Bradford and Sunderland. In Manchester in 1843 the Guardian newspaper recorded a review of the Distin concert of the previous night, directly after a letter from Charles Dickens. The review of the concert at the Athenaum, notes that the five Distin men were accompanied by Mrs Distin at the piano.[422]

Saturday 28 October in 1843 offers a mark in the sand for Matilda – it is the final time that records show that she played the piano for the group for certain. This was in Preston. The rest of the Distins continue to play in Leeds, Manchester, Derby, Ashbourne and Nottingham in November. The press records are then silent on the role and whereabouts of Mrs Distin.

A sideways look at Matilda's daughter Marian

Matilda's adult daughter, Marian certainly needed a helping hand in the 1830s. Marian's mother in law stepped in to provide income opportunities for couple - pubs and shops to manage. Things appear to have gone from bad to worse over the dozen or so years for the couple Thomas and Marian Elliott. In the early 1830s Thomas left Bristol and went to London and led a 'dissolute' life, while she stayed in Bristol teaching music. From the start of 1832 she spent three years in Edinburgh,[423] followed by a four month stint in Belfast. Marian and her children later went to Bristol, for around six years (c1835 – 1841).

Reflections of seven years as a member of a travelling band

In retrospect the late 1830s and 1840s were not the best of times to launch a new musical act. The 1840s were known as the 'hungry forties.' Despite that label the 1840s were good years for the band.[424] There were some good harvests in the early 1840s, but in 1845 the Irish potato crop failed and the bad harvest produced a crisis. Many people emigrated to America and there were a series of political crises.[425]

The seven years, 1837 to 1843, had been a whirlwind of activity for the Distins. When they boarded the boat for France in December 1843, they had behind them seven years travelling throughout the UK. They rarely stopped in one town for more than a few weeks, excepting their two Dublin visits. Matilda was 53 and John 50 as they set sail, their four sons aged from 20 to 26. The tides of the culture were changing, and so too was the economy. The Victorian values of thrift, independence and strong character were beginning to be shaped. The Distin sojourn in Ireland had fortunately been just before the big potato famine. They had had seven years of success, and they were appreciated by the public commanding good ticket prices. They had developed their repertoire, polished their act and their music had hit a popular chord with the Victorian public.

But this life on the road must have taken its toll on the family. John appears to be keen to drive his career forward, and in this he may have been aided and abetted by Matilda. They had, however, no home and their young daughter was being cared for by strangers in Bath. They could be described as a Victorian version of wandering minstrels, not an ideal situation for a middle aged bandswoman. Evidence shows they were strapped for cash and perhaps the forthcoming continental tour was not so well planned as it looked it retrospect.

The Distin band arrive in Paris, 1844: Matilda is out of the limelight

Asking for a loan of £20 John Distin wrote to Lord Newborough on 2nd January. He wrote that he given up his intention of visiting Russia. The following day, John wrote again to Lord Newborough apologising for not providing an address, which he noted was 'J.Distin, the Distin family, Post Office, Paris.[426] From this time Matilda is missing from any contemporary reports of the band, it is not certain whether she remained in London, with relatives, kept company with the family band or followed another unknown option. As she had elected to be with John through what can be imagined as stressful times, leaving her first husband and family and then following a young bandsman on the move, it is most likely that she accompanied the rest of the Distins to the continent in 1844, but it is not known for sure. Her role may have been a travel manager, sorting out the iterinaries, sourcing provisions, managing whatever servants had accompanied them and attempting to broker translation services – presuming none of the family spoke other languages than English. She may have continued to coach her sons and to take part in the continual rehearsals. She may have continued to play the piano for the band in public, and just have been ignored by the media of the time.

Illustration X. c. 1843—England: A print depicting the Distin Family Brass Quintet.[427]

.

Reasons why she becomes invisible in 1844 are myriad and are partly explained by her health three years later. She may have invalided herself out, intensive times on the piano stool may have led to arthritic fingers and other ailments. Society was rarely kind to older women and Matilda and her family may have thought that the key role of pianist needed to go to a younger person. She may have been determined to walk out of the limelight, or just have been pushed into the shadows. One way or another, her departure from the press reports coincided with a time when the band started to take off in a spectacular way.

Career defining events for John Distin: Albert Sax and European aristocracy

Early in 1844 the Distins attended a performance where a saxhorn was played by Jean-Baptiste Arban and the saxophone by Adolphe Sax.[428] John Distin was interested in setting up his own instrument making business in London and using an interpreter, he visited the major instrument makers in Paris. He visited Sax the day after the performance. Some commentators made negative remarks.

> 'The Distin family did not achieve the same critical
> acceptance in the rest of Europe that they had previously
> been used to in England. This was especially true in
> Vienne. There they performed terribly in an audition. Their
> shoddy execution was a direct result of their crude

instruments. On February 4, 1844 they met Sax at the Rue-Saint-Georges workshop after hearing the saxhorn for the first time the night before.'[129]

The Distins ordered a new set of saxhorns which the family used in their concerts. All the new instruments were bell-front saxhorns and were of different sizes and pitches. The Distins are credited with coining the term, 'saxhorn.'[430] Later in 1844 the Distins returned to Britain with their new saxhorns and made the instruments widely known. The first successful introduction of the saxhorns to the British public took place in November 1844 by the Distins. There must have been some rivalry as Sax himself had attempted to introduce the saxhorn about a month before the Distins in an unsuccessful series of concerts.[431]

Arguably the crescendo of John's career came in the Spring and Summer of 1844 when he and his sons performed to European aristrocrats. In May the Distins performed in the Tuilleries, Paris before 'the King of the French.'[432] There were at least two concerts involved, the family played at a concert organised by the composer Hector Berlioz before the French King and several members of his family. John also performed at a grand concert that was held at the Royal Conservatoire with great success and there he was presented with a silver medal.[433]   This was a career pinnacle moment and it possible to imagine Matilda bristling with uxorious pride from the front row with four of her offspring, but these moments – if they happened - were unrecorded.The Distins made a tour of Germany in September. They were to return to Germany later, but on this occasion Baden-Baden was on their tour.[434]

The fantastic year of international fame and discovery came to a magnificent autumn and winter for the band. They introduced the new saxhorn instruments to the British public in Brighton in November. The fact that they performed a few concerts in the Newburgh Rooms may not be coincidental. Maybe this was part of the agreement with Lord Newborough, for the loan of £20 in January. It is hard to know for sure as the facts in the 21st century may have been lost in the debris of time. A concert reviewer noted,

'the saxhorn unites the power of the French Horn to those of the cornet-a-pistons; with the mellowness and sweetness of the former, and the brilliance of the latter, its tone is richer, and less metallic than that of the cornet-a-piston, though possessing the same flexibility and power of execution'. The following issue commented 'Of the performances on the saxhorns it is impossible to speak too highly. The performance of Mr. Distin, sen. on the alto-horn, excited surprise among the musicians in Paris, when

Mr. D. had the honour of performing before the King of the French.' [435]

Brighton would have been the place where the family stayed for a few weeks, and in November and December the band played three times to the aristocrats at Arundel Castle. Arundel is the ancestral home of the Dukes of Norfolk and a prestigious venue for any musician. John had arrived. The performance on 11th December is the first one which names another piano accompanist, the 'Distin family and Messrs Smith (voice and piano)', marking, perhaps a formal change when Matilda had definitely departed from the stage.[436]

Then came the 'command' performance. In mid December the Distins played for royalty at Windsor Castle,

'In the evening the Distin family attended, by command, at the Castle, and had the honour of performing before Her Majesty and Prince Albert and the Royal circle.'[437]

John found time in these days to make his first appearance at M. Julien's concerts and an illustration of him appears in the Illustrated London News.[438] In the following few days the band played on several occasions at St James Theatre in London and Arundel Castle. Their 1844 tour culminated in another performance at Windsor Castle on Boxing Day. The Distin quintette was accompanied by the Misses Smith, and their brother Mr F.Smith took Matilda's old position at the piano. The performance at Arundel was a special bonanza,

'Arundel Castle. An entertainment given by the Duke and Duchess of Norfolk for the Duke and Duchess of Cambridge – 200 'of the nobility and gentry of the Western part of Sussex were invited'. Distins, 'performers on the new instrument, the Saxhorn'.[439]

Matilda and the Distins were likely to have stayed in Windsor over the Christmas and New Year period, as the band is noted as again playing before the Queen in January 1845 at a Grand Fete.[440]

Quibbling and quarrelling in 1845

Besides the glory of regal demand for his talents 1845 ushered in a potentially stressful few weeks in which John engaged in a verbal battle with Albert Sax.

'A very interesting a series of letters was published in The Musical World in January 1845 sent by a "foreign artist resident in London" believed to be Sax, and by John Distin.'[441]

In these letters Sax complains that he has not been given credit on the concert programmes as the inventor of the saxhorn. Distin counters, mentioning his family's experience at Windsor where they tried Sax's instrument which Distin maintained, was different,

'it has not the same mechanism, but it is a very old German or Italian invention, called the "double cylinder", [not manufactured by M. Sax]'.[442]

Later John made peace with Albert and signed an agreement, but this fracas must have left its mark. In the future John and his sons, especially Henry would spend considerable effort on developing patents for instruments and their technology.

1845: another busy year for the Distin band and the creation of a business

While the band were tuning up for royalty at the start of the year, there is an echo of adverse criticism in the press, with the Distin family, 'sometimes faring well and sometimes badly.'[443] It may be far fetched to consider that this statement links with the retirement from the stage of Matilda, but it is possible that the band had to start adjusting to a team of new and perhaps untried pianists on their busy touring times. The changes of pianist could have had a negative effect on the band's performance for a short while.

In late January the group were performing in Wolverhampton, and, at the end of January to the Queen Dowager, Queen Adelaide, in Worcestershire at Whitley Court. The band then were back in London for a couple of weeks and in February John gave a London address in his correspondence about the Sax affair.[444] After some more appearances at Whitley Court, the Distin menfolk continued their touring as they had done in the early years of the 1840s: London, Manchester, Liverpool, Chester, Preston, Oldham, London, Liverpool and London, before travelling to Germany again to perform in the Palace at Hanover before the King of Hanover in mid May. A week later they appeared before Queen Victoria for a fourth time at a soiree of the Duchess of Kent.[445] The relentless schedule of performing continued in London and in May they advertised the start of their sales business,

'Distins' registered sax horns. THE DISTIN FAMILY beg to inform the Professors, Military Band Masters, and Amateurs, they now have a Stock of the ABOVE SPLENDID INSTRUMENTS ON SALE, at their residence No. 49, Manchester Street, Manchester Square, London.'[446]

In 1845 the Distins set up their business in London selling printed music and musical instruments, although at that time they were only dealers and were not involved in any instrument making activity. They first started selling instruments from their residence in Manchester Street, the earliest known advertisement for this address dates from May 1845.[447] At a similar time they appear at an Opera Concert Room in London for Mrs Anderson's Grand Morning Concert.[448] Mrs Anderson appeared regularly in the musical world and in 1845 was probably working closely with her pupil, the budding pianist, Kate Loder, Matilda's niece, who made her debut performance around this time.

Many more London concerts are reported for the Distins including the Philharmonic Concerts in June, led by Matilda's brother, John David Loder.[449] It is noteworthy that they performed to support the Royal Dispensary for the Diseases of the Ear also in June.[450] This performance may have been linked to the later problems George Distin had with his ear in 1848. The band is off to Dublin for six concerts in June and July, but whether Matilda stayed back to manage the business at Manchester Square or she stuck to the sides of the family is unknown. In July the band played in London and Liverpool. In August there was a trace of the relationship between John and his sponsor, Lord Newborough. John wrote to Newborough explaining he was unable to visit Glynllifon because he arrived home late. This correspondence demonstrates how important it was at the time to keep in close contact with the investors.[451]

The band, with or without Matilda, performed in Bristol, Bath, Carnarvon, Bangor, Beaumaris and Shrewsbury. They were particularly busy in August and gave a private concert at the end of the month at Penrhyn Castle. In Liverpool they performed to 2,500 people.[452] More venues quickly followed; Scarborough, York, Liverpool and Wolverhampton before the band announced a visit Germany and Russia in October.[453] They appeared in October in Liverpool and other places, Newcastle under Lyme, and then in Glasgow in November, when Matilda's nephew, Mr A.T. Loder took Matilda's former place with the band.[454]

Henry Distin   **George Distin**

William Distin...............Theodore Distin

Illustration XI. Named images of the four Distin sons from a Distin Jug. Information from Professor Arnold Myers, based on 1845 Baugniet print, identification made by Crosscup & West, Philadelphia.

For the rest of the month they performed in Glasgow and Edinburgh and then returned to London to prepare for their heralded continental tour. They had impressive letters of support.

> 'The Distin Family have just returned to town from North. They will soon proceed to the continent. They have letters from H. R. H. the Duchess of Kent to the King of the

Belgians, the Duchess of Neumours, the Grand Duke of
Saxe Cobourg Gotha, the Duke of Saxe Weimar and other
illustrious personages.'[455]

As far as surviving press reports go 1845 was an extremely busy year for the
Distin band. Mrs Distin remains absent from the newspapers.

*Illustration XII. A Distin Jug. There is an inscription on the base, 'The Distin
Family. The Sax Horn Performers'.*

1846: a significant year for the Distin band, but what was Matilda doing?

The year kicked off with another international tour for the Distin menfolk for
four months. They played in Paris and Germany. In Paris there was a political
statement made by the French King, Louis Philippe who 'expressed himself

highly delighted with the performance, and requested that it might close with 'God Save the Queen.'[456]

In Germany they achieved recognition by the musical fraternity as well as the aristrocratic elite, 'Meyerbeer presented the Distins with selections from his operas arranged for their own instruments.'[457]

They played in Berlin, Hanover, Brunswick and arrived back to spend a couple of months performing in London. After London the band made its usual sort of tour around England, performing at Bath, Bristol, York and Liverpool among other places. In most newspaper reports there is no mention of a pianist; once Mr Negri is mentioned as pianist, although he also conducted. In December their tour ended on another high note with a performance in Arundel Castle for the Queen with Matilda's niece, Kate Loder accompanying the band. This may have been one of Kate's earliest public appearances. She was an exceedingly talented musician and aged 21 for this concert.

> 'The Distin family performed their favourite airs on the Sax horns, much to the gratification of the company; and a very young lady, Miss Kate Loder (a relative of the composer), distinguished herself in a brilliant fantasia on the pianoforte … Her Majesty was so pleased with the performances of the Distin family, that she commanded a repetition of one of the airs after the whole had been concluded.'[458]

The Distin manufacturing business also was started in 1846. Distin & Sons was created in London, 1846-1850, by John and this was the inception of what was to be known as one of the most important manufacturing companies for the cornet in the19th century, although what was made when is not absolutely clear.

There was a reconciliation with Sax, and the Distins became Sax's sole official agents in Britain in 1846. According to an advertisement the family only sold 'registered saxhorns' at the time. The earliest known advertisement stating this, is from August 1846 when it was announced that, 'registered saxhorns, sax-cornets, horns, tubas and others' were offered for sale at the Distins' musical instrument warehouse at 31, Cranbourn Street in London.[459]

It is hard to know the precise instruments sold, Distin & Sons had already registered a design for a saxhorn in Britain and no surviving instrument known is made according to that design. It appears that the family was not involved in any instrument making activity at the time and it is not known who was making the instruments sold at their premises at this early date. For a short time they held the saxhorn monopoly in Britain, and from 1847 "saxtubas" were added in the list of instruments offered for sale, this was a term used by the Distins to denote upright saxhorns.[460]

The fact that the Distin boys were amassing great fame in performance and were creating a business begs the question as to what was Matilda doing. The year 1846 started badly for Matilda; her brother, John David, died in early 1846, at the age of 57.[461] He had had Masonic connections and the Freemason's Quarterly Review named the cause of her brother's death as 'dropsy.' The musical establishment rallied round and Sir George Smart organised a benefit for his widow and daughters in Bath – even though they were living in London. Sir George travelled by the recently opened railway and he stayed with musician Dominick Hervey, who married into the Loder family, and later was buried alongside John David in Kensal Green Cemetery. The local paper reported that 'a metropolitan and resident talent provided their Gratuitous Services' in front of six hundred people in Bath. Three of his sons John, Edward and William attended the burial at Kensal Green.[462]

Reflections on parallel lives: John David Loder

The star of the Loder children in the 1790s was John David, two years older than Matilda. An able violist, he had succeeded in making not only a decent living, but a moderate name for himself, by performing, teaching, writing and publishing. John David's life was closely connected with his sister's, both in the musical world and in personal life.

In 1841 he wrote the fifth edition of his classic instruction book for violists, the first had been in 1814. In 1840 this was famous enough to be mentioned by Richard Doyle, later of the Punch magazine. He had established a business in Bath with his cousin Andrew in 1813, until this was proclaimed bankrupt. He was in business as a music publisher at 46 Milsom Street Bath. He was a stalwart of many prominent musical institutions and his name appeared on the list of Professors at the Royal Academy of Music from 1822. John David Loder was a member of the Philharmonic Society Orchestra in both 1819 and 1840, listed in both as a 'leader' earning £52.10 in 1840 for eight concerts and £31.10 in 1819.[463] Overall John was in demand and commanded a reasonable income.[464]

John was an active musician for instance he led the second performance of Beethoven's ninth symphony in London. He appeared to be frenetically busy playing in Festivals in the 1820s and 30s, but this had a downside as he spent a lot of his time on the road from his base in Bath. Ultimately, in 1841, he quitted Bath to live in Chelsea with his family, probably following his bankruptcy in

Bath. Contemporary accounts of him mention his warmth, kindness and humour, these factors were probably mixed with sensitivity and may account for his breakdown in 1822. He appears to have had a happy married life with Rose, they had some 12 children, most of whom were musically talented.[465]

John David played professionally with the Distins and there was a strong personal relationship between brother and sister.[466] It may have been John David who supported Matilda through the early days of her separation from Thomas Ridgway. His death would have been a blow to her, at a time when she was no longer playing for the Distin band. His widow and offspring would have needed support following his death.

Matilda in 1847: behind the scenes, on the sidelines

What happened in 1847 to Matilda goes a long way to explain what may have invalided her out of an active role with the family fame in the previous couple of years. She was a grieving sister in 1846 but it is not known if Matilda had been left in London to coordinate the new Distin business activities in the mid 1840s. She may have continued a quasi musical role with her sons and husband on the continent and on the road. She may have sat in the front row watching them with amazement, with pride and maybe envy. There is no evidence.

1847 was another magnificent crowd puller for her husband and four sons. The year saw the band continue with its exhausting schedule including trips to play in Scotland, Boulogne, Dublin, Liverpool and Manchester. There were times when the band played at a different venue each day, but the players spent a good amount of time in London. While the Distin band moved from strength to strength, perhaps gaining the status of 'superstars' of their time, their mother, Matilda was not well. There may have been many contributing reasons for her not joining the family on stage after 1844. Certainty one reason for her opting out of the family band was that she was losing her sight. It is likely that her eyesight was failing for a year or more before she was a patient for eye surgery – in July 1847. The contemporary press reports noted,

> 'Blindness from Cataract. On Saturday Mrs Distin, the mother of the eminent artistes who perform on the Sax horns underwent the operation for cataract in both eyes with complete success under the skilful hand of Dr F.H Brett. Her case excited peculiar interest in scientific circles as it was considered incurable by that celebrated oculist, Juncken of Berlin. Mrs Distin declared very little inconvenience after the operation.'[467]

To have to undergo such an operation in both eyes Matilda must have been virtually blind, it would have been a risky procedure. It would seem likely that she was exceedingly brave, stupid or desperate. The surgeon she chose, Dr Brett had published a book just weeks before her operation. Matilda must have been in contact with the medical specialists of the time and jumped at the opportunity described in Brett's eight volumes. Matilda would have been chloroformed for this operation and following it she would have had to wear very thick magnifying lensed spectacles to see reasonably.[468] A few years later Brett was suspected of being an imposter.

Whilst Matilda was part of a risky operation the Distins began to manufacture instruments as well as sell musical paraphernalia. Some of this manufacturing was dubious business practice,

> 'The fact that the Distins were now making their own
> instruments might have contravened their contract with
> Sax. Also, by the end of 1847 they were supplying cornets
> by Courtois, and (later) cornets by Besson, alongside
> cornets and other instruments from Sax's workshop.'[469]

The Distin men continued to travel and entertain in later 1847. The occupation of the piano stool changed a little. The typical line up in the band in 1847 and 1848 were the five Distin men accompanied by Mr Willy, for example at concert at the Mechanics Institute in Manchester in November 1847 the five Distin men were accompanied by Mr Willy at the piano and Miss O'Connor as a vocalist.[470]

1848 – Challenges, changes and Matilda's last days

1848 rang in with seismic changes for Europe. The year saw monarchies collapse in France, Austria, Italy and Poland. The nearest the UK came to active revolution was a rally organised by the Chartists on Kennington Common, whilst at the same time Karl Marx was busy in the British Museum writing the Communist Manifesto.[471] While massive revolution was brewing in Europe things were going badly wrong for the Distin family. There is a hint of the family's movements from their ever travelling programme and their work in Banbury. On the 4th April, 1848, there was noted, 'A Grand Concert by Mr. Distin and his Four Sons, 'the original and unrivalled performers on those extraordinary instruments, the sax-horns and sax tubas.'[472]

This was the day George, the oldest Distin son, died in April.[473] He was aged 30. It seems that he had a significant ear condition which affected him for over a year. It must have been both painful and difficult for him to perform on a brass instrument in the previous months and his condition may explain the performance by the band in 1845 for the Royal Dispensary for Disease of the Ear. George was initially buried in his uncle's, John David Loder's, grave in Kensal Green Cemetery.

Illustration XIII. 31 Cranbourne Street, London in 2013

The family stopped performing for a couple of weeks, and resumed in early May. According to John Distin's letter to The Musical World, the bass that was played by George was taken up by the brother who used to play second alto. John Distin had to rearrange all their music for a quartet with piano accompaniment.[474] Initially reviews were not so favourable on the new arrangement of the music, but within a short time they resumed their former enthusiasm.[475]

On 13th June there was noted 'The Distins' Sax-Horn Concerts' and on the 27th October: 'The Distins' Farewell Concert, with Miss Moriatt [Harriett] O'Connor, Mr H. Distin, Mr W. Distin and Mr Theodore Distin, accompanied by Mr Willy Jun.[476]

The final curtain call

Matilda was not a well woman. From the beginning of June she began to suffer from a carbuncle – not uncommon in the days before antibiotics. This type of infection was likely to strike those with a low immune system and Matilda had had a series of body blows: her operation a year before on her eyes, the death of George in the Spring of 1848. Matilda died from a carbuncle on the 23 June 1848, at 31 Cranbourn Street. Her death was reported in the Times. 'On the 23 instant, after a severe illness of 21 days, Ann Matilda Distin, aged 57 wife of Mr John Distin, the celebrated Saxhorn performer, deeply and sincerely regretted by her family and a numerous circle of friends.' The informant was Ann Latham, acting as a nurse and present at the death. The death was also reported in other newspapers.[477]

On 23 June 1848, the day she died, John bought plot number 7639 in Kensal Green Cemetery in which several family members were to be buried. The burial took place two days later, on 25 June. It is likely that men were the only mourners, as was traditional at the time, the custom was for a funeral carriage and horses to carry the coffin across London to the new cemetery of Kensal Green.[478]

It is not known how the Distin family reacted in her final days. During the three weeks before her death the band played in London, and five Distin concert appearances appear in the press.

Tying up the loose ends

The band played on

After barely a pause, the four Distin menfolk continued their previous touring programmes. On the personal front things changed rapidly and the dynamics of the band were different. Henry married Jayne Baynes in September at Marylebone.[479] Jane Distin, as she became, was almost certainly the composer of the melody of 'Listen to the Curfew Bell', 1862[480]. There were a couple of London based concerts and in mid August the band played in Swansea and Bristol. The latter performance generated a sad press comment,

> 'A fortnight ago we had the Distin family here, whose concerts were tolerably well attended, although it did not escape general notice how much their performances suffered through the death of one of the brothers.'[481]

In October they were aiming for a major American tour, and gave a Grand Farewell Concert at the Theatre Royal, Drury Lane, 'Under the special patronage of Her Most gracious majesty the Queen and His Royal Highness Prince Albert'; Pianoforte – Miss Kate Loder.'[482] A review of this concert, emphasised the Distins' popularity, and also mentioned that one of the Loders, probably one of the sons of John David was the leader.

> 'Messrs. Distin were received with vehement applause, and that the entertainment, long as it was, did not appear to fatigue more than half the company – an incontrovertible sign that excellence was the prevailing feature of the concert. Mr. Loder was the leader.'[483]

After more farewell concerts in the south of England the four men departed for America –with Louisa Distin and Harriet O'Connor in toe – five months after Matilda's death.[484]

There were some ups and downs in their North American tour. Their initial venue, at the old Park Theatre, in New York had been destroyed by fire when they reached the city on 1st January 1849 and other catastrophes followed.[485] However in general the band received good and eulogistic reviews over the following months, and while they were there they changed their style a little, to include singing. They were supported by Louisa and Harriet as vocalists.[486] By November they returned to England and performed along with Louisa and Harriet.[487] In the next year John continued his correspondence with his sponsor, Lord Breadalbine, informing him that the sons were singing in a letter from

London.[488] The following year, 1851, John wrote to his other sponsor, Lord Newborough, requesting a loan of up to £50 to patent 'a great improvement on the principle of brass instruments.'[489] In 1857 John wrote a final begging letter to Lord Breadalbine for a loan and informing of a farewell concert.[490]

The Distin business

The legal partnership between the brothers and their father was formally ended four months after Matilda's death.

> 'NOTICE is hereby given, that the Co partnership between John Distin, Henry John Distin, William Alfred Distin, and Theodore Distin, of No. 31, Cranbourn-street, in the county of Middlesex, Music and Musical Instrument Sellers, under the style-or firm of Distin and Sons, was this day dissolved by- mutual consent.-Dated this 27th day of November 1848.'[491]

The men were not wealthy. 'Despite their financial success, it is said that, at times, the members were financially embarrassed.'[492]

In a nutshell what happened to the Distins

John Distin

John never married again. He apparently focused his energy on continuing to play with the band. In 1851 he was living in Charlotte Square, St Pancras, in London with William and Theodore, all calling themselves musicians, 'Saxehorn'. He retired from active performance in1857 and lived with William. In the1861 census he lived in Aldershot, at 18, Wellington Street, calling himself a widower and 'Professor of Music aged 69 of Plympton St Mary, Devonshire'. He wrote a little music and three of his publications are to be found in the British Library in 2013. He died at 9 Great Newport Street, the street behind Cranbourn Street where his son Henry had built the Distin factory in the 1850s, so it is likely that he lived with Henry and the growing new business at the time of his death.[493] He was buried in the family plot in Kensal Green in 1863, aged 69.

Henry Distin

Henry was the showman in the family concerts and frequently mentioned in contemporary press reports in the 1830s and 40s. He outlived his brothers and led a long and complex life. He received early training at the Royal Academy of Music became a keen entrepreneur and took over the family firm in 1850. Henry and Jane had several children, some of whom died young and were buried with their grandmother, Ann Matilda. His travels took him from London, New York (c.1877-1882), Philadelphia (c.1882-1890), and Williamsport, in Pennsylvania (c.1886-1909).

By 1850, Henry became the sole owner of the company, manufacturing brass instruments under his own name and by 1851 the arrangement with Sax ceased. In Henry's business ventures things did not go smoothly, his work ethics were criticised and in 1856 a workman from Austria called Tischendorf sued him.[494]

Overall it is possible to view Henry as an ambitious wheeler dealer and showman, rather than a top class performance musician. He was described as having 'plenty of self reliance' and when he set up the Cranbourn Street shop in 1850, he had 'scarcely a stiver in his pocket after paying initial expenses'. A near contemporary story was that a new customer arrived while Henry was unpacking and asked for a cornet. Henry took a cab to the wholesale dealers and in twenty minutes made £9 profit on the deal.[495]

Either the inventor or perhaps developer of the ideas of others he started to register patents in several directions. He developed the famous Distin drum which is shown in publications from 1857.[496]He opened the business premises at 9 Great Newport Street in 1857 and in 1859 the Cranbourn Street premises were given up and the new premises were expanded three years later in 1862.

The business published music in a Distin's Band Journal and also manufactured brass instruments for the Army and Navy. The firm was sold to Boosey and Co. in 1868. Henry then lost money in business ventures and emigrated to New York in 1877. Again he created a business, selling instruments and moved to Philadelphia establishing the Henry Distin Manufacturing Co. He spoke to a reporter for the New York Times in 1881 and much of the information on the band is based on this article. Some of the facts in the article are incorrect – for instance his father's year of birth is four years out. Three publications in his name are to be found in the British Library. Henry retired in 1890 and died in 1903.[497]

William Distin

William Alfred Distin, the third Distin son, started his career on the natural horn in the family band and then took up the saxhorn. He, like Henry, had received training at the Royal Academy of Music and was an excellent bass singer. It is recorded that on one occasion, William was deputising at the Chapel Royal,

Windsor, when the Prince Consort [Albert], was 'struck by his voice and asked who it was who sang so beautifully. William was consequently presented to his Royal Highness.'[498]

William composed songs that included 'The United Volunteers', which was published in London in 1860. In 1855, he independently patented (GB# 2688) a crank added to the piston rod to give a rotary action to the piston, which returned by means of a spring.[499] In 1861 he lived with his father in Aldershot, and described himself as a Professor of Music aged 39 of Westminster, London. It is possible that he also travelled to Australia.[500] He also 'found fame as a singer with a fine bass voice' until he died in December 1879 in Southwark. He never married and was buried alongside his parents in Kensal Green.[501]

Theodore Distin

Theodore was the most prolific composer of the brothers: the British Library has 59 of his publications, most of which are sheet music for songs. He married twice and fathered several children. There were several obituaries for Theodore, who died in 1893.[502]

One described the vocalist and composer, giving his father's credentials, 'trumpeter to George IV' and noting that Theodore studied the French horn and when he was thirteen he played with his father and brother in the newly formed Distin quintet band which later played at Windsor Castle. From 1844 Theodore studied singing and he was for a considerable time a baritone. He became better known as a vocalist than as an instrumentalist in the latter years of his life, 'he had a fine resonant voice and a clear enunciation, and he sang with great expression.' The obituary praises Theodore 'as a prolific composer of songs' carrying off a number of prizes. He was also known as a popular musical lecturer. 'He used to tell some most amusing and interesting stories of his travels with the Distin family.' It continues by mentioning Ann Matilda,

> 'Mr Distin whose mother, Miss Loder, was an aunt of that charming Kate Loder, who became Lady Thompson was a link which bound this musical generation to a greater generation, in which his father was not one of the least distinguished figures. A fellow of infinite jest, he was full of anecdote.'

Theodore appears to have been a respected musician and person. Theodore left to his widow Annie Distin, effects of £979 17s 4d, a good sum for those days.[503]

Louisa Distin

The 1851 UK Census taken on 31st March states 'Louisa Distin, 19yrs, musician – unwed' as a 'niece' at the home of Rosamund Loder (Rose, widow of John David Loder), 36 Manchester Street, Marylebone. This seems peculiar as she was married Nugent Varley in February 1851, her marriage apparently was some kind of secret, unless there was a record error. She was only 19 when she married it may be that she did not have her father's permission. Louisa was only 16 when her mother died and whilst touring with her father she may have had an opportunity to meet Nugent as he was around at some of these concerts. Nugent was the manager of the Corn Exchange in Nottingham when the Distins performed there in 1850. He was also involved with the Loders.[504] Later in 1851 she and Varley had their first son. Another daughter died early in life.

The Varleys sailed to Australia and seven of her nine children were born in Victoria, Australia, at various gold mining towns: Fryers Creek, Talbot, Lamplough, Amherst and Ballarat East. Nugent's role appears to have been travelling around the gold mines selling provisions. At one stage a poignant advert appeared in the press, apparently from her,

> 'Nugent Varley, Ararat - should this meet his eye, or any of his mates, his wife earnestly requests his writing to her. She has written 9 times and no answer.'

Nugent and Louisa probably separated around 1871. Her second marriage certificate (to Robert McKindlay) stated that her first husband had died in 1880.[505]

Louisa must have kept in contact with her brother Henry. A torn newspaper article from 1881, the New York Times interview with Henry Distin, was in the possession of a member of the Distin family in the 21st century. Louisa also took to Australia a momento of her mother – the copy of the compositions Matilda made in Windsor in the 1820s dedicated to Lady Coyningham.[506] Louisa worked as a pianist in Australia and died in Melbourne in 1908, outliving one of her talented daughters, Violet, a singer on the Melbourne stage who died in childbirth in 1895.[507]

The fate of the Ridgway relatives[508]

Ann Matilda's five Ridgway children all made it onto the stage, but like their mother, their appearances in the 'limelight' were short lived and they were not leading performers.

Thomas Frederick Ridgway performed, probably as a boy with his father, and was known as 'Tom'. He was a popular performer and an incident is recorded of him performing a stunt, when the carpenters were not in place to catch him. He grabbed a handful of hair of one of the assistants as he sailed past, making sure he did not let go.[509] He continued his career as a 'Comedian' and 'Teacher of Dancing.' He married but had no children and died in Southampton in 1879.

George Norman Ridgway had started the rounds of theatre life but died young of consumption – probably in Scotland in 1832 at the age of 23. Although the evidence is not absolute he may be the Ridgway to have been described as, 'the best clown we have seen since the days of the celebrated Grimaldi.'[510]

The third young brother **John Henry Ridgway** continued life in the same vein as his oldest brother. He was a 'Comedian' in 1841 and a 'Professor of Dancing' later and little else is recorded about him and his career. He also married and remained childless. He died in Birmingham in 1878 and is remarkable as is one of the few of Ann Matilda's relatives to leave a will. His fortune was less than £300 and it went to his widow.[511]

Marian Ridgway married at 16 and had three surviving children. She became an actress and pianist, like her mother. Similarly, her first marriage was unhappy and she and her husband separated. She became a manager for a hat manufacturers where she met her second husband. She was one of the first divorcees under the new legislation in England a decade after her mother's death. She died at a similar age to her mother in1869.

Charles Ridgway was the youngest of Matilda and Thomas' children. He became a theatrical tailor and later a disabled pantomimist. He outlived his siblings by a long way and spent his life, according to census information, in South London, not far from where he was born in Southwark. He married and fathered 12 children many of whose names are those of his Ridgway siblings. Not one of the three daughters is named after his mother. He died in Lambeth in 1893.

Three of Matilda's close Loder relatives achieve fame

Interwoven into Matilda's story is the importance of close family connections. Musicians needed the supportive resources of like minded relatives to survive and thrive. The Distins had given a leg up professionally to Matilda's nephew Abraham, who had been apprenticed initially as a barber. Two of her other Loder nephews and one niece achieved more spectacular fame, with their careers developing during Matilda's lifetime.

Edward Loder

Edward James and his twin John Fawcett, born 1810,[512] were the first children of John David and Rose Loder, Matilda's brother and sister in law. Edward was a talented composer and musician. As a boy he studied with his father, and then with F. Ries at Frankfurt in 1826-28. In 1828 he returned to England, then went back to Frankfurt to study with Ries. He was a Conductor at Princess Theatre, London and also worked in Manchester where he was musical director for the Theatre Royal. In the mid 1830s he found himself in financial difficulties and had to write new songs frequently for commercial purposes to make ends meet. Despite having composed some nine operas, he never seemed to fulfil his potential and much of his work remained unpublished. In 1856 he had the first signs of a brain disease and died in London 1865.[513]Much has been written about him and his unfulfilled musical abilities, one review summarises Edward's career.

> 'It is a sad reflection that only two operas give an adequate impression of Loder's [Edward] talents He was forced to spend the majority of his compositional life on hack work that allowed little chance for his creative abilities to flourish. No composer was immune from the pressures that forced this upon him, but in Loder's case it is a particular cause for regret.'[514]

George Loder (junior)

George Patrick Henry was Matilda's nephew and the son of her younger brother George. Born in 1816 in Bath he led a rich and eventful life. At the age of 13 he was apprenticed to Frances, his cousin Andrew Loder's wife, following the death of his father that year. He left Bath in the 1830s and spent much of his life working and travelling in North America and Australia. Like his first cousin Edward, George was another extremely talented musician who did not leave an enormous musical legacy. In 1836 he visited America, staying for some time in Baltimore, and in 1844 he was principal of the New York Vocal Institute, and member of the Philharmonic and Vocal Societies, which he had helped to establish there. About 1856 George went to Adelaide, South Australia, with Madame Anna Bishop, and afterwards with Lyster's opera troupe as a conductor. About 1860 he was again practising his profession, as organist, vocalist, conductor, and composer, in London. In 1861 he published there 'Pets of the Parterre,' a comic operetta, which had been produced at the Lyceum, and in 1862 'The Old House at Home,' a musical entertainment. Loder's music was more popular in America than in his own country. 'The New York Glee Book,' 1844 (republished as 'The Philadelphia and New York Glee Book' in 1904), contains several of his original part-songs. He also issued 'The Middle Voice,' 12 solfeggi, London, 1860, and various separate songs by him were published both in England and America. George paid a second visit to Australia, and died after a long illness in Adelaide in 1868. [515]

Kate Loder

Kate Fanny Loder was the daughter of Ann Matilda's younger brother, George and his second wife who was indirectly related to Mrs Anderson, the pianist who worked for the Royal family. George (junior) was her half brother. Despite the early deaths of her parents, Kate became an amazing and highly talented woman. She received accolades from the contemporary press and many have written about her. Her early career is intertwined with the Distins, playing the piano for key events for the band in the later 1840s. In the 1851 census she is staying with her Uncle John's widow, Rose Loder, along with her first cousins, including Louisa Distin.[516] A summary of her achievements is given below,

> 'Member of a professional musical family in Bath.
> Attended the RAM 1839-44, where she studied with her
> aunt, Lucy Anderson, and with Charles Lucas. In 1844
> made her debut playing parts of the Mendelssohn Concerto
> in G Minor at Lucy Anderson's concert (at which the
> composer was present). Became professor of harmony at
> the RAM. Performed Mendelssohn and Weber piano
> concertos at the Philharmonic Society. Associate of the
> Philharmonic Society. Joined Royal Society of Female
> Musicians in 1848. Married in 1851 and retired from
> public concerts in 1854. Continued to compose (including
> an opera, overture, two string quartets, a piano trio. piano
> sonatas, two books of organ voluntaries, songs, violin
> sonatas, and arrangements) until 1899.' [517]

Epilogue and spotlight on Ann Matilda: what was her real legacy?

It is debatable what kind of legacy women leave for the future. For Ann Matilda three types of legacy are possible: the personal, the professional and the impact of her role as a woman.

Ann Matilda the mother: the genetic legacy

It is amazing that so many of Ann Matilda's mother Bathsheba's nine children made it into adult life – six or seven. Ann Matilda was similar, ten of her children survived the gruelling 19th century childhood, with only one known casualty in early adulthood. Three out of the four of her daughter Marian's children grew into old age and only one of Louisa's nine children failed to make it to adult life.[518] In London in the mid 18th century 49% of all recorded children were dead by the age of two, and 60% by the age of five. In Victorian times the rate had fallen and 15% of babies did not reach their first birthday. This rate doubled in the poor slum areas.[519] Henry Distin's children did not do so well, three of them died young and were buried – with one of Theodore's young children alongside their grandmother in the family plot in Kensal Green cemetery in London. Louisa Distin and Charles Ridgway had large families. Matilda's grand offspring ensured that a trace of her DNA is around – probably carried by hundreds of people in the UK, Australia, the USA and elsewhere in the 21st century. In the early 21st century at least four of her descendants are professionally engaged with the stage.

What did Matilda do for her children, if anything?

Some would consider Ann Matilda's extraordinarily busy life, a sign of both immense energy and potential obsessive behaviour. Evidence is thin on the ground, but it would seem certain that she had some time for her offspring and that all her children received a reasonable education. The evidence of business activities, letters, legal activities, publications and reports show that at minimum Marian, Louisa, Henry, William and Theodore were well educated and skilled in music, and probably other fields too. Maybe the image of their mother's dilemmas helped her two daughters prepare for the vicissitudes of life that came their way. These were substantial for both daughters.

Matilda was a dubious role model to her two daughters. Marian's marriage story was a repeat of her mother's, an unhappy marriage followed by a second apparently happy one. Louisa's life pattern was longer but arguably similar to her mother's and her half sister's. Louisa made the adventurous, brave or perhaps desperate decision to depart for Australia soon after her mother's death. Both daughters were pianists like their mother.

Certainly there was no financial legacy for her children. Ann Matilda spent her life on a shoestring. Her uncle, cousin, brother and probably mother all went bankrupt. Suggestions of an easy life by her first husband never materialised and her second husband was often asking his sponsors for loans, for more money. She lived within a family which was supported by and possibly beholden to wealthy patrons. The Distin family income from continual concerting must have been good, but it was soon spent, leaving nothing of note from her for the next generation, except perhaps her role model, and, in the case of Louisa, a copy of her compositions.

Discordant relationships and dysfunctional families

It is impossible to explore Ann Matilda's relationship with her 10 children. It is only possible to surmise. Ann Matilda's exodus from Tower Street around 1816 might have brought about a schism with at least some of her children. While Charles, the Ridgway baby and theatrical tailor, fathered about a dozen children none of the girls were given the names Matilda nor Ann, whereas his choices for his sons reflected Ridgway family names. Likewise Matilda does not appear in the names of her other grandchildren although Louisa gave one daughter a middle name of 'Anne'. It would have been common practice for the time for granddaughters to have been given one of the names of their grandmother.

Similarly the feelings of Ann Matilda's offspring, can only be surmised, no evidence exists. The Ridgway children could have taken the brunt of local gossip and professional sneers as they pushed forward with their stage careers in the 1820s. However marriage breakdown was relatively common in the theatre at that time so it might not have caused particular problems in the streets of Southwark. In the 1830s and 40s when the Distins began to make the national news and cause a stir in royal circles it would have been understandable if the Ridgway offspring had felt anger, resentment and jealousy about their mother's apparent behaviour to them. These kind of feelings, if they existed, could have touched the next generation. Some of her Ridgway grandchildren may have known her, if they did their stories remained untold and the Ann Matilda myths and fables were not created for the future.[520]

For the Distin sons – if they had known about their Ridgway connections– there may have been an issue about accepting their illegitimacy. It might have concerned the Distin musicians that around the London stage there were clowns and dancers who were their half brothers. For the three surviving Distin sons it could have been highly embarrassing to see that their half sister made the headline news with details of her divorce case, only a decade after their mother's death. An investigative reporter of the mid 19th century could have easily linked the threads together and made a dint in the careers of the Distins, but this didn't happen. The presumption is that everyone in the know kept quiet or couldn't be bothered.

In memoriam

The family graves in Kensal Green were cheap and insignificant. They are located away from the main paths, unvisited, unremembered. Surrounded by the magnificent monuments of Victorian architecture and sculpture the Loder and Distin graves are of very plain stone, the inscriptions almost obliterated. In a good light, when the cemetery gardener lifts the turf, you can make out the words, 'Matilda, Distin, Ruddock' and parts of other words. Despite the enormous investment the Distins made in placing adverts in newspapers to promote themselves a minimal amount was invested in providing a memorial for their memory. Her descendants in the UK knew nothing her 150 years after her death. The fate of Ann Matilda Distin was a century and a half of oblivion.

The lights went out for Ann Matilda

For Ann Matilda the lights dimmed on her stage career as her eyesight failed around 1844. Until then she was on the record as the pianist for the Distin band, the only pianist recorded. After that the band employed a series of intermittent pianists playing that essential role.

Today it is impossible to know and understand what happened to Ann Matilda and how she felt during her twilight years 1844 – 48. The fading loss of her vision may have become a hazard. Visually impaired people can play the piano, so Ann Matilda may have continued at the piano stool for some time while her sight deteriorated. However the challenging lifestyle associated with the band may have put an end to her career. The punishing regime of constant, uncomfortable travel, new venues, new accommodation would have been difficult for the able bodied, let alone for a visually impaired middle aged woman wearing long and bulky dresses typical of her time.

In those final four twilight years it is not known whether she travelled with the band or whether she stayed in London attempting to help set up the new Distin business. She left the band at the time of their greatest achievements in 1845 and beyond. For many people in her situation, suffering from a condition with no guaranteed remedy, it would be a time of unhappiness and frustration. She may reminisced that her stage career had started in Bath with her rendition of Arthur's loss of sight.

Basking in reflected glory; deserving a place in the limelight

The Distin band was an extraordinary phenomenon. A 19th century comment on the band encapsulates their attraction,

> 'Their soft playing and ability to make delightful crescendos and diminuendos, were, 'tis said, the chief charms of the performance of the Distins. In brass instrumental music, it is delicate phrasing, intelligent light and shade, and refined quality of tone, and emphatically not the exhibitions of lung-power, which are most befitting.'[521]

It is doubtful whether this genre of brass band could be developed without the foundations of an empathetic and able pianist. For seven years Matilda provided that essential cornerstone to the band, the harmony, continuity and warmth of a piano. She must have spent some time and energy managing strong egos and talents of the five Distin men. She may have done more, it is not known.

The Distin band can be seen as an early prototype for small brass bands and having similarities to popular and jazz groups of the 20th century. They performed all over the UK, in Europe and in North America. They played to large audiences and created their own 'fanbase'. There was also the paraphernalia of fame, in the Distins' case these were locally produced mugs and jugs showing their images. In the 21st century these mugs are significant collector's pieces as they were in the later 19th century.[522] Likewise the Distin instruments are sought after in the 21st century. Ann Matilda was there for seven years from the band's inception. She was key to its establishment and development. She deserves recognition for being a founding part of this iconoclastic music phenomenon. But her vital contribution to the band has been ignored.

A tribute to Ann Matilda's uncelebrated and forgotten talents

Ann Matilda travelled through her time primarily in the shadows. She was the unseen woman and wife behind two moderately well known men. She was the daughter and sister of other minor male celebrities, she had two talented nephews and a highly skilled niece. She mothered eight sons and two daughters who all appeared on the stage. The hopes and ambitions for all of these people were high, but only the Distins really made a significant mark on their stage.

She had an extraordinarily full life. Chosen to take leading theatrical roles in her early teens, Ann Matilda made her mark on the London stage in her own right before becoming hidden in the background. So much of Ann Matilda's energy was taken in producing and nurturing children. Pregnancy and recovery must have accounted for a full 10 years of her life and for three decades she may have lived continually surrounded by her own young family. Concurrent with some of her motherhood years were the two decades she spent on the stage, 14 years as an actress and dancer and 7 seven as a pianist.

Ultimately perhaps she chose a mixture of security over risk. Her life can be seen as a compromised set of decisions based on fame versus privacy. She and her families must have felt the ever present allure of a life on the road seeking applause, fame and fortune. The decisions to travel those roads were taken by others, her husbands.

Imprisoned by the language of the time

As a woman Ann Matilda was a minor role model for other women. She was frequently mentioned in the media of the times, in newspapers from Scotland, Ireland and most parts of England. From the start of her career as a girl, when she was the' budding flower of histrionic art', she entered her husband's, Ridgway's, shadow with 'a sweet and plaintive expression in [her] countenance which gave much interest to the subordinate character which she personated.'

From her appearance in the press as Mrs Distin, in the mid 1830s, descriptions of her are minimal. Mostly she is recorded as the pianist, occasionally as the sister of Mr Loder, musician from Bath. The word 'subordinate' is attributed to her more than once. Attributes and phrases like 'able', 'sweetness and taste', 'excellence and quality', 'admirable', 'charming' and 'so efficient an auxiliary' flow from the pens of the reporters of the time about her.

The Distins used the newspapers ruthlessly to promote themselves and their forthcoming concerts by investing in advertising space. The newspapers helped to reflect on Matilda's expertise and to reconstitute her to fit into society's mold. The few existing reports of her give an image of a woman of sweetness and light, not a limelighter or a women's rights revolutionary.

The petticoat revolutionary?

There were many seismic shifts in society during Ann Matilda's lifetime, but she wasn't a leading light in these changes. Despite being on the stage at the time when there was an increasing recognition and success of serious performing women, it is not clear that she was a major advocate of women's theatrical matters. She joined into the 'revolution', performing in public for most of her life from the age of 12, but she wasn't a leading light of either the bubbling women's movement or in the position of women as performers. She may have shied away from an active front line role in the whispering juvenile women's liberation movements of her time. It would be her daughter Marian and her niece Kate who made significant contributions to these movements.

Illuminating the real Ann Matilda

She may or may not have been a woman with a dazzling attraction, a magnetic personality and outstanding looks. She certainly had a powerful personality, she took amazing risks and was full of energy. She had a significant career as both an actress and pianist and spent years travelling around in stressful conditions, while devoting decades of her life in child production. Eventually she retired from the stage when she was in her fifties. Beneath the surface of respectability of her life as a professional pianist in her latter years, there lay the whiff of scandal. Perhaps to cover this she did what was expected, she stayed in the background, tinkling the piano keys.

She played them all: the chosen dancing pupil to the Professor of Dancing, dancer and actress of the Bath Theatre Company, the principal actress and Columbine, the wife of a middle ranking clown and Harlequin, a travelling actress, the mistress of a Grenadier Guards and Royal Bandsman, a composer, the pianist for a new type of band and mother to 10 children. At the end of the day, she was an actress par excellence inventing a new life, changing identities and slipping silently out of the limelight.

Appendix 1. Women of the Petticoat Revolution: 11 women who shook the stage in Ann Matilda's lifetime

Francis Abington (1737 -1815),[523] two generations older than Ann Matilda, was an actress from a poor background, starting as a flower girl and street singer and progressing as a significant actress for nearly two decades at Drury Lane. She was an intelligent woman and became a leader in fashion, her headdress known as the Abington cap. She had an unhappy marriage to her music teacher, a royal trumpeter.

Elizabeth Inchbald (1753 – 1821)[524] was a well known novelist, actress, critic and dramatist and a highly talented person. She wrote 11 diaries. These are rare documents which illustrate a unique view of Romantic Britain. Her career introduced her to a wide group of movers and shakers of the time, and she counted William Godwin, Thomas Holcroft, Maria Edgeworth, Sarah Siddons and John Philip Kemble among her friends. Like Ann Matilda, Elizabeth was low down the family pecking order and her father died when she was young. Elizabeth was the eighth of the nine children of a farmer, John Simpson, who died when she was around eight. Elizabeth was educated with her sisters at home. She went to London to act when she was 19, and apparently was the victim of sexual harassment. She married fellow Catholic actor Joseph Inchbald (1735 – 1779) possibly for protection. The marriage was reportedly difficult. Together they toured Scotland and then moved around England. After Joseph Inchbald's death in 1779, Inchbald continued to act for several years, in Dublin, London, and elsewhere. Her acting career, only moderately successful, spanned seventeen years and she appeared in many classical roles, as well as in new plays such as Hannah Cowley's 'The Belle's Stratagem.'

Between 1784 and 1805 she had nineteen of her comedies, sentimental dramas, many of which were translations from the French, performed at London theatres. Eighteen of her plays were published, though she wrote several more: possibly between 21 and 23. Her two novels have been frequently reprinted. She also did considerable editorial and critical work. A four volume autobiography was destroyed before her death upon the advice of her confessor, but she left some of her diaries. Her play Lovers' Vows (1798) was featured by Jane Austen in her novel Mansfield Park – a play which was shown in Bath when Ann Matilda made her debut performance there with her dance tutor in 1803. Elizabeth's political beliefs can more easily be found in her novels than in her plays due to the constrictive environment of the patent theatres of Georgian London. She quarrelled publicly with Mary Wollstonecraft in 1797.

'Inchbald's life was marked by tensions between, on the
one hand, political radicalism, a passionate nature
evidently attracted to a number of her admirers, and a love
of independence, and on the other hand, a desire for social
respectability and a strong sense of the emotional
attraction of authority figures'.[525]

It is unlikely that Ann Matilda met the former resident of her road in Bath,
Elizabeth Linley, but tongues may well have been wagging about the Linley's
star daughter when Ann Matilda was a girl. Certainly her Loder father and
Uncle would have known the work of Mr Linley. Elizabeth Linley Sheridan
[1754 -1792] was the daughter of Thomas Linley, [526] singing master, composer
and conductor in Bath two decades before Ann Matilda was baptised. Before the
Loders lived in Orchard Street near the Bath theatre the Linleys had lived a few
houses away from the theatre.[527] Like the Loders a good proportion of the
Linley family made it onto the stage; seven of the twelve Linley children
entered musical or theatrical careers. Elizabeth, was a talented musician and
wife of the playwright and politician Richard Brinsley Sheridan.

Trained by her father at an early age, her first performance was at Covent
Garden Theatre aged 12, alongside her brother in 'Fairy Favour' on 31 January
1767 and, like Ann Matilda, she was a child performer. In May 1767 Elizabeth
sang and Thomas played the violin in a concert at Bath. Despite her growing
reputation, her father forced her to promise to marry Walter Long, after much
protest, to prevent her taking a theatrical career and to bring wealth into the
Linley family. On 26 June 1771, a new comedy, called 'The Maid of Bath,'
opened at the Haymarket Theatre, dramatizing and illustrating her story. She
eloped with Richard Sheridan to France in 1772. They were both underage and
so the marriage was invalid until Elizabeth's father eventually consented
officially, later in 1772, on the day after her last public appearance. In 1772
Sheridan fought a famous duel against Captain Thomas Mathews in defence of
Elizabeth's character, which Mathews had defamed her in a newspaper article.
In marrying Sheridan she agreed to give up the stage, although she still sung
informally.

Sarah Siddons, another iconoclastic actress and contemporary of Ann Matilda,
(1755 – 1831), was a serious actress. She was a potential role model with a
strong connection to Bath.[528] Sarah had developed her career on the stone stage
of the Bath Orchard Street Theatre around the time that Ann Matilda's sister
Mary had been born. From a theatrical family, Sarah pursued the stage against
the initial wishes of her father. Her personal life was mixed. She began as a
lady's maid in 1773, then at the age of 18, married William Siddons, an actor.
She gave birth to seven children but outlived five of them, and her marriage to

William became strained and ended in an informal separation. Her most famous role was Lady Macbeth. For two decades she was the queen of the London theatre. Her last performance was in 1819, when Ann Matilda was back in London. She is considered by some to be the greatest British actress of all time.

Dora Jordan,[529] (1761 - 1816) was a prime example of a popular actress who shook the theatrical establishment at the time. After two relationships and three children, she had a long term affair with the third son of George III, later to be King William IV. The couple had 10 children during their two decade relationship, and she nursed the first of these, George, for five months before returning to the stage, where she took the baby along with her. After they separated Dora continued to act. Dora and William's story was very public and certainly broke many of the taboos of the role of women, the social acceptability of the stage and the image of royalty.

Mary Wells was also known as Leah Sumbel and Mary Davies (1762 – 1829).[530] Another woman older than Ann Matilda she is a rare woman in the theatre who wrote her own story at that time, in 1811. Mary Wells wrote her 'Memoirs of the Life of Mrs Sumbel' reflecting on her own life. It is a well written book, by a woman with a mission. She, like Ann Matilda, started work as a child actress. Mary experienced domestic violence and moved to London. One of her early roles, like Ann Matilda, was that of Prince Arthur, in Shakespeare's 'King John' which she played in Birmingham. She married twice and moved around the country a lot. She was disinherited for continuing her stage career. Mary also contributed to the newspaper the 'World' owned by her second husband. She was alienated from at least some of her children and grandchildren.

Elizabeth [Eliza] Billington,[531] (1765 or 68 – 1818) was a British opera singer and another who wrote her own story, 'Memoirs of Mrs Billington' (1792).[532] She overcame the disadvantages of a difficult childhood (possibly both her father and brother were abusive) to become a professional performer and a fine musician. She had two unhappy marriages. James Ridgway was the author of most of the memoirs. Typical of time Ridgway, in the supposed interests of defending the rights of the publisher and the moral probity of the stage, portrays himself as a hero and Mrs Billington a villain. He documents his refusal to be intimidated by husbands and lawyers, who, at her request, attempted to block publication. He published her letters to her mother, unwittingly showing Eliza's own moving and educated voice. It is not known whether this James Ridgway was related to Thomas Ridgway, Ann Matilda's husband.

Maria Theresa Kemble (1774–1838)[533], née Marie Thérèse Du Camp, [spelt in different ways, for example Ducamp] was an actress and dancer on the English stage and wife of Charles Kemble, a brother of Sarah Siddons. She wrote a number of comedies. She was born in Vienna into a family of musicians and dancers. Brought to England, she appeared when six years old at the Opera House, as Cupid in a ballet. After playing at the age of eight in a theatre directed by M. Le Texier Zélie, she was engaged for the Royal Circus. She worked in the Haymarket Theatre and Drury Lane. Her father left her in England for Germany, where he died while she was still young; she picked up English, and played juvenile and small parts. She married Charles in 1806 but kept up her stage career with occasional breaks for many years.

Jane Scott[534] (1779–1839) was a British theatre manager, performer, and playwright. Her father, John Scott, supported Jane to develop the Sans Pareil Theatre, where they offered music and light shows. They gathered a theatrical company and by 1809 the theatre was licensed for musical entertainments, pantomime, and burletta. She wrote more than fifty stage pieces in an array of genres: melodramas, pantomimes, farces, comic operettas, historical dramas, and adaptations, as well as translations. She significantly moved to change the theatrical culture of the time and the Sans Pareil attempted to make a move towards free theatre unfettered by the monopolies of theatrical licenses. She retired in 1819 and married John Davies Middleton and lived in Surrey until her death, aged 59 or 60.

Maria Foote (1797(?) - 1867)[535] had a father who managed in the theatre. She, like Ann Matilda, was a 'child' actress and appeared on the Plymouth stage in 1810, and Covent Garden in 1814. At the age of 18 she played Fanny in the Inchbald play 'The Clandestine Marriage'. She toured Ireland, Scotland and Paris and played every season at Covent Garden for a decade, but often in minor parts. Her personal life was complicated, she had two children in a relationship with William Berkeley whom she sued for breach of promise of marriage. She is said to have travelled England, Ireland, and Scotland every year for five years, an estimated twenty five thousand miles.

Lucia Elizabeth, or Madame Vestris (1797 – 1856)[536] was a close contemporary of Ann Matilda, with a similar life span.[537] From a European background, Lucia's mother was a noted pianist and her father a musician and art dealer who had lost property in the French revolution. Her parents separated and her mother supported her daughters by teaching the piano. Lucia was married to a French dancer at the age of 16. She sung and acted, and after four years he deserted her. She excelled in breeches parts as well as taking leading roles in opera. In 1830, having made a fortune from her performing, she leased the Olympic Theatre where she presented burlesques and extravaganzas.

She married in 1838 for the second time, to the British actor Charles James Mathews and accompanied him on tour to America. She helped him in managerial ventures, including the management of the Lyceum Theatre and Covent Garden. Interestingly she has the same 'labels' given to her as sometimes given to Ann Matilda, singer, dancer, actress. She too married twice, and seemed to have had a successful second marriage for some decades to the end of her life.

Appendix 2. Outline family tree: the Loders

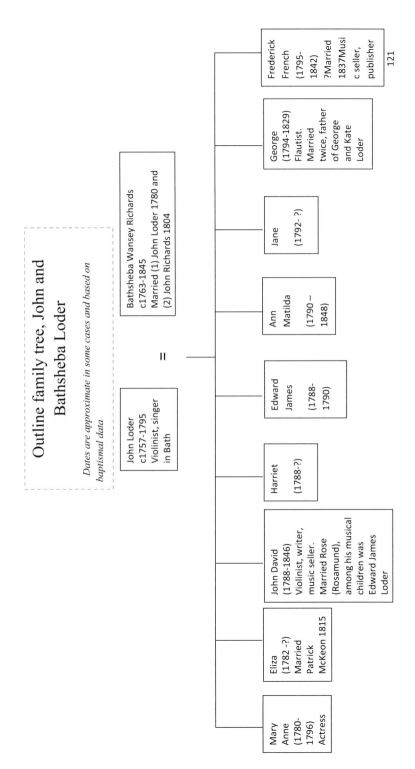

Outline family tree, John and Bathsheba Loder

Dates are approximate in some cases and based on baptismal data

John Loder
c1757-1795
Violinist, singer
in Bath

=

Bathsheba Wansey Richards
c1763-1845
Married (1) John Loder 1780 and
(2) John Richards 1804

Mary Anne
(1780-1796)
Actress

Eliza
(1782 - ?)
Married
Patrick
McKeon 1815

John David
(1788-1846)
Violinist, writer,
music seller.
Married Rose
(Rosamund),
among his musical
children was
Edward James
Loder

Harriet
(1788-?)

Edward
James
(1788-1790)

Ann
Matilda
(1790 –
1848)

Jane
(1792- ?)

George
(1794-1829)
Flautist.
Married
twice, father
of George
and Kate
Loder

Frederick
French
(1795-1842)
?Married
1837 Music
seller, publisher

Appendix 3. Outline family tree: the Ridgways

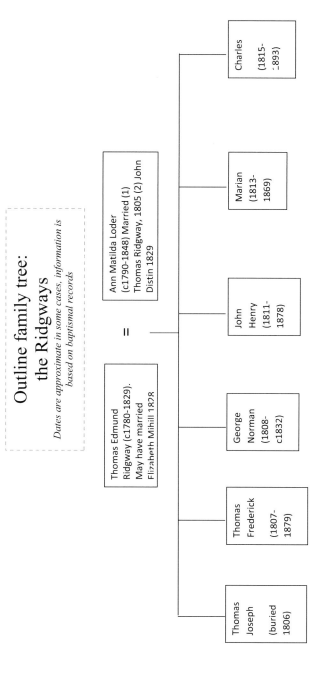

Outline family tree: the Ridgways

Dates are approximate in some cases, information is based on baptismal records

Thomas Edmund Ridgway (c1780-1829). May have married Elizabeth Mihill 1828

=

Ann Matilda Loder (c1790-1848) Married (1) Thomas Ridgway, 1805 (2) John Distin 1829

Thomas Joseph (buried 1806)

Thomas Frederick (1807-1879)

George Norman (1808-c1832)

John Henry (1811-1878)

Marian (1813-1869)

Charles (1815-1893)

Appendix 4. Outline family tree: the Distins

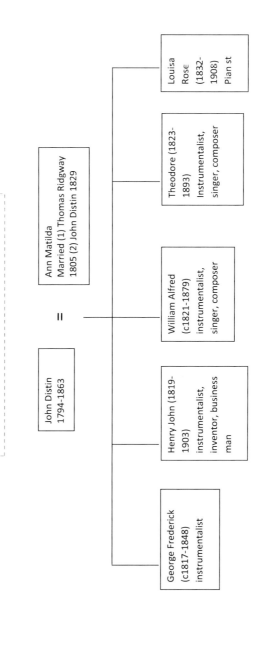

Outline family tree: the Distins
Dates are approximate in some cases, information is based on baptismal records

John Distin
1794-1863

=

Ann Matilda
Married (1) Thomas Ridgway 1805 (2) John Distin 1829

George Frederick (c1817-1848) instrumentalist

Henry John (1819-1903) instrumentalist, inventor, business man

William Alfred (c1821-1879) instrumentalist, singer, composer

Theodore (1823-1893) Instrumentalist, singer, composer

Louisa Rose (1832-1908) Pian st

A note on sources and evidence used

Sources and researcher surnames are given in the Endnotes section. Books and websites are detailed in the Bibliography. Websites consulted are dated but details may change from day to day. To aid the Ann Matilda research I have developed an Ann Matilda chronological database which is unpublished and a work in progress. Three highly valued components of this are the databases from Dr Carole Hooper (unpublished), from Professor Myers and Eugenia Mitroulia (Appendix 1 from their 2011 article in the Scottish Music Review) and from the British Newspaper Archive. Currently this has some 468 items.

The content of Ann Matilda's story has come from my own research using primary evidence sources, similar research done by others - especially relatives - and books and websites describing findings by other authors. As this publication is a synthesis of data, wherever possible I give the name of the researcher who has unearthed information used. From time to time some of the findings are in conflict and the evidence source material is identified in different ways, dependant on how it was recorded. The occasional anonymous authors of wikipedia have helped occasionally to provide a little contextual colour to sometimes inaccessible areas of research.

The story of Ann Matilda is necessarily limited by the available evidence. In general this is scant. Pre 1837 British evidence is often thin, spelling was flexible, street numbers unfixed and generations of family were often given similar names (for example Andrew Loder). A particular problem is the paucity of evidence relating to the lives of ordinary women of her time. It would be impossible to write a life story of any of her three Loder sisters, Eliza, Harriet or Jane, for instance. The evidence for their lives is virtually non existant. Ann Matilda though made the newspapers because she was on the stage; the lives of her contemporaries largely went unremarked and unrecorded. For the women who made the newspapers of her times their lives would inevitably be constructed and reconstructed to fit in with the cultural images of Victorian times.

A second point that hampers research into women like Ann Matilda is that the existing evidence is often confusing and incomplete. Theatre records, for instance usually only refer to Miss Loder or Mrs Ridgway, and it is possible, but unlikely, that there were others with the same name. Lastly much of the 'contemporary' evidence is unreliable – much of what has been written about the Distins has relied on the article in the New York Times of 1881, quoting

Henry Distin. History is written by survivors and they may be mistaken. Certainly either Henry or the reporter or the printer got at least one fundamental detail wrong in this article. The date of birth for John is incorrect by four years. Thus other 'facts' in this article are suspect. Similarly there are areas in which the evidence about Ann Matilda is uncertain or open to several interpretations. Where this is apparent the issues are discussed in the Endnotes. New sources of information about the past are opened up regularly and some future evidence sources may shed new light on Ann Matilda. New views and information on Ann Matilda will clarify what is fiction, fable, or fantasy. This life story is based on the 2013 facts as they are understood.

Bibliography

(This contains a list of specific reference publications, followed by subsection on general sources of relevant information).

Ambrose, Tom, 2005 'The King and Vice Queen: George IV's last Scandalous Affair' Sutton Publishing Stroud.

Austen, Jane. Jane Austen Society. http://www.janeaustensoci.freeuk.com/index.htm.

Austen, Jane 1990 edition 'Northanger Abbey' Oxford University Press.

Austen, Jane, website. http://www.austen.com/mans/vows/

Baines, Anthony, 1976 'Brass Instruments, Their History and Development' Faber and Faber, London.

Baker, Kenneth, 1995 'The Prime Ministers' Thames and Hudson London.

Barker, Kathleen, 1974 'The Theatre Royal, Bristol 1766 – 1966' The Society for Theatre Research.

Bate, Philip, 1972 'The Trumpet and the Trombone' Ernest Benn Limited London.

Bath Central Library collection of playbills for Bath Theatre Royal.

Bath Georgian newspaper project. http://www.bathnes.gov.uk/services/libraries-and-archives/archives/georgian-newspaper-project.

Bath Old Theatre Royal. http://www.bath-heritage.co.uk/theatre-royal-old.html

Bath records office: collection of Rate books for Orchard Street, Bath, business directories. Bath and North East Somerset Council. http://www.batharchives.co.uk/.

Beedell, A.V.,1992 'The Decline of the English Musician' Clarendon Press Oxford.

Biddlecombe, George, 1994 'English Opera from 1834 to 1864'. Garland Publishing Inc New York and London.

Bingham, Tony, Antique Musical Instruments, London. www.oldmusicalinstruments.co.uk. [Further details in subsection bibliography general]

Boaden, James, 1825 'Memoirs of the life of J.P.Kemble. volume 1'. Philadephia, Small et al.

Bor, M. and Clelland, L., 1962 'Still the Lark, a biography of Elizabeth Linley' Merlin Press London.

Borsay, Peter, 2000 'The Image of Georgian Bath, 1700 – 2000' Oxford University Press.

Broadbent, R.J., 1901 London. 'Two aspirins and a comedy.' Ch XVIII History of the Pantomime. London. http://archive.twoaspirinsandacomedy.com/index.php?post=s1160238015

Broard, John, Nelson, A., Cross, G., Donohue, J., Ellis, J., The Sans Pareil Theatre 1806 – 1900 calendar. See Donohue, Joseph.

Brown, J., and Stratton, Stephen, (1971 and various editions since 1897) 'British musical biography: A dictionary of musical artists, authors, and composers born in Britain and its colonies.' Da Capo Press New York.

Buchanan, Anne 2012. Verbal and email information. Local studies Librarian, Bath NES library (Bath Central Library) 2012. Local_studies@Bathnes.gov.uk

Burroughs, Catherine, ed. 2000 'Women in the British Romantic Theatre 1790 – 1840' CUP Cambridge.

Byrne, Paula. 2013 'The Real Jane Austen' Harper Collins London.

Carse, Adam, 1946 'The Prince Regents Band' in Oxford Journal Music and Letters XXV11 (3) pp 147 -155.

Christopoulos, Margaret, 2013. Unpublished. 'Chronology of life events of Ann Matilda Distin.'

Clarke, Andrew Cunningham, 2011 Bath and its Musical Diaspora, 1788 – 1868, Three Case Studies, University of Bristol, Dept of Music MPhil dissertation. Bristol.

Cowan, Lorna http://wc.rootsweb.ancestry.com/cgi-bin/igm.cgi?op=GET&db=haydencowan&id [accessed between November 2012 and January 2012]. In April 2013 this website facility is being updated and is not available.

Darlington, Ida, 1954 'Survey of London' London County Council, volume XXV.

Davis, Graham and Bonsall, Penny 2006 'A History of Bath: Image and Reality' Lancaster.

Dibdin, Charles the Younger: see Speaight.

Dibdin, Thomas, 'Theatrical Biography of all the Principal Actors and Actresses in 1824' http://archive.org/stream/biographybritis00unkngoog#page/n6/mode/2up .

Dibdin, Thomas 1837 'The Reminiscences of Thomas Dibdin of the Theatres Royal, Covent Garden, Drury Lane, Haymarket etc' 2 volumes.

Distin, Henry New York Times p.10, interview 7th August 1881 With Henry Distin. 'The Famed Distin Family. Career of the Great Saxhorn Quintet.'

Doane, Joseph 1794 'A Musical Directory for the Year 1794' London.

Donohue, Joseph (Editor) Professor of English, University of Massachusetts, and Cross, Gilbert B., and Nelson, Alfred (General Editors) http://www.umass.edu/AdelphiTheatreCalendar/actr.htm 'The London Stage Project 1800 – 1900.'

Dudgeon Ralph T., 2004 'The Keyed Bugle' Scarecrow Press Maryland USA.

H. Earle Johnson, 1953 'The Germania Musical Society', The Musical Quarterly, vol. 39, no. 1, Jan. 1953, pp. 75-93.

Elliot, Kirsten & Swift, Andrew 2003 'Bath Pubs', Akeman Press, Bath.

Fawcett, Trevor 1995 'Voices of Eighteenth Century Bath: An Anthology of Contemporary Text Illustrating Events.' Ruton Bath.

Fawcett, Trevor 1998 'Bath Entertain'd: amusements, recreations & gambling at the 18th-century Spa' Ruton Bath.

Forsyth, Michael, 2003 'Bath' New Haven and London.

Foster, Miles Birket, 1912 The History of the Philharmonic Society of London 1813 -1912 London.

Hare, Arnold (Editor) et al. 1977 'The Orchard Street Calendar 1750 – 1805' Kingsmead Press, Bath.

Highfill, P.H., Burnim, K.A. and Langhans E.A.,(eds.), 1984 'A Biographical Dictionary of Actors, Actresses, Dancers, Managers, & Other Stage Personnel in London, 1660-1800', Southern University Press.

Hyman, Robert and Nicola, 2011 'The Pump Room Orchestra, Bath: Three Centuries of Music and Social History', Hobnob Press Salisbury.

Greer, Germaine, 1979 'The Obstacle Race' Picador Pan Books London.

James, Kenneth Edward, 'Concert Life in Eighteenth-Century Bath' (PhD Thesis, Royal Holloway College, University of London, 1987).

Jenkins, Rebecca, 2006 'Fanny Kemble the reluctant celebrity' Simon and Schuster London.

Jenkins, Simon, 2011 'A Short History of England', Profile Books London.

Mitroulia, Eugenia & Myers, Arnold, 2011 'The Distin Family as Instrument Makers and Dealers 1845-1874' Scottish Musical Review No 1 vol 2. http://www.scottishmusicreview.org/index.php/SMR/article/viewFile/20/18 Mitroulia/Myers 2011 supplementary data for appendix 1 http://www.scottishmusicreview.org/index.php/SMR/article/view/20.

McConnell Stott, Andrew, 2009 'The Pantomime Life of Joseph Grimaldi' Canongate Edinburgh.

McVeigh, Simon, 1993 'Concert life in London from Mozart to Haydn' Cambridge University Press.

Matthew, H.C.G., and Harrison, Brian, Ed 2004 'Oxford Dictionary of National Biography' Oxford.
New Grove Dictionary of Music and Musicians. Oxford University Press. Various editions, including 2001.

Nottingham and Notts Radical History Group ND 'Home of the Infuriated Rabble'. Peopleshistreh.wordpress.com.

Perry, Gill with Roach, J., and West, S., 2012 'The First Actresses', National Portrait Gallery, London.

Porter, Roy, 1991 'English Society in the Eighteenth Century' Penguin'.

Reilly, Leonard 2009 'The Story of the Borough' Neighbourhood History 7. London Borough of Southwark.

Reitzel, William, 1933 'Oxford Journals Review of English Studies' os-I 451-456

Rohr, D., 2001 'The Careers of British Musicians 1750- 1850' Cambridge University Press Cambridge.

Royal Academy of Music (RAM) http://apollo.ram.ac.uk/emuweb/pages/ram/display.php?irn=20829 .

Rose, Algernon, S., Circa 1890. 'Talks with Bandsmen' Republished by Tony Bingham London.

Scheider, B. 1979 The Index to the London Stage, 1660 – 1800 Southern Illinois Press.

Shakespeare on line. http://www.shakespeare-online.com/plays/characters/arthurbio.html .

Smallwood, Angela, 'Women Playwrights, Politics and Convention: the Case of Elizabeth Inchbald's "Seditious" Comedy, Every One Has His Fault (1793)' http://www2.shu.ac.uk/corvey/cw3journal/issues/smallwood.html .

Speaight, George, Editor (1956) 'Memoirs of Charles Dibdin the Younger' The Society for Theatre Research, London.

Steinbach, S., 2005 'Women in England 1760 – 1914 A Social History' Phoenix, London.

Sumbel, Mary 1811 'Memoirs of the Life of Mrs. Sumbel, Late Wells: Of the Theatres-Royal, Drury-Lane, Covent-Garden, and Haymarket' , Written by herself. Also known as Leah Wells, Mary Wells and Mary Davis [Accessed through the University of Nottingham Special Collections].

Temperley, N.,ed. 1981 'The Romantic Age 1800 – 1914' Blackwell History of Music Athlone Press.

Tomalin, Claire, 1994 'Mrs Jordan's Profession' Penguin London.

Toogood, M , 2010 'Bath's Old Orchard Street Theatre' Cepenpark Publishing Chippenham.

Uglow, Jenny 2003 'The lunar men: the friends who made the future 1730 - 1820' Faber and Faber London.

Venning, Annabel, 2006 'Following the Drum, the lives of Army Wives and Daughters' Headline Book Publishing London.

Walford, Edward, 1878 'St George's Fields', Old and New London: Volume 6 (1878), pp. 341-368. From http://www.britishhistory.ac.uk/report.aspx?compid=45286.

Warbis, J., 1988 'Southwark Streets and Alleys up to 1860.' [From Southwark Library].

Wilson, Ben, 2007 'Decency and Disorder 1789 – 1837' Faber and Faber London.

General and additional sources of information

Bath in 1790s http://visitbath.co.uk/spa-and-wellbeing/history-of-baths-spa .

Bath in time. Images of Bath www.bathintime.co.uk [accessed May 2012].

Bate Collection, Music Department, University of Oxford. www.bate.ox.ac.uk/.

Bingham, Tony, Antique Musical Instruments, London. www.oldmusicalinstruments.co.uk/

List of European venues taken from Tony Bingham's print (October 2006 and April 2013) M. Christopoulos from T. Bingham's print.

Adelphi Theatre: Joseph Donohue, (Editor) Professor of English, University of Massachusetts, and Cross, Gilbert B., and Nelson, Alfred (General Editors) http://www.umass.edu/AdelphiTheatreCalendar/actr.htm [accessed 1st November 2012, December – March 2013].
'The London Stage Project 1800 – 1900.' Resources affliated or produced by the Project include:
The Adelphi Theatre Calendar, a complete calendar documenting the day to day history of the Adelphi Theatre; Paul Buczkowski's bibliographical lists of Periodicals in London from 1800 to 1810; a databank of basic information concerning theatres in operation between 1800 and 1810.

Ray Farr, conductor in Residence, University of Durham. Regrettably it has not been possible to include information from Farr's new book on the Distin Band (2013). It has proved to be unavailable February – April 2013. The author has contributed some information to Ray for his book before its publication. The Endnotes include references to Ray's comments.

Holburne Museum Bath
http://www.holburne.org/muse/search/item.cfm?MuseumNumber=A169
The Holburne Museum has art from the 18th and 19th centuries including some related to the Bath Theatre.

New York Public Library website has a large collection of images, including (a) one of the Distin Band showing Mrs Distin, (b)Theodore Distin. (c) one of 'John Loder'

University of Edinburgh, Musical Instrument Museum
http://www.music.ed.ac.uk/euchmi/galpin/gxkta.html

Topic Index

Matilda: change in direction, change of name. The early Distin years 1816-1829

Matilda: the Distin years of fame 1829-1848

Tying up the loose ends

Epilogue and spotlight on Ann Matilda: what was her real legacy?

Appendix1 :11 women who shook the stage

Endnotes[a selection of topics]

Endnotes and references

[1] The introduction to limelight is given by several named sources including: Faraday, Michael; James, Frank A. J. L (1999). The Correspondence of Michael Faraday. p. 11. ISBN 978-0-86341-251-6. Almqvist, Ebbe (2003). History of industrial gases. pp. 72–73. ISBN 978-0-306-47277-0, Reid, Francis (2001).The Stage Lighting Handbook (Stage and Costume). U.K: A & C Black Publishers Ltd; 6Rev Ed edition (31 May 2001). pp. 1224 pages. ISBN 0-7136-5396-5. From wikipedia [accessed 27.03.13].

[2] Tony Bingham, proprietor of 'Old Musical Instruments' business, London. Verbal information 2008.

[3] New York Times, p.10, interview 7th August 1881 With Henry Distin. 'The Famed Distin Family. Career of the Great Saxhorn Quintet.' A copy of this was given to the author by B. & R. Kearin, the copy was transcribed by Joan McMaster who had access to a copy of a very old copy of this article, in Australia, probably taken from an original 1881 newspaper.

[4] Graham Davis and Penny Bonsall, 2006 'A History of Bath: Image and Reality' Lancaster. P.83.Quoted by Clarke, p. 9.

[5] **The name: Ann Matilda.** It is difficult to know what name she was known by, for her early life I presume she was known as Ann. Her name will be considered later.

[6] Fawcett, Trevor, 1998 'Bath Entertain'd: amusements, recreations & gambling at the 18th-century Spa' Ruton Bath. Fawcett and other authors write extensively about the history and development of Bath in the 18th Century. An outline summary of the city can be found on the website, http://visitbath.co.uk/media/information-sheets/history-and-heritage [accessed 24.08.12].

[7] The Hanoverian Georges ruled from 1714 – 1820 http://www.britroyals.com [accessed 27.08.12].

[8] Information on Baldwin and Woods the younger from: http://www.cotswolds.info/places/bath/famous-people.shtml [accessed 24.08.12];

[9] http://www.cotswolds.info/places/bath/famous-people.shtml [accessed 24.03.13].

[10] Borsay, Peter, 2000 'The Image of Georgian Bath, 1700 – 2000' Oxford. p.136. Quoted by Clarke p.12.

[11] Clarke, Andrew Cunningham, 2011. 'Bath and its Musical Diaspora, 1788-1868, Three Case Studies', MPhil Thesis, University of Bristol. p.9.

[12] Clarke p.9.

[13] The William Herschel Society . http://www.williamherschel.org.uk/ [accessed 24.08.12]. Also verbal information from staff at the Herschel Museum, Bath, May 2012.

[14] Herschel Museum Bath, verbal information May 2012.

[15] **Loders of Bath.** There are Loders, Loaders, Lowders and Louders to be found in the records for Bath and the surrounding area of Somerset. There is also a James Loder who is recorded marrying a Mary Powell at Bath St James 8th January 1784. (Bath Record Office, Microfiche of Parish records).

[16] **Loder information.** The four main sources used are Clarke 2011, the Rootsweb family tree website facility built up by Lorna Cowan with major contributions from Debra Smith and others http://wc.rootsweb.ancestry.com and my own original research. The information on the rootsweb facility has developed over time (2008-12). The Biographical Dictionary of Actors, Actresses, Musicians, Dancers, Managers and other Stage personnel in London1660 -1800 P.Highfill, K.Burnim and E.Langhans (several editions, 1973-1993) South Illinois University Press was also consulted. These sources are not always consistent with each other.

[17] Cowan.

[18] McVeigh, Simon, 1993 'Concert life in London from Mozart to Haydn' Cambridge University Press. pp.182 -205.

[19] Clarke, p.13.

[20] P. H. Highfill, Jr, K. A. Burnim, and E. A. Langhans (eds.), 1984 'A Biographical Dictionary of Actors, Actresses, Dancers, Managers, & Other Stage Personnel in London, 1660-1800', Southern University Press. (1973 – 1993).

[21] Highfill et al.

[22] James, Kenneth Edward, 1987, 'Concert Life in Eighteenth-Century Bath' (PhD Thesis, Royal Holloway College, University of London, 1987) p.777, quoted by Clarke p.29. Highfill et al. note that in 1784 Andrew and John were instrumentalists in concerts in Bristol and maybe John was the singer who sang as a treble at the Handel memorial concerts at Westminster Abbey in 1784. Bath Chronicle 1st May 1788, quoted by Clarke, states that in 1788 John Loder played in a benefit for Mr Cantelo with others including William Herschel.

[23] English Chronicle or Universal Evening Post 12 September 1789, quoted by Clarke p.29. Stourton Caundle is 30 miles from Weymouth.

[24] James p.777-9 and quoted by Clarke. p.29. Clarke gives the example of the three day Somerset Music Meeting at Wells, Bath Chronicle 14 August 1788. James notes that John played the viola in a number of string quartets.

[25] St James's Chronicle or the British Evening Post 29th April, 1773. Quoted by Clarke p.31.

[26] Clarke p.31.

[27] Clarke p.31.

[28] Joseph Doane: A Musical Directory for the year 1794. Facsimile copies are available, for instance, from the RCM www.RCM.ac.uk.

[29] Clarke p.31 An open letter to the Bath Chronicle 3 January 1799, implored the Church Officers and the inhabitants of the parish to 'decline giving a promise to any Candidate until the pretensions of each have been duly investigated.'

[30] Bath Chronicle, 4th December 1806. Quoted by Clarke p.31.

[31] Andrew Loder Senior was baptised in Stourton Caundle in 1721, Andrew junior in 1752 in Stourton Caundle. Cowan.

[32] Kirsten Elliot and Andrew Swift, 2003 'Bath Pubs' Bath p.117 – 122. There are only three known pubs in England with this name. The Bath directories for the period cite only one family with the name Loder.

[33] Bath Chronicle 11 August 1785 and quoted by Clarke. The notice describes a property of three cellars and five stables and gardens. Bath Chronicle, 15th September 1785. 'Music: breakfast concert - for benefit for Mr Loder (who labours under severe illness). At Great Room, Spring Gardens, on 15 Sep. Tickets 3s 6d. (inc breakfast) at Mr Lintern's music shop, Church Yard, Bath. Ball follows.' Quoted by Clarke.

[34] London Gazette, 11th October 1785. He was ordered to surrender himself at the Bush Tavern, Bristol.

[35] Clarke p.32.

[36] One example of this is that of Caroline Herschel, sister of the astronomer and musician William, whose reputation was dwarfed besides that of her brother, despite being very able in the same field. From Brown, Frank, 2000, 'Caroline Herschel as a Musician', William Herschel Museum, Bath.

[37] Baptism of Bathsheba Richards. 13 May 1763, St Marys Redcliffe, Bristol. Cowan.

[38] John and Bathsheba Loder appear as witnesses at the marriage of Mary Richards [Ann Matilda's maternal grandmother] and John Henrard, 1784. AncestryLibrary.com. Cowan.

[39] Mr Richards appears later as a music tutor to John David Loder, Clarke p.11.

[40] Bathsheba's signature is given on the register for her 2 marriages. AncestryLibrary.com. Cowan.

[41] Records of Births, Marriages and Deaths, BM+D (Debra Smith, recorded by Cowan) have verified that there is no direct connection with the Cantelo family, and the entry in the Highfill et al. Dictionary for Hezekiah Cantelo is incorrect.

[42] Cowan.

[43] 6 May 1782 in St Swithin's, Walcot, Bath, Somerset. Cowan.

[44] Mary was baptised in January 1783 at St Swithins, Walcot, Bath. Cowan. Her birth was noted in the press. The Bath Chronicle of the 26 December 1782 records, 'Births: wife of John Loder, musician of Bath , delivered of a daughter last Tuesday morning. The baby's great great grandmother is Mrs Cantel now living in Bristol.' This newspaper item does not square with the data researched for the Cowan data, the 'Bersheba' (no known surname) who married Thomas Cantle in February 1739(?) in St Marys Redcliffe, Bristol, would have been Bathsheba Wansey's great grandmother. There is a slim chance that there was ongoing intermarriage in the Cantle family in Bristol in the earlier 1700s.

[45] Bathsheba died 31 December 1845 at 2 Nelson Close, Lansdown, Bath of heart disease. In the census in 1841 she is recorded as a widow of independent means living in Kingsmead Street, Bath. Cowan.

[46] It was noted that John Loder had been the owner of a shop on Orchard Street, Bath – related to a later bankruptcy in 1798, Clarke p.30. It is possible that this had come from his father, Andrew Loder senior. Alternatively it may have been given in some way to Bathsheba and because of the prevailing law – that husbands were in control of much of their wives' property it was in John Loder's name.

[47] Various newspapers note that theatre tickets could be purchased at the Loders, 5, Orchard Street. (also 3, Orchard Street) See note above re bankruptcy in 1798. Georgian Newspaper Project, Bath. http://www.bathnes.gov.uk/services/libraries-and-archives/archives/georgian-newspaper-project [accessed several times 2011 -2013].

[48] London Chronicle Issue 4069, 26th December 1782.

[49] Cowan.

[50] For the Loder children it is convenient to surmise that they were born within 30 days of their baptism, this was only a social convention and the actual dates of birth of the children may never be known. Discussion of some of the nine children's baptisms is given consideration in the text, including that of Ann Matilda. Eliza was baptised at St James Bath 12 December 1784. Nothing much is known of her life, an Eliza Loder marries a Patrick McKeon at St James Bath on 18 April 1815, aged about 30.

[51] Marriage of John Henrard and Mary Richards, Bath Abbey (St Peter and Paul), 16 February 1784. Parish Records, microfilms.

[52] Horse Street was given as the address for tickets for A. Loder and Orchard Street for 'Loder' in the 1780s and 1790s. Georgian Newspaper Project.

[53] These three were baptised 14th August, 1788, at Bath Abbey, recorded in the Parish Register probably reflecting their birth order, John David, Harriet and Edward James. Clarke p. 29 – 33.

[54] Clarke p. 29 – 33.

[55] Clarke p.33.

[56] Doane directory of 1794.

[57] Wendeborn, a view of England p. 239, quoted by D.Rohr, p.157 Rohr, D., 2001 'The Careers of British Musicians 1750- 1850' Cambridge University Press Cambridge.

[58] Verbal information from Ann Buchanan, Bath Local Studies Librarian, August 2012.

[59] Verbal information from Anne Buchanan.

[60] **French revolution.** http://europeanhistory.about.com/od/thefrenchrevolution [accessed 17th September 2012]. There are many publications giving a timescale of events for the French Revolution and impact on the UK.

[61] Uglow, Jenny, 2003 'The lunar men: the friends who made the future 1730 -1820' Faber and Faber London. p.505.

[62] Uglow p.463.

[63] **Baptism record for Ann Matilda Loder (and consequent debate about her paternity and her birthdate).** I visited the Somerset records office 15th august 2012 and with the help of two senior members of their research staff studied the original Parish register for 1790 for Bath Saint James. The baptism record is located out of date sequence in the register, written at the base of the page after entries for mid December 1790. Out of sequence entries are relatively common in the Somerset area. The actual words [except one 'XXX'] for Ann's baptism record are clear and written over three 'lines'.

> 'Daughter of John x Bathsheba
> Ann Matilda Loder was baptised October 20th
> XXX omitted to be inserted in its proper place'

There is an inverted 'v' indicating an insertion under and between the words Matilda and Loder. The word XXX is not clear, it probably has three letters and the research staff members' best guess is 'was'. In addition a line has been drawn in the first 'line', effectively crossing through from 'Daughter of John' and the cross between the words John and Bathsheba. The word 'Bathsheba' is relatively clear and is not crossed through. Elsewhere on the same page the ampersands are 'fancy' and traditional, however on thumbing through the register there are other pages where the ampersand is like a simple 'x'. The research staff studied in depth the issue and went so far as looking up other records as below. There are two sets of theories, either way Bathsheba is the mother.

i. Accidental line drawn: the line was meant to mark the end of the previous entry and AM's out of order entry, but missed and the x could mark a 'deletion' of the line OR the line was an accident OR the clerk/vicar thought he had got muddled up.

ii. Purposeful deletion: that John Loder was not the father of AM, or thought not to be the father, and that someone made a fuss and requested that the name John was deleted. This is interesting because Somerset research staff consider that the crossing out was made at the time of insertion of the record, in the same hand as the person who wrote the other entries for 1790, the vicar or parish clerk. Bathsheba is the given mother whatever. As the previous and consequent children all had clear 'John and Bathsheba - or variations of 'Bathsheba' as parents if this latter is the case there would have been some contemporary evidence/belief of a short term affair - possibly while John was out of town playing his violin. Research colleagues searched all the quarterly court records and the bastardy orders (for Loder, Loader, Lowder, Louder etc) and there was none. The research staff considered that both options were possible but on balance this second option was more likely. If this second theory is accepted, at least one party to the baptism, John, Bathsheba or the vicar believed that John was not Ann Matilda's father.

The register contains contemporary records of other children/babies being recorded as 'bastard', not the case with Ann Matilda's registration. If a person wished to inspect the register there was not - apparently - a problem. The vicar/clerk would probably allow limited regular access to the records - the paper is beautiful and tough and parchment like and would probably have routinely been kept under lock and key.

Another theory has been suggested: that Ann Matilda was the illegitimate daughter of Bathsheba before her marriage to John Loder and baptised at the age of 11, or earlier. I have rejected this theory as the balance of evidence is weighted in favour of a birthdate of around the end of September 1790. A significantly earlier date of birth does not tally with other data, namely Ann Matilda's early performances at the Theatre Royal – which were made at the same age as her elder sister Mary (circa 13 years), and her recorded age of death, age 57 in 1848. But this remains a mystery in 2013.

The only conclusion that can be made [2013] is that if John wished his name to be deleted as AnnMatilda's father he took no recorded legal action. Thus it would appear that John recognised Ann Matilda as his daughter legally. Her baptism date is midway between her older siblings (triple baptism in August 1788) and younger sibling (November 1792). Somerset Heritage [Ref. D/P/ba.ja 2/1/5]. Margaret Christopoulos.

[64] Debra Smith, family historian, 16 May 2012 notes: 'The majority of children were baptised before their 30th day of age because parents believed to not do so would mean they were not recognised by God as having a name as they entered Heaven, should they die in those first few days/weeks. It is why ill babies (or those they thought would not last the night) were quickly baptised at home, then a 2nd ceremony held at the church to recognise the godparents should the child survive to the 30th day. Remembering too that mothers were "laying-in" for at least the first 2 weeks of the child's life, so the minimum time frame for a church baptism would be 14 days of age. It is possible that Ann was a 'sickly' baby and thus originally baptised in her home, with the church ceremony held around her 30th day but we shall never know as it is not written as such in the entry.'

[65] Records consulted, Somerset Heritage Centre. 29 August 2012. The Bath St James register, ref: D/P/ba ja 2/1/5, covers baptisms and burials 1782 to 1812. The entries are inserted from each end towards the middle, i.e one has to reverse the volume to change from baptisms to burials. The Bath St James register, ref: D/P/ba ja 2/1/5, covers baptisms and burials 1782 to 1812. P.Hocking of the Somerset Heritage Centre confirmed that the burial was in the 'yard', 29 August 2012. Edward James, possibly a twin or triplet, was buried on 26th December 1790 in the yard of St James Church.

[66] It is unclear what the fate of 'Harriet' was. It has been impossible to trace verifiable records of her.

[67] Register of Baptisms April, 1790, the surname is unclear, another Ann(a) Matilda baptised 10th april 1790 daughter of James and Elizabeth Kittell (or Mittell, Millett.) in St James, parish Bath.

[68] Rohr, p.17.

[69] Clarke, p.24. Also Rohr p.8.

[70] Cowan.

[71] Greer, Germaine, 1979. 'The Obstacle Race' Picador Pan Books London. p.12.

[72] Rohr p.119.

[73] Rohr p.120.

[74] Rohr p.133.

[75] Clarke p.16.

[76] **Records of rate books in Bath (Bath Records office).** There is an incomplete record of the Bath Rate books. Inevitably Rate books only record the ratepayer and not necessarily the resident of a property. Both City and Parish rate books exist in the Bath records office for some of the years 1790 to 1800, but not all. The City Rate book for 1790 lists no 'Loder' for Orchard Street. It lists other people associated with the Theatre, like Mr French and Mr

Quick. It also notes the Theatre and the third name following 'The Theatre' is a Mr Wingrove, with a 'Prynn' written separately in a column to the right. Two other names are given after Mr Wingrove. The Rate book for the quarter ending 4 June 1793 notes a Mr Lowder in place of Mr Wingrove, but the positioning of the name in the rate book is the same. Similarly the quarter ending 15 January 1795 has Mr Lowder in the same listing. If the rate books listings are consistent they probably relate to the relevant dwellings. The St James Poor rate book for 1796 lists a Mrs Loder and a Mrs Prynne at the same part of the list for Orchard Street. Interestingly further down Orchard Street, 14 properties away is 'Mr The Cantel Richard'. The Rate book for the quarter ending Christmas 1797 lists Mr (s?) Loder with Mr (s) Prynne in a column to the right at the same address, and lists Mr Richards at the same presumed residence as in the 1796 rate book. Mrs Loder is listed in the 1799 rate book (Christmas to Lady Day, 21st March) in Orchard Street, but the previous position in the 'address' listing has been taken by a Mr Edwin, Mrs Loder is listed paying rates towards the other end of the short street, but as the actual listings are named and are inconsistent it would not appear that she lived in Mr Richards' dwelling at that time, his name is no longer in Orchard Street. She appears to be at this same address in the following quarter (to 27th June 1799), again no Mr Richards. In the latter Rate book Mrs Loder's name is on the same line as 'Tebay Void'. The next extant Rate book for St James (July, 1801, 42466/9) shows no Mrs Loder, but in the position in the book her name appeared in the 1799 book is listed a Mr Tebay (numbered 204).

[77] This topic will be examined further in a later section.

[78] Toogood, verbal information May 2012.

[79] Rate books for the parish of St James, Bath Record Office.

[80] Graham Davis email 12 sept 12.

[81] The Rate books indicate a fast turnover of rate payers in the 1790s in this street.

[82] Toogood, verbal information May 2012 and published information 2010. Malcolm Toogood is a Bath historian and has supported the theatre for many years. He has studied the deeds of theTheatre Royal. He is of the opinion (Toogood 2012) that the street numbering system of the 1790s was informal and difficult to link to 21st Century surviving buildings. Adjacent to the Theatre (on its left if viewing from the opposite side of the road) was a building which was officially located in Pierrepoint Street, he considers it unlikely that there were any residential properties in the same side of the road as the theatre in Orchard Street in the 1790s (Toogood, 2010, page 21 Map of Bath 1795). The residential properties were on the opposite side of the road from the Theatre Royal and from current evidence (Toogood 2012) considers that number 3 Orchard Street would have been located on the opposite side somewhere between the theatre and St James Street, and in 2013 this is a Marks and Spencers lorry depot.

[83] Uglow p. 464.

[84] Uglow p.464.

[85] There were food riots (bread and meat) recorded in Nottingham for instance, April and July 1795 Nottingham and Notts Radical History Group.

[86] Clarke, p. 30 'Bath Journal,' 14, September, 1795; 'Morning Post and Fashionable World,' 19 September, 1795.

[87] The Bath Chronicle records the following 4 press notices:
17 Sep 1795 Deaths: Mr John Loder, musician of Bath, in Weymouth on Wed [16 Sept]. Leaves a widow & seven young children.
22 Oct 1795 Music: concert in New Assembly Rooms on 4 Nov for benefit of widow & children of Mr John Loder, musician. Vocalists Miss Gopell, Mr Braham, Messrs Taylor, Williamson, Tuck, Russell, J. Ashley, A. Loder; etc. Tickets 5s.

5 Nov 1795 Music: young Loder, 8 yrs old is playing a violin concerto at the approaching concert for benefit of a widow in great distress left with 7 small children.

5 Nov 1795 Music: benefit concert for the widow & 7 young children of late John Loder, musician. Postponed from 4th Nov to Wed 11 Nov at New Assembly Rooms on Wed 11 Nov. Violin concertos played by Mr Richards & by Master J. Loder aged 8; Mrs Miles playing concerto on piano; Symphony by Haydn; songs, etc. Tickets 5s from Mrs Loder, 5 Orchard St, Bath; etc.

It is not clear who the seven 'small' or young Loder children were. To date it has been impossible to trace the life of 'Harriet'. She may have died early as an infant. The oldest daughter, Mary, was 12 years 9 months at the time of her father's death and would not have been regarded as a 'young child'.

[88] Report on the benefit concert for Mrs Loder and her family, Bath Herald, 14th November 1795. The benefit concert was advertised to be 11 November 1795. A copy of this item is also available in © Bath in Time - Bath Central Library Collection Image Reference 34211.

[89] Clarke p.11 notes that this was David Richards.

[90] Hare, Arnold (Editor) et al.. 1977 'The Orchard Street Calendar 1750 – 1805' Kingsmead Press, Bath p.226 1795/6, 1796/7 and 1797/8.

[91] Bath Library playbill, there is only one playbill in the Bath Library collection that mentions a Miss Loder at this time, in the 1790s. The play concerned was written by Mrs Inchbald and was performed Tuesday 14 March 1797. In the cast was Mr Cunningham (as Mr Placid), he later married Mary's cousin, Andrew Loder's daughter, Amy.

[92] Smallwood , Angela, 'Women Playwrights, Politics and Convention: the Case of Elizabeth Inchbald's "Seditious" Comedy, Every One Has His Fault 1793' http://www2.shu.ac.uk/corvey/cw3journal/issues/smallwood.html [accessed 1st October 2012].

[93] Smallwood.

[94] Clarke, pp. 31,32 quoting James Concert Life p.779-782.

[95] Oracle and Public Advertiser, 16 September, 1796.

[96] Oracle and Public Advertiser, 2 March, 1797.

[97] The Duke of York had heard John David Loder play at his mother's benefit. (Clarke and newspaper reports).

[98] Clarke p.32.

[99] Clarke p.11 quoting the Bath Chronicle of 16th January, 1800.

[100] Clarke p. 33 quoting Bath Journal, 27 January, 1800; 3 February, 1800; 10 February, 1800; 17 February, 1800. Master Pinto played in two further seasons (1803-4, 1804-5) before his untimely death in 1806.

[101] Clarke p.33 Bath Journal, 2 June, 1800.

[102] Clarke p. 33 George Frederick Pinto (1785-1806).

[103] Verbal information from Anne Buchanan, Bath Library May 2012.

[104] Rohr p.62.

[105] Rohr p.71.

[106] Fawcett, Trevor 1995 'Voices of Eighteenth Century Bath: An Anthology of Contemporary Text Illustrating Events.' Bath Ruton. p.130.

[107] Fawcett 1995 quoting from Sibbald Memoirs. p.128-9.

[108] Fawcett 1995 p.127.

[109] Jenkins, Rebecca, 2006 'Fanny Kemble the reluctant celebrity' Simon and Schuster London. p.50 Miss Decamp was the mother of Fanny Kemble, and wife of Charles Kemble – Fanny's father . Miss Decamp [various spellings] made her first stage appearance aged 8 in 1783 at the Kings Theatre – she danced as a diminutive cupid in a ballet by Noverre that

followed the main opera. Fawcett, 1998 p.83 mentions children appearing on stage at the Theatre Royal Bath.

[110] **Clara Fisher child actress**
Clara Fisher was born in London England, on July 14, 1811. Her father was Frederick George Fisher, a librarian and well-known amateur actor. Her earliest memories were of attending concerts and plays with her family. At the age of five her father enrolled her in acting lessons. Her first performance was on December 10, 1817 at the Drury Lane Theatre as Lord Flimnap in the production of David Garrick's Lilliput, where she 'astonished the audience with her great talent'. After her success at Drury Lane, Clara moved on to successful engagements at Covent Garden. By her teens she had successfully performed Richard III, Shylock, Douglas, and Dr. Pangloss. She was hailed as Britain's 'child wonder' and was regarded as the most successful child actor of her time. Two relevant references are given on wikipedia, Maeder, Clara Fisher; Douglas Taylor (1897). Autobiography of Clara Fisher Maeder. New York: The Dunlap society. pp. 1–5. ISBN 0-8337-2180-1 and Percy, Reuben; Sholto Percy (1839). The Percy Anecdotes, New York: Harper. p. 34.Information from: http://en.wikipedia.org/wiki/Clara_Fisher . [accessed 27 March 13].

[111] Forsyth, Michael, 2003 'Bath' New Haven and London, quoted by Clarke p.20.

[112] Toogood, Malcolm, 2010 ' Bath's Old Orchard Street Theatre' Cepenpark Publishing Chippenham p.9, and Toogood verbal information May 2012.

[113] Fawcett, 1998 p.83. Further general information on the Theatre Royal Bath can be found on: http://www.bath-heritage.co.uk/theatre-royal-old.html .

[114] Fawcett 1998 p.83.

[115] Fawcett 1998 p.83.

[116] Barker, Kathleen, 1974 'The Theatre Royal, Bristol 1766 – 1966,' The Society for Theatre Research. p.71.

[117] Fawcett 1998 p.83 describes the triumphal return of Sarah Siddons in 1799. The theatre performances were sold out and people crowded the avenues near the Theatre Royal to catch a glimpse of her, quoting Bath Herald 2 Feb 1799.

[118] Fawcett 1998 p.83.

[119] Barker p.53 quoting from Felix Farley's Bristol Journal 26.10.1782.

[120] Barker p.63, quoting Sarah Farley's Bristol Journal 11.5.1799 re Blue Beard. French died 6th September 1803 and his son continued as scene painter for a while, but disappeared after 1806, Barker p.71.

[121] Barker p.61.

[122] Barker p.62.

[123] Malcolm Toogood verbal information Mary 2012.

[124] Barker p.77.

[125] Barker, p.74.

[126] James, Kenneth Edward, 'Concert Life in Eighteenth-Century Bath' (PhD Thesis, Royal Holloway College, University of London, 1987). quoted by Clarke p.23.

[127] James quoted by Clarke p.23.

[128] Clarke p.23.

[129] Burial of Mary Henrard (born Mary Cantle or Cantel, later Mary Richards) in Bath, St James 2nd September 1797. Cowan.

[130] Bath Chronicle, 13 September, 1798 and quoted by Clarke p.30.

[131] Morning Post and Gazetteer, announcement, 10 September, 1798, Clarke p.30.

[132] **Bathsheba and bankruptcy and Mr Prynn**: there is a tangled web of evidence. Clarke p.30 states that Bathsheba was declared bankrupt, quoting the press report, Oracle and Daily Advertiser, 19 September, 1798. This short notice states, 'At Guildhall, on Tuesday, the 16th

October next, at Ten O'clock, by the direction of the commissioners under a commission of bankrupt awarded against Richard Prynn, Linen Draper. A neat freehold dwelling house and premises, desirably situate the corner of Orchard Street, near the Theatre &c. late in the possession of Mr. Loder, and of annual value of Twenty Five Pounds. The premises are in good, substantial repair, and are built on a part of the Abbey Orchard: situation eligible and pleasant, and may be entered on immediately after sale '. Prynn [or Prynne] is a name listed at the side, and in a separate column, of the name 'Loder' [or Lowder] in some of the rate books of the 1790s.

Colin Johnson, Bath record office, 28 September 2012, notes, 'The Rate books at this period are very basic in format and provide very little information. There is no indication given of the nature of premises, whether residence or business. The narrow left hand column only occasionally shows a name, and this is believed to be the agent or landlord through whom the rate was paid. I have no evidence to confirm this but other researchers have told me this is their opinion. I can only assume that Prynne had this role in relation to Mr & Mrs Lowder.'

A number of quotations from the Georgian Newspaper Project tell the story of Mr Prynn and his business activities [http://www.bathnes.gov.uk/services/libraries-and-archives/archives/georgian-newspaper-project accessed 27 March 2013].

7 May 1789 Fashion: partnership between Richard Prynn & William Collins has expired so all their stock of materials at Bengal Warehouse, 26 Markt Pl will be sold cheaply. After stock disposal, business will be continued by Richard Prynn. Bath Chronicle.

13 Aug 1789 Notices: public apology - Richard Prynn, linen draper, confessed to defaming the character of Mr Robert Minchin in a conversation at the Cross Keys. Action against him dropped on his agreeing to pay costs of the suit & make public acknowledgement. Bath Chronicle 1221/1789 article:3 c.

26 Apr 1792 Goods: Richard Prynn, draper of Bengal warehouse, 26 Market Pl, Bath can supply dimities at 18d/yd, counterpanes 11s ea, white calicoes at 13d/yd, printed furniture cottons 17d & 18d, etc as a result of recent fall in price of cotton (wool) [list of products/prices] Bath Chronicle 857/1792 article:3 c.

15 Nov 1792 Fashion: bargains in cheap linen drapery, muslins etc at Mr Prynn's Bengal warehouse, 26 Market Pl, Bath. Inc. tambours2s/yd, worked cravats 2s, gown pieces 10s ea, flannels 10d/yd, dimities 16d, pocket handkerchiefs 1d etc. Bath Chronicle 2024/1792 article:3.c.

20 Mar 1794 Goods: J Stafford has let his front shop to Mr Prynn, linen draper, & erected warerooms in his extensive premises up the adjacent court. Bath Chronicle 863/1794 article:3c.

16 Oct 1794 Notices: Richard Prynn has left Old Bengal Warehouse in Market Place & moved to No 23 opp. the Corn Market. Muslins - good 4 qtr plains 9d/yd, books 15d/, India mails 12d/, clear handkerchiefs 10d-8s each, tick do 9d upwards, 6 qtr wide India books 12d/ry, pocket handkerchiefs [linen] 1d each Bath Chronicle 2694/1794 article:3 c.

24 Sep 1795 Marriages: Mr Prynn, linen draper [of Bath] to Miss Jane Cantelo, in the Abbey Church on Sat [19 Sept] Bath Chronicle 1859/1795 article:3 b.

8 Oct 1795 Goods: sale of prime Irish linen by Richard Prynn at Bengal warehouse, 23 Market Place, Bath. Bath Chronicle 1948/1795 article:3.d.

13 Jun 1799 Deaths: Mr Richard Prynn, linen draper in Market Pl, Bath, Monday Bath Chronicle.

5 Dec 1799 Finance: bankruptcy - Richard Prynn, haberdasher, Bath dividend 21 Dec; J Anstie, clothier, Devizes dividend on 30 Dec Bath Chronicle 2528/1799 article:4,c.

One interpretation of this set of events is that John Loder had purchased the property in Orchard Street in around 1792/3. With his death Bathsheba sold or handed over the freehold of the property to a managing agent, Richard Prynn, who was a local draper and businessman. She might well have done this to release money for herself and the family, while maintaining somewhere to live. Things did not go well for Mr Prynn and his businesses and he was declared bankrupt in September 1798, forcing her out of her home when the property was sold possibly to a Mr Edwin if the rate book for 1799 is to be believed.

[133] Bath Theatre Royal Playbills, for example 3 May 1803, and 28 January 1804 when Mr Tebay performs along with both Miss Tebay and Miss S. Tebay.

[134] Clarke, pp 29-47.

[135] Cowan. There is a record of an Eliza Loder marriage later in the 1800s in Bath, when Bathsheba's daughter Eliza would have been around 30. A Jane Loder signs as witness for the first of the marriages of the brother George. The records of an illiterate Jane Loder give a marriage record. There is no evidence of another performing Miss Loder.

[136] Bath Library Theatre Royal Playbill, for 2 June 1803. There is a perennial caveat, that Miss Loder was in fact Ann Matilda. This evidence is best viewed in retrospect, given the information from the Theatre Royal in 1804/5, and that Miss Loder clearly then refers to Ann Matilda. If another Miss Loder appeared on the stage at that time one of them would have been given an initial - as in the case of the Misses Tebay, see earlier note.

[137] Clarke p.33. Clarke notes, 'There was increased frequentation of the Sydney Gardens to the east of the city now accessible along Great Pulteney Street, completed towards the end of the 18th century. The introduction of the Grand Gala provided the opportunity for a diverse mix of entertainment from music, both military and orchestral, to fireworks and acrobatics in these gardens.' p.19.

[138] **The play, 'Lovers Vows.** http://www.austen.com/mans/vows/ [accessed 27 March 2013].'The play opens with a woman, Agatha, begging for help on a road. A soldier, Frederick, comes along and, without her even asking him for help, he offers her some of the little money he has. She recognizes him immediately as her son, who has been away in the army for five years. He is so distraught at finding her in such a bad condition, he immediately spends the remainder of his money to buy her some wine to revive her. He tells her that he has come home for a copy of his birth certificate, because he wants to change to a different career, but no one will hire him without it. This then leads to the mother's confession that he is a 'natural son', that is to say, an illegitimate child, and because of this, she was not permitted to register his birth in the church. He demands to know who his father is and how she had been abandoned by him.'

'Central to the play is the fact that the baron and Agatha had pre-marital relations which produced a bastard son. Though such topics were well known, and certainly Jane Austen used characters such as Harriet Smith in her work, to have a genteel household perform a play centering on such issues could cause a problem, and with a father such as Sir Thomas, who was a strong advocate for proper decorum, it could certainly cause problems within the family upon his return, when he discovered what had been occurring. The character Edmund's (from Mansfield Park) objections were that respectable ladies did not involve themselves in the theater. From the time of Shakespeare into our own century, the theater was not considered an appropriate place for a lady to earn her living, but a place for loose women. Another of his objections was to the plot of the play itself and the illicit act at the heart of it.'

[139] Jane Austen Society. http://www.janeaustensoci.freeuk.com/index.htm [accessed 27 March 2013].

[140] Austen, Jane 1990 edition 'Northanger Abbey,' 1990 p.70 Oxford University Press.

[141] William Reitzel 1933, notes that Mansfield Park was written between 1811 and 1813 p.453 Oxford Journals Review of English Studies 1933 os-I 451-456.

[142] William Reitzel p.454.

[143] Hare, A., Ed p.226.

[144] Hare pviii quoting Bath Journal 11 oct 1779 and J. Winston: the theatrical tourist (1805) p. 5.

[145] Hare, p.212.

[146] S. Kemble appeared in John Bull and Henry IV on 12th October and 13th October 1804. Hare, Calendar p.212.

[147] Bath Central Library collection of playbills, for example, those dated on 26 January 1804.

[148] **Miss Loder appears in the playbills (Bath Central Library collection 2013)** The playbills with a reference to Miss Loder are listed in this endnote.

2nd June 1803: Ann Matilda's debut – as far as is known - Mingaud, Professor of Dancing in this City, 'Le Grand Ballet des Cerceaux' – Performed by himself and his pupil Miss Loder.

26 January 1804: first known performance by Ann Matilda– for the Company - (always referred to as Miss Loder) in 'Hero of the North', in the chorus of Nuns.

28 January 1804: Sadak and Kalasade: 'Genius of the Fountain of Oblivion, Miss Loder'. And also 'A Fancy dance by Miss Loder.'

February, 2, 9, 11, 1804: Miss Loder's name on playbills.

15 March 1804: Much ado about nothing. In act II – a masquerade, 'A fancy dance by Miss Loder.'

12 April 1804: 'King John 'Shakespeare's', Miss Loder plays the part of Prince Arthur.

17 April 1804: 'Wife of two husbands' in act I 'a hornpipe incidental to the piece by Miss Loder in character of a British Sailor.' In the same day's playbill is Sadak and Kalasade with the Genius of the Fountain of Oblivion as described in playbills of January 1804.

19 May 1804: Cymbaline was the play, at the end of the play 'a favourite hornpipe in the character of a British Sailor by Miss Loder.' Plus on the same day's playbill 'Paul and Virginia' Miss Loder was one of the young women of 'The island.'

24 May 1804: 'The Will', 'An entire new fancy dance by Miss Loder.'

5 June 1804: Between the play and the farce there was a ballet 'L'Heureux Moment' by Miss Loder [and others].

[**13 October 1804** S Kemble is mentioned as having played in Shakespeare's Henry 1V]. NB S Kemble is not listed in the index of the performances at the theatre for that time.

22 December 1804: 'Hunter of the Alps' dancers Mr Ridgway and Miss Loder.

5 January 1805: 'Magic of Hope' Harlequin Mr Ridgway, Clown Mr Gomery, Columbine, Miss Loder.

29 January 1805: Hunter of the Alps' dancing by Mr Ridgway and Miss Loder.

31 January 1805: 'Don Juan' Dancing by Mr Ridgway and Miss Loder.

2 February 1805: 'Provok'd Husband' (comedy) Miss Jenny played by Miss Loder.

7 February 1805: 'Magic of Hope' 'pantomine invented and produced by Mr Gomery.' The three main roles were the same as on 5 January 1805.

9 February 1805: several performances were held, (example 1) 'The Coat and Badge' 'got up under the direction of Mr Ridgway.' Tom Tug – Mr Ridgway, Wilhelmina – Miss Loder. (Example 2) 'Raising the Wind' (farce), Peggy – Miss Loder.

14 February 1805: 'Magic of Hope' (Comic Pantomime) Three main roles as on 5th January.

16 February 1805: (2) 'The coat and badge' Wilhelmina – Miss Loder (3) 'Hunter of the Alps', dancing by Mr Ridgway And Miss Loder.

18 February 1805: 'Hero of the North' chorus of nuns including Miss Loder.

21 February 1805: 'Magic of Hope', three main roles as on 5th January.

26 February 1805: 'Magic of Hope' as on 5th January.

2 March 1805: 'Don Juan' dancing by Mr Ridgway and Miss Loder.

6 April 1805 last night of Magic of Hope, Miss Loder as Columbine.

References in local newspapers include:

1804 March Bristol Infirmary: 'charming little girl' who personated Prince John (Henry IV Shakespeare) – 'Miss Loder', and, 'and who so correctly personated Prince Arthur, on Monday last (Miss Loder); and we trust that the Managers will foster, by the sunshine of their patronage, this budding flower of histrionic art.'

1804 June and July: Swansea where Miss Loder played Fanny in the 'Lock and Key' in the Swansea Theatre. Varley and Cowan.

[149] Bath Library playbill for Thursday 12 April 1804, showing cast list, with Miss Loder as Prince Arthur.

[150] Bristol Journal, Bonner & Middleton 24 March1804.

[151] From The Works of William Shakespeare. Vol. 12. Ed. Evangeline Maria O'Connor. J.D. Morris and Co. http://www.shakespeare-online.com/plays/characters/arthurbio.html

[152] Of 11 Theatre Royal Bath Playbills, which mention 'Miss Loder' studied, from the Bath Library, dated January to June 1804, 7 mention a solo dance routine by Miss Loder, some note two different dances.

[153] Playbill for 28 January 1804.

[154] Playbill for 17 April 1804.

[155] Playbill 22nd December 1804.

[156] **Note on Harlequin and Columbine**, 'Harlequinade is a comic theatrical genre, defined by the Oxford English Dictionary as "that part of a pantomime in which the harlequin and clown play the principal parts". It developed in England between the 17th and mid-19th centuries. It was originally a slapstick adaptation or variant of the Commedia dell'arte, which originated in Italy and reached its apogee there in the 16th and 17th centuries. The story of the Harlequinade revolves around a comic incident in the lives of its five main characters: Harlequin, who loves Columbine; Columbine's greedy father Pantaloon, who tries to separate the lovers in league with the mischievous Clown; and the servant, Pierrot, often involving a chase scene with a policeman.

Originally a mime (silent) act with music and stylised dance, the harlequinade later employed some dialogue, but it remained primarily a visual spectacle. Early in its development, it achieved great popularity as the comic closing part of a longer evening of entertainment, following a more serious presentation with operatic and balletic elements. In the 18th and '19th centuries, it was presented with increasingly elaborate stage effects as the closing part of pantomimes. A fairy initiated a "transformation scene" that transformed the pantomime characters and scenes into the harlequinade. It lost popularity towards the end of the 19th century and disappeared altogether in the middle of the 20th century, although pantomimes continue to be presented without the harlequinade.' From several references, including Early Pantomime", Victoria and Albert Museum, accessed 21 October 2011, Hartnoll, Phyllis and Peter Found (eds). "Harlequinade", The Concise Oxford Companion to the Theatre, Oxford Reference Online, Oxford University Press, 1996, and Mayer, David. "Pantomime, British", Oxford Encyclopedia of Theatre and Performance, Oxford University Press, 2003, information from wikipedia   http://en.wikipedia.org/wiki/Harlequinade [accessed 4 October 2012].

[157] Playbill 5th January 1805, playbills also exist for the same play with Mr Ridgway and Miss Loder for 14, 16, 21, and 26 February, 1805.

[158] Playbill 9 February, 1805.

[159] Barker p.72.

[160] Playbill for 2 March 1805, dancing in 'Don Juan'.

[161] Felix Farley's Bristol Journal on 19.1.1805 reviewed a new pantomime, 'The Magic of Hope'.

[162] Felix Farley's Bristol Journal, 26 January1805.

[163] Clarke, p.33 quoting Bath Chronicle 17 May 1804, - Theatre Royal Bath - Benefit for Mr Lovegrove & Miss Loder - Tuesday next 22 May - "The Clandestine Marriage" Tickets etc Miss Loder, Lower James St, Bath. The relevant playbill from the Bath Library was not available/temporarily missing August 2012.

[164] Barker p.59.

[165] Bath Chronicle 30 June 1804 Swansea theatre (their first appearance) Mrs. Johnstone, Mrs. Phillips, Miss Loder. p.3. Cowan.

[166] Cowan.

[167] Bathsheba Loder Second marriage to John Richards. 30 Jul 1804 in St George, Bristol, Gloucestershire. Cowan and Highfills et al. **John Richards:** Birth: Abt 1754 in Worcester, Worcestershire. Burial: 17 Mar 1836 St Swithin's, Walcot, Bath, Somerset (although there are other possible John Richards at this time). Two occupations are given: Band leader and Captain Paymaster of the 43rd Foot. Marriage: 21 Nov 1771 Mr John Richards, to Miss Maxfield, of Bristol (stage name was Richardson).
Bristol Gazette, 22.11.1804 'Married. Lately, Mr Richardson, formerly of this Theatre, to Mrs Loder, wife of the late Mr John Loder, of Bath.' John, who was born in Worcester, first appeared on the Bath stage in 1790, and later at Covent Garden. Bathsheba was his second wife. He was 'formerly of this theatre' in Bath Abbey. Cowan, Highfill et al.

[168] Clarke , p.33 quoting Bath Chronicle 17 May 1804, - Theatre Royal Bath - Benefit for Mr Lovegrove & Miss Loder - Tuesday next 22 May - 'The Clandestine Marriage' Tickets etc Miss Loder, Lower James St, Bath. There is no evidence of a Lower James Street Bath. The Local Studies Librarian, Anne Buchanan, reviewed the Harcourt maps of the city, for example the Harcourt map of 1794 and at that time there were two James Streets, one in the North of the City and one in the South, the latter was adjacent to Orchard Street, where the Theatre was located and was more likely to have been named 'Lower', not only was it the Southerly one, but it was nearer to the River and thus 'lower'.

[169] It is impossible to know the date the couple met. Both joined the Company for the season 1804/5 and would have been acting and rehearsing together from some time in the autumn 1804. All the company members were thrown together, in the coach travel arrangements to and from Bristol and possibly in the accommodation arrangements in Bath and Bristol.

[170] A "Ridgway," possibly Thomas, acted and danced in the spectacles at the Royal Circus from the summer of 1802 or earlier. Cowan quoting the website, lists several occasions in which Ridgway performed. http://sites.google.com/site/hughwilliamwilliams/home/mr-williams-scene-painter-chronology. Similar information in Highfills et al.
(a) Ismael in Gonsalvo de Cordovain August 1802.
(b) One of several warriors in Zamor and Zamona or The Peruvian Boy.
(c) The principal character in The Jubilee of 1802; or Preston Guild in September 1802.
(d) Lucioc in Louisa of Lombardy; or The Secret Nuptials in April 1803.
(e) A participant in "new and appropriate Combats" in The Black Forest; or The Natural Child from June through to mid-November 1803.
(f) A principal character in The Wild Girl; or La Belle Sauvage on 14 May.[1804?]
(g) Dagobert in an alteration of The Jubilee called Haste to the Wedding on 18 June 1804.

Barker, 1974, p.259 notes Ridgway (Dancer/Harlequin) as a special engagement of performers 26 November1804 – 7 January1805, presumably this was in Bristol.
[171] Anne Willis, local historian, Bradford on Avon notes, 'There was plenty happening in the parish at that time. The Napoleonic Wars had led to a recession in the cloth trade which badly affected the town. The Kennet and Avon canal was near completion, the Caen Hill Locks which connected the east and west sections being opened in 1810. Before then there was a tramway between the two sections.'
[172] Information about the travel to and from Bath and Bradford on Avon and discussions of theories of why Thomas may have been resident in Bradford on Avon with Anne Buchanan, Bath Central Library, August, 2012. 'The K&A Canal didn't officially open until 1810 – when the Widcombe Locks and Caen Hill flights were completed. It seems as if there was use of the canal before these locks were complete – I can't be certain how they crossed the Avon as I find conflicting information on the building of the Dundas Aqueduct, which may have been in use from 1801, although it wasn't 'opened' until 1805. The River Avon has never been a navigable waterway above Bath for the movement of cargo or passengers. I don't think this would have been a viable option for travelling between the towns.' Anne Buchanan, 24 August 2012.
[173] Information from the Wiltshire County Records Office, 2012. The marriage register notes that the marriage was performed by a curate, a man named J. D.Nicklin.
[174] Felix Farley's Bristol Journal for 23 March 1805 reported that 'Last week was married at Bradford [on Avon], Mr Ridgway, to Miss Ann Loder, both of our [Bristol] Theatre.'
[175] Bristol Mirror, 16 March 1805.
[176] **The marriage between Ann Matilda and Thomas Ridgway.** There are three key issues/mysteries about this marriage: (a) how would parental permission for the under aged be recorded in Wiltshire in the early 1800s. (b) Marriages in Lent. In many parishes the vicar would refuse to carry out marriages in Lent, because it was seen as inappropriate to be celebrating in Lent. (c) Marriages which are not in the 'bride's' parish. It was normal practice for the bride's home parish church to hold the marriage ceremony. The following records discussions with the Archivist, Wiltshire Records Office. (21 November 2012, verbal information) and with a vicar/historian, D.Grigor, (3 October 2012) to attempt to resolve some of these points. There is no clear answer.

Bradford on Avon didn't have a banns book until 1810. The licensed marriages might have stated this information. This wedding, though, was one 'by Banns'. The Archivist confirmed that in Wiltshire in the early 1800s there were no separate proformas, and it was not until 1824 that marriage practices were formalised with stricter regulations concerning the recording of marriages in which one of the parties was under 21. As for the bride's parish as the usual venue for a marriage, there were no absolutes in this matter, only one of the couple had to have some base in the parish for the previous three weeks.

The Ridgway couple could have lied about her age, and potentially his proper address, although in a small town like Bradford on Avon it was likely that two actors performing in the New year pantomimes etc in nearby Bath would be recognised and so it is most likely that parental permission was given verbally when the Banns were read. From Thomas' apparent baptismal date in Southwark, he would have been in his mid 20s, and required no parental permission for marriage. The law at this time permitted young people to be married from the age of 12. They should have permission of parents. (Information related to Bride's home parish and marriage from Anne Buchanan Bath Central Library August 2012.) Often this was written as a signature on the register, or in some cases there was a separate proforma.

According to several record offices contacted in connection with this research the practice was mixed from place to place, some vicars would, for instance, consider verbal permission sufficient, perhaps as a separate event or through the reading of the Banns. Banns had to be read on the three Sundays before the wedding, in this case starting on 24 February (and 3 and 10 March). As Easter Sunday was 14 April in 1805 the wedding day was actually in Lent. Lent was, and is, a very serious time for the Church of England. At that time it was frowned upon to have a wedding during Lent, and if a wedding took place any celebrations and festivities were not permitted in normal circumstances. The Rev D. Grigor, has confirmed, even if the Bishop forbad any weddings or celebratory events, ultimately it was up to local Vicar to do as he wished, he was all powerful in his parish. Lent marriages were good for nonconformists - but there is no evidence of this in the case of the Ridgways The vicar who performed the wedding may have been a 'laissez faire' priest. Ann Matilda and Thomas, being actors, may have lied about her age. The Reverend Edward Bowles, who was probably the vicar responsible for the parish at the time, may have been a free thinker, he had only started at the parish of Bradford on Avon in December 1804, maybe he turned a blind eye to the underage marriage issue or left it all to the curate. There may have been a public and verbal announcement and Bathsheba made no objection to her 14 year old daughter's marriage. The actual ceremony was carried out by the curate, J. Nicklin (copy of the marriage register, Wiltshire records office, from R & B Kearin). If the marriage had not been carried out 'legally', it is possible that Ann Matilda and Thomas would have be able to use this information to hasten their later separation, but there is no record that they attempted this.

[177] Bristol Gazette, 28 March 1805.

[178] Felix Farley's Bristol Journal 30 March1805.

[179] Monday 1 April 1805.

[180] **John Richards** John's life story is unclear. Highfills et al. 1987, pages 367 to 369. It is not clear when John died and there may have been more than one John Richards around Bath at this period of time. There are several candidates for the death and burial of John. As the Richards family, of which Bathsheba was a member, was reported in the 'European Magazine' of January 1812. Cowan suggests another possibility of Burial: 17 Mar 1836 St Swithin's, Walcot, Bath, Somerset. His occupation Band leader and Captain Paymaster of the 43rd Foot, as well as an actor.

[181] Cowan.

[182]

http://www.poetsgraves.co.uk/Classic%20Poems/Wordsworth/composed_upon_westminster_bridge.htm[accessed 3rd January 2013].

[183] Clarke p.38.

[184] Rohr, p.11.

[185] **The Ridgway Records in Southwark**. AncestryLibrary.com and the Southwark original records and additional information by B.Kearin, indicate that a Ridgway [Ridgway is sometimes spelt Ridgeway] was baptised at St Mary Newington on 9th March, 1780, his parents being Thomas and Mary Ridgway. Thomas and Mary have another son, Joseph, baptised 28th April 1782 at St George the Martyr. A marriage record shows a Thomas Ridgway marrying Mary Downing 17th January 1779 at St George the Martyr, by Banns, she signs her name with a cross. There is a burial record of a Thomas Ridgeway on 29th January 1795. Although Mary Downing could have been born anywhere (so too Thomas the elder), there is a probable candidate for the woman who becomes Mary Ridgway in 1779, who is described at the time as a widow. A widow, Mary Downing, could be the Mary Ridgway whose age at burial in 1815 is given as 76. This widow, Mary Downing, was born Coles and baptised 19 August 1739 from Cartwright Street, St Botolph without Aldgate. As Mary Coles

she married Joseph Downing, a bricklayer, 16 September 1771, in Finsbury, signing her name. This Downing couple had two sons, William (baptised 17 February 1773) and John, (baptised 22 November 1778). If it is the same Mary she gave birth to the two Ridgway boys in 1780 and 1782, in her late 30s and early 40s.

Mary Ridgway was buried in 1815 at the given age of 76, (burial record), if this is accurate, which it may not be, she would have been born around 1740. In 1791 Thomas Ridgway is paying the rates in St Georges Row (which later becomes Tower Street and/or is the same road). Later, in 1801, Mary is a recorded ratepayer there.

The rate books for Southwark, confirm some information about Thomas senior and Mary Ridgway. The rate book indexes are for 5 or 10 year periods. The first time a Ridgway is recorded is 1760, when a Thomas Ridgway is noted. In 1768 a Thomas Ridgway is recorded as 'poor'. In 1774 – 7 Thomas Ridgway is again recorded as 'poor'. In 1781 two Ridgways are included at separate addresses, John and Martha. In 1791 a Thomas, who is probably Thomas Edmund's father and married to Mary, is recorded as paying rates on St George Row in the parish of St George the Martyr. A Directory of street names in Southwark [Southwark Streets and Alleys up to 1860'], notes that St George Row changes its name to Tower Street 'by 1814'. Thomas senior's name is listed 18th in the Row, with 21 names following his. The family's address is later (for example for Marian Ridgway's baptism in 1813) given as 17 Tower Street). In 1801 Mary Ridgway is a ratepayer in St George Row and in 1811 she pays rates in Tower Street. One theory that fits these facts is that Thomas senior from Southwark was unable to maintain a reasonable income, perhaps he was on the stage or in some intermittent work, and married an older woman with money – Mary Downing. They had two late children, the oldest of whom was encouraged to go on the stage. If Thomas senior was the same ratepayer in 1760, he might have been a similar age to Mary, and around 50 when he died in 1795.

Records of Thomas' burial, 15 February 1829 note he was 42. Often such records are unreliable, this would give his birth year around 1786/7. Highfills directory (p. 380, notes of a 'Mr Ridgway' appearing at the Haymarket Theatre in 1792, and also a Drury Lane company list shows a Mr Ridgway as at 1st October 1799 as a member, it is unclear up to what age a boy would be described as 'Master' rather than Mr. Thomas's birth date, close to his baptismal date of 1780, is taken as the most likely for this publication, and the presumption is that his age of death was incorrect by a few years. However the information is unclear and contradictory. It is unlikely, but possible, that other Ridgways were performing in London at the same time as actors with the same surname seem, from Playbills, to insert their initial to differentiate themselves.

[186] Scheider, B. 1979 The Index to the London Stage, 1660 – 1800 Southern Illinois Press. Scheider 1800 lists a Ridgway as an actor appearing on 16 April, 1792 at the Haymarket theatre.
[187] http://sites.google.com/site/hughwilliamwilliams/home/mr-williams-scene-painter-chronology, also Highfills et al.
[188] As in earlier endnote, Highfills and Cowan. (a) Ismael in Gonsalvo de Cordovain August 1802.
(b) One of several warriors in Zamor and Zamona or The Peruvian Boy.
(c) The principal character in The Jubilee of 1802; or Preston Guild in September 1802.
(d) Lucioc in Louisa of Lombardy; or The Secret Nuptials in April 1803.

(e) A participant in "new and appropriate Combats" in The Black Forest; or The Natural Child from June through to mid-November 1803.

(f) A principal character in The Wild Girl; or La Belle Sauvage on 14 May.

(g) Dagobert in an alteration of The Jubilee called Haste to the Wedding on 18 June 1804.

[189] Southwark local history and archive centre, original rate books and indexes. In 1760 a Thomas pays rates in Queen Street. In 1768 and 1774-7 a Thomas Ridgway is classified as poor living in Grange Walk Bermondsey Landside. If this is the same person he could be the father of Thomas Edmund, and have been born around the late 1730s and fallen on hard times in the late 1760s, the whole area was well known for an area which offered cheap accommodation and plenty of casual work to newcomers. However there is no clear evidence in 2013 (Reilly, 2009 'The Story of the Borough').

[190] 'Blackfriars Road: The Surrey Theatre and Surrey Chapel', Old and New London: Volume 6 (1878), pp. 368-383. URL: http://www.british-history.ac.uk/report.aspx?compid=45287 The information on the history of the Surrey Theatre is taken primarily from this source [accessed 26 October 2012].

[191] 'Blackfriars Road: The Surrey Theatre and Surrey Chapel', Old and New London: Volume 6 (1878), pp. 368-383. St Georges' Fields:
'The circus and obelisk provided a formal termination of Blackfriars Road, a mile long boulevard from the recently constructed Blackfriars Bridge. At the circus, Blackfriars Road intersected with new and existing highways to Lambeth, Newington, Westminster Bridge and The Borough at Southwark. In local parlance the area was known as the "obliss", it was a destination point for both trams and busses, so passengers, - if they so wished - could ask for a "tuppeny to the obliss please guv." An Act for Improving St George's Fields of 1812 required that all new building around the circus should have concave fronts and should be consistent with a minimum diameter across the Circus of 240 ft. It also specified that no houses "inferior to the 3rd building rate should be erected on the frontages of Borough Road and St. George's Circus".' http://en.wikipedia.org/wiki/St_George%27s_Circus, a source quoted is Ward, Robert (2007) The Man Who Buried Nelson: The Surprising Life of Robert Mylne. London: Tempus Publishing. ISBN 978-0-7524-3922-8. p.76 [accessed 2nd November 2012]. The Surrey Theatre information is from:
URL: http://www.british-history.ac.uk/report.aspx?compid=45287 The information on the history of the Surrey Theatre is taken primarily from this source [Date accessed: 26 October 2012].

[192] Speaight, George, 1956, editor of 'Memoirs of Charles Dibdin the Younger.' The original memoirs were written in 1830.

[193] McConnell Stott, Andrew, 2009 'The Pantomime Life of Joseph Grimaldi' Canongate Edinburgh. p.225.

[194] http://www.british-history.ac.uk/report.aspx?compid=45287 Blackfriars Road and Surrey Theatre.

[195] Southwark Local Library publication, the Surrey Theatre, 1(ii), copy of a playbill for 30 January 1826.

[196] Southwark Local Library: later history of the Surrey: at around 1833 when Elliston was lessee of the Surrey and the Olympic Theatres, the actors, who were common to both houses, had to hurry from St. George's Fields over Blackfriars Bridge to Wych Street, and sometimes back again the same evening. Often the permitted 'legitimate drama' was performed in a pragmatic way, as the law only allowed musical performances at the minor theatres often a piano or another instrument played in the background to accompany Hamlet or similar. The Lord Chamberlain's powers did not extend to St George's Fields. Political plays were forbidden on the Middlesex side of the Thames and these types of acts became attractive

because they were forbidden. After the death of Elliston, the lesseeship was held in succession by others and but it never rose far above mediocrity. The building was burnt down a second time in January, 1865, but rebuilt and re-opened in the same year.

[197] Lockie's Typography 1810, http://www.google.co.uk/books?id=nZwHAAAAQAAJ&printsec=titlepage#v=onepage&q&f =false [accessed 2nd November 2012]. This directory states, 'Tower St. St. Georges Fields – the fourth on the R. from the Obelsik towards the asylum.' Mary Ridgway paid the rates on a Tower Street property for several years, from 1811 until her death in 1815, (rates books, Southwark Library) several of Ann Matilda and Thomas' children were noted as being from this address in the Baptism records of St George the Martyr. A later trade directory notes this address for Thomas as a gentleman. This information was uncovered initially by Bert and Peggy Hooper in the Library records. Additional information from the Southwark Library.

[198] Morning Post 15th April 1805, p.2 . [British Newspaper Archive, BNA]

[199] **Harlequin**

'Harlequinade is a comic theatrical genre, defined by the Oxford English Dictionary as "that part of a pantomime in which the harlequin and clown play the principal parts". It developed in England between the 17th and mid-19th centuries. It was originally a slapstick adaptation or variant of the Commedia dell'arte, which originated in Italy and reached its apogee there in the 16th and 17th centuries. The story of the Harlequinade revolves around a comic incident in the lives of its five main characters: Harlequin, who loves Columbine; Columbine's greedy father Pantaloon, who tries to separate the lovers in league with the mischievous Clown; and the servant, Pierrot, often involving a chase scene with a policeman.

Originally a mime (silent) act with music and stylised dance, the harlequinade later employed some dialogue, but it remained primarily a visual spectacle. Early in its development, it achieved great popularity as the comic closing part of a longer evening of entertainment, following a more serious presentation with operatic and balletic elements. In the 18th and 19th centuries, it was presented with increasingly elaborate stage effects as the closing part of pantomimes. A fairy initiated a "transformation scene" that transformed the pantomime characters and scenes into the harlequinade. It lost popularity towards the end of the 19th century and disappeared altogether in the middle of the 20th century, although pantomimes continue to be presented without the harlequinade.' This information is from several references, 'Early pantomime', Victoria and Albert Museum, Hartnoll, Phyllis and Peter Found (eds). "Harlequinade", The Concise Oxford Companion to the Theatre, Oxford Reference Online, Oxford University Press, 1996, Mayer, David. 'Pantomime, British', Oxford Encyclopedia of Theatre and Performance, Oxford University Press, 2003, from: http://en.wikipedia.org/wiki/Harlequinade [accessed 29th october 2012].

[200] **Theatre Royal Covent Garden, an outline history**

'In 1728, John Rich, actor-manager of the Duke's Company at Lincoln's Inn Fields Theatre, commissioned The Beggar's Opera from John Gay. The success of this venture provided him with the capital to build the Theatre Royal (designed by Edward Shepherd) at the site of an ancient convent garden, part of which had been developed by Inigo Jones in the 1630s with a piazza and church. In addition, a Royal Charter had created a fruit and vegetable market in the area, a market which survived in that location until 1974. At its opening on 7 December 1732, Rich was carried by his actors in processional triumph into the theatre for its opening production of William Congreve's The Way of the World.

During the first hundred years or so of its history, the theatre was primarily a playhouse, with the Letters Patent granted by Charles II giving Covent Garden and Theatre Royal, Drury Lane exclusive rights to present spoken drama in London. Despite the frequent interchangeability between the Covent Garden and Drury Lane companies, competition was intense, often presenting the same plays at the same time. Rich introduced pantomime to the repertoire, himself performing (under the stage name John Lun, as Harlequin) and a tradition of seasonal pantomime continued at the modern theatre, until 1939.

In 1734, Covent Garden presented its first ballet, Pygmalion. Marie Sallé discarded tradition and her corset and danced in diaphanous robes. George Frideric Handel was named musical director of the company, at Lincoln's Inn Fields, in 1719, but his first season of opera, at Covent garden, was not presented until 1734. There was a royal performance of Messiah in 1743. From 1735 until his death in 1759 he gave regular seasons there, and many of his operas and oratorios were written for Covent Garden or had their first London performances there. He bequeathed his organ to John Rich, and it was placed in a prominent position on the stage, but was among many valuable items lost in a fire that destroyed the theatre in 1808. In 1792 the architect Henry Holland rebuilt the auditorium, within the existing shell of the building but deeper and wider than the old auditorium, thus increasing capacity.

Rebuilding began in December 1808, and the second Theatre Royal, Covent Garden (designed by Robert Smirke) opened on 18 September 1809 with a performance of Macbeth followed by a musical entertainment called The Quaker. The actor-manager John Philip Kemble, raised seat prices to help recoup the cost of rebuilding, but the move was so unpopular that audiences disrupted performances by beating sticks, hissing, booing and dancing. The Old Price Riots lasted over two months, and the management was finally forced to accede to the audience's demands. During this time, entertainments were varied; opera and ballet were presented, but not exclusively. Kemble engaged a variety of acts, including the child performer Master Betty; the great clown Joseph Grimaldi made his name at Covent Garden. Many famous actors of the day appeared at the theatre, including the tragediennes Sarah Siddons and Eliza O'Neill, the Shakespearean actors William Charles Macready, Edmund Kean and his son Charles. On 25 March 1833 Edmund Kean collapsed on stage while playing Othello, and died two months later.

In 1806, the pantomime clown Joseph Grimaldi (The Garrick of Clowns) had performed his greatest success in Harlequin and Mother Goose; or the Golden Egg at Covent Garden, and this was subsequently revived, at the new theatre. Grimaldi was an innovator: his performance as Joey introduced the clown to the world, building on the existing role of Harlequin derived from the Commedia dell'arte. His father had been ballet-master at Drury Lane, and his physical comedy, his ability to invent visual tricks and buffoonery, and his ability to poke fun at the audience were extraordinary.

Early pantomimes were performed as mimes accompanied by music, but as Music hall became popular, Grimaldi introduced the pantomime dame to the theatre and was responsible for the tradition of audience singing. By 1821 dance and clowning had taken such a physical toll on Grimaldi that he could barely walk, and he retired from the theatre.[8] By 1828, he was penniless, and Covent Garden held a benefit concert for him.

In 1817, bare flame gaslight had replaced the former candles and oil lamps that lighted the Covent Garden stage. This was an improvement, but in 1837 Macready employed limelight in the theatre for the first time, during a performance of a pantomime, Peeping Tom of Coventry. Limelight used a block of quicklime heated by an oxygen and hydrogen flame. This allowed the use of spotlights to highlight performers on the stage…..The Theatres Act 1843 broke the patent theatres' monopoly of drama. Covent Garden.' Information from: http://en.wikipedia.org/wiki/Royal_Opera_House [accessed 5th nov 12].

[201] **Theatre Royal Drury Lane, a brief history**

The Theatre Royal, Drury Lane, commonly known as Drury Lane, is a West End theatre in Covent Garden, in the London borough of Westminster. The building faces Catherine Street (earlier named Bridges or Brydges Street) and backs onto Drury Lane. The current building is the most recent in a line of four theatres which were built at the same location, the earliest of which dates back to 1663, making it the oldest theatre site in London. For its first two centuries, Drury Lane could 'reasonably have claimed to be London's leading theatre'. For most of that time, it was one of a handful of patent theatres, granted monopoly rights to the production of 'legitimate" (meaning spoken plays, rather than opera, dance, concerts, or plays with music] drama in London. …In 1672 the theatre caught fire and Killigrew built a larger theatre on the same plot, designed by Sir Christopher Wren; renamed the "Theatre Royal in Drury Lane," it opened in 1674. This building lasted nearly 120 years, under the leaderships of Colley Cibber, David Garrick and Richard Brinsley Sheridan, the last of whom employed Joseph Grimaldi as the theatre's resident Clown.

In 1791, under Sheridan's management, the building was demolished to make way for a larger theatre which opened in 1794. This enormous new Drury Lane survived for only 15 years before burning down in 1809. The building that stands today opened in 1812. It has been the residency of a number of well known actors including; Edmund Kean, child actress Clara Fisher, comedian Dan Lenolt is a Grade I listed building.'
http://en.wikipedia.org/wiki/Theatre_Royal,_Drury_Lane [accessed 5th nov 12].

[202] **Astley's Amphitheatre…Philip Astley**

'My Royal Amphitheatre opened in 1795 after the previous building had burnt to the ground. The Amphitheatre had a stage with a proscenium arch in addition to the circus ring and the two were interlinked by ramps so that the horses could run on to the stage from the ring. I thought this an ingenious design, which heightened the possibilities for tricks and dramatic effect. Oh, the excitement of sitting close to the ring with horses swishing past your face as they cantered up a ramp just a few inches away! Unfortunately the wooden building was lit by candles - a terrible fire hazard. The circus burnt down again in 1803 much to my chagrin. The fire started in the lamp room where some fireworks from the previous evening's performance had been carelessly discarded. The fire started in the lamp room where some fireworks from the previous evening's performance had been carelessly discarded.

In 1804 Astley's was rebuilt for a third time. Each time the theatre was rebuilt the interior became more ornate; we had more money for the finer details of taste! I even ensured that the stages were strengthened to take the weight of more horses and increase the dramatic potential of my acts. I continued to collect new acts from home and abroad. Clowns, ropewalkers and tumblers complemented the equestrian entertainment. Despite the privilege of our royal title the press were not always so flattering about our entertainment at Astley's.' Astleys was later known as Davis' Amphitheatre.
http://www.vam.ac.uk/content/articles/t/the-first-circus/ [accessed 1st November 2012].

[203] McConnell Scott, illustration opposite p. 276, illustration 17, British Library. Charles Dibdin is shown holding a speaking trumpet calling, 'there is no fire', 15 October 1807.

[204] James Boaden, 1825 'Memoirs of the life of J P Kemble. volume 1.' Philadephia, Small et al.

[205] Barker p.70 There was a dislocation due to the burning down of Covent Garden in 1808, followed by Drury Lane in 1809. Exodus of Bath leading players to London for example Egerton, Mrs Charlotte Mardyn (the latter claimed an affair with Byron).

[206] 'Theatrical Biography of all the Principal Actors and Actresses in 1824' Thomas Dibdin (University of Nottingham special archive collections). This is also available to view on line at: http://archive.org/stream/biographybritis00unkngoog#page/n6/mode/2up [accessed 6th nov 12].

[207] The London Morning Chronicle notes a performing Mrs Ridgway on 22 July 1805 and later on 25 September 1805 (British Newspaper Archives, BNA).Both performances were at the Royal Amphitheatre, Astleys. In July Mrs Ridgway was part of the performance, as Secalia, 'this evening and every evening this week'. The September performance was a benefit night for Mr Robert La Toise, Mr Gounet and Mr Ridgway. Mrs Ridgway was a principal character, and in addition, 'Mrs Ridgway for this night only will dance a hornpipe in the character of a British Sailor'. Mr Ridgway played Harlequin Albion, and Mrs Ridgway plays not only Columbine but the part of Harlequin, unless the paper made a mistake.

[208] Morning Chronicle for 22 July and 25 September 1805. [BNA]

[209] Morning Chronicle, 7 May 1806, p.1 and Morning Chronicle 8 September 1806 p.3 [BNA].

[210] Morning Chronicle, 20 October 1806, p.3, 'Royalty Theatre Well Street, Goodman's Fields,' Principal character Ridgway, also includes the three Miss Giroux. In the Harlequin of Scotland the Harlequin is Mr Ridgway and Columbine, Mrs Ridgway' [BNA]. The burial of Thomas Joseph at St George the Martyr church is recorded on AncestryLibrary.com. The burial record has the omission sign and a note recording 'of Tower Street'. The first letter of the word Tower is not clear, and could be 'Lower' (thanks to the Local History Staff, Southwark Library, February 2013 for help with interpretation.) Burial 26 October St George the Martyr Southwark.

[211] Reilly, Leonard 2009 The Story of the Borough London Borough of Southwark p.1, 43, 48.

[212] Harper House was mentioned in the letter of admon [administration] following Thomas' death in 1829.

[213] Reilly, pp. 48, 59, 70, 83, 85, 99, 101.

[214] Information from Southwark Library, February 2013.

[215] Quoted in, Walford, Edward, 1878 'St George's Fields', Old and New London: Volume 6 (1878), pp. 341-368. From http://www.british-history.ac.uk/report.aspx?compid=45286 [accessed 12 April 2013].

[216] AncestryLibrary.com and Cowan. Baptism records Thomas Frederick Ridgway born (b): 9 Sep 1807 in Lambeth, Surrey christened (c): 4 Oct 1807 in St Mary, Newington, Kennington Park Road, Surrey. George Norman Ridgway b: 7 Nov 1808 in Lambeth, Surrey c: 14 May 1809 in St Mary, Newington, Kennington Park Road, Surrey. John Henry Ridgway b: 19 Aug 1811 in 17, Tower Street, St. George's Fields, Lambeth, Southwark c: 10 Nov 1811 in St George The Martyr, Southwark, London. Marian Ridgway b: 2 Jul 1813 in 17, Tower Street, St. George's Fields, Lambeth, Southwark c: 9 Aug 1815 in St George The Martyr, Southwark, London. Charles Ridgway b: 24 Jul 1815 in 17, Tower Street, St. George's Fields, Lambeth, Southwark c: 4 Aug 1815 in St George The Martyr, Southwark, London.

[217] The name of Tower Street was changed and is in 2012, Morley Street (information from B. Kearin). It is located between Waterloo Road and Westminster Bridge Road, and close to St George's Circus.

[218] The rate book indexes for Southwark show that a Thomas Ridgway (probably Thomas Edmund's father) paid rates on a property on St Georges Row Southwark in 1791, this Row is joined to Tower Street and later is called Tower Street for its whole length, J. Warbis, 1988, 'Southwark Streets and Alleys up to 1860.' Mary Ridgway is the ratepayer on St George Row in 1801 and in 1811 she is the rate payer on 17 Tower Street. Southwark Local History and Archive department.

[219] Marian's place of birth is listed in the 1851 census as Kent Road, her age is given as 33.Cowan.

[220] Speaight/ Charles Dibdin p.90.

[221] Speaight/ Charles Dibdin p.90.

[222] Morning Chronicle, 7 May and 6 September 1806. [BNA]

[223] McConnell Stott p.224.

[224] http://www.umass.edu/AdelphiTheatreCalendar/ [accessed Autumn 2012 – March 2013, also accessed in 2010 and earlier when this facility was connected to Eastern Michigan University.

[225] Theatre Royal Bath Playbill for February 9th, 1805. Bath Central Library.

[226] Highfill et al. p.380 quoting Charles Dibdin theYounger's Memoirs.

[227] Speaight/ Charles Dibdin p.102.

[228] Times digital archive, Friday 26 July 1811.

[229] Speaight/ Charles Dibdin p.106.

[230] Times digital archive 6 July 1813.

[231] London Sadlers Wells, 28 June 1813. Cowan.

[232] 'On November 28, 1813, the Circus in Liverpool was opened by Messrs. Astley, Davis, and Parker as the New Olympic Circus. 'Dickie ' Usher was the equestrian clown, Ridgway the pantomimic ' Joey,' and Blanchard the pantaloons. Quoted by Cowan.

[233] McConnell Stott p.230.

[234] McConnell Stott p.220.

[235] **The Sans Pareil Theatre**
http://www.umass.edu/AdelphiTheatreCalendar/actr.htm [accessed 1st November 2012].
The following information is taken from this website and is part of the 'The London Stage Project 1800 – 1900. Resources affiliated or produced by the Project include:
The Adelphi Theatre Calendar, a complete calendar documenting the day to day history of the Adelphi Theatre; Paul Buczkowski's bibliographical lists of Periodicals in London from 1800 to 1810; a databank of basic information concerning theatres in operation between 1800 and 1810. The editor is Joseph Donohue, Professor of English, University of Massachusetts, USA.' Thanks to Gilbert Cross for permission to use materials from this website.

'The Sans Pareil opened late this season but remained open for more than 140 evenings between 3 December 1808 and 13 July 1809. Two companies performed at the theatre during this time. The resident Sans Pareil Company, under the management of Gabriel Giroux, ended its season 25 March (advertisement, 25 March LTM Collection). Holland of Covent Garden then took the house, as he had in the previous summer. However, there was no interval between winter and summer seasons and there was overlap in the repertory and the performer rosters. The Bashaw, The Magistrate, and Mother White Cap were given under both managements, Mother White Cap running for two months after March 25. In the absence of sufficient playbills, it is impossible to know all the actors who stayed on from the winter season, but advertisements tell that Jane M. Scott herself performed for the first month of the second season. James Kirby, making his first appearance at the Sans Pareil on 4 March, played Clown to the end of the summer, and Madame Louis danced Columbine in both February and July.

A small group of mature, skilled actors succeeded the largely juvenile company of the 1807-08 season this year. …... Mrs. Ridgway was Columbine this summer, as she had been in the previous year.

Most of the pieces given through April were the work of Jane Scott. The Magistrate, her successful play of the preceding season, returned in December 1808, for thirty-five performances. She performed The Rout, a song and recitation piece from the 1806-07 season, at her March 1809 benefit. Miss Scott also wrote at least three new pieces for the present season. ……... Miss Scott's first pantomime, Mother White Cap; or, Hey Up the Chimney, played from February to May. Kirby was Clown and Lardner Pantaloon. Hunt and Lewin played Harlequin and Madame Louis and Mrs. Ridgway Columbine.

The Sans Pareil was a lively variety house once again. …… Goodwin, later ballet master at this house for a season, danced on the same program with Mrs. Ridgway, and he danced with Miss Twamley from the Opera House. Though Giroux's dance pupils of the preceding season had departed, several children performed. Master Aubun, an "infant phenomenon" whom Dibdin introduced at Sadler's Wells the previous spring, helped open the season on 3 December. He was advertised as a self-taught violinist, five years of age. Master Whale, "under seven years of age," danced a pas seul in January. Master James Wallack, 'late of the Theatre Royal Drury Lane,' performed in July.

This season the Sans Pareil enjoyed some stability in its staffing. Gabriel Giroux was now an experienced manager. James Sanderson was returning for his second season as bandleader and composer. Morris again designed and built the scenery. John Scott, free from day to day managing, concentrated on the stage machinery and on his 'splendid artificial fireworks, unequalled in Europe' (news clip, 31 December 1808).'

[236] Morning Chronicle 8 June 1808 p.1 and 9 June 1808 p.3 [BNA].

[237] Ann Matilda is described as Mrs Thomas E. Ridgway and Mrs Ridgway. http://www.umass.edu/AdelphiTheatreCalendar/m10cgd.htm [accessed 1st November 2012].

[238] McConnell Stott p.234-5.

[239] **John and Jane Scott and the Sans Pareil**
http://www.umass.edu/AdelphiTheatreCalendar/m06d.htm#Label001 [accessed 1st November 2012]. 'The merchant John Scott, founder of the Sans Pareil, made his fortune with a washing blue of his invention, "Old True Blue," "for bluing stockings, fine and family linen and cotton ... also for dying silk, tiffeny [sic], gauze ... and for writing and drawing a most transparent blue" (advertisement qtd. in Alfred L. Nelson's "'True Blue' Scott and His Daughter at the Sans Pareil," p. 1). Scott also sold magic lanterns……. John Scott's daughter Jane, a pupil of Dr. Arne at one time, gave singing and pianoforte lessons in the years preceding her Sans Pareil debut and wrote songs, some of which she offered for sale. She had also, in the words of W. C. Forman, "a passion for the stage, and a good deal of native talent" (W. Forman, "The Story of The Adelphi," Notes and Queries, June, 1930, p. 419). The Theatrical Observer made the same points about Miss Scott and described the obstacles she faced and the support her father gave her.

Miss Scott developed strong symptoms of [the] dramatic disease and though her extraordinary talent was undoubted by her father and friends,........ Now Miss Scott, in addition to some natural defects had the smallpox and rickets unfavourably, but as genius comes in all disguises, she really had great talent, both as an actress and a writer. Scott was induced to gut the back of his warehouse in The Strand, and fit it up as a theatre where his daughter might safely indulge her predilection for the stage. Here for some two or three years, assisted by some young people, her pupils, she dramatised and acted away to a subscription party of her own friends (December 11, 1844).

Scott must have been convinced by these amateur theatricals, for he decided to replace the makeshift building with a small new private theatre, probably constructed in 1804, which was transformed into a well-appointed house in 1806. .....the shrewd Scott was well equipped for his venture: Scott "had the ingredients for a theatre: the magic lantern, his knowledge of fabrics such as those used in curtains, drapes, and screens; his skill as a dyer and colourer; and a talented daughter who could sing and play" (p. 3).

"Old Scott," the Theatrical Observer said, "very wisely obtained a license for a minor performance chiefly provided by his clever daughter and, thinking of her alone, called [his theatre] The Sans Pareil and opened the doors to chance customers." The Theatre, a small house without a gallery, was built in 1806 ...... A notice of November 21, 1806 informs the public that 'the theatre is perfectly dry, having been finished upwards of two years in a manner, the proprietors trust, will meet their approbation' (Adelphi Scrapbook).
The Sans Pareil opened on 17 November--not 27 November, the date most historians give. Jane M. Scott, this evening when she was making "her first appearance on any [public] stage" and every evening of the season, was the only performer.

In his discussion of one-man shows, Richard L. Klepac places Miss Scott in a long line of English solo actors: Samuel Foote, George Alexander Stevens, Charles Lee Lewes, John Palmer, John Collins, Charles Dibdin (who would give one performance at The Sans Pareil in 1808), Rees, Jack Bannister, and later and also at the Sans Pareil/Adelphi, Charles Mathews (Mr. Mathews at Home, pp. 9-11). An evening at the Sans Pareil this season consisted of songs and recitations "written, composed ... spoken, sung, and accompanied by Miss Scott," followed by "an optical exhibition of visionary objects" and then a shadow play which included fireworks.....

Strictly speaking, none of the entertainments this season was dramatic. .....The "optical exhibition of visionary objects" was described as 'something in the manner of the Phantasmagorias.' It was, like the Paris and Lyceum Phantasmagorias, a ghost show, calling up the famous dead'.

[240] The British Stage, 1817, of the Sans Pareil. Quoted by Burroughs, p.188. 'Women in the British Romantic Theatre 1790 – 1840' Ed Catherine Burroughs 2000 CUP Cambridge.
[241] Victoria and Albert Museum Archive Theatre collection, London. (V&A) Original press cutting.
[242] http://www.umass.edu/AdelphiTheatreCalendar/hist.htm#intro [accessed 1st November 2012].
[243] Liverpool Mercury February 1812 p.1 notes, New Olympic Circus. In the course of the evening a favourite ballad called the Fortune Teller, by Mr Ridgway. Also involves Mrs Ridgway. The Liverpool Mercury of 27 November 1812 p.1, notes New Olympic Circus, for the season from Sadlers Wells, Astleys and the Surrey. Includes a 'new dance composed by

Mr Ridgway called the Miser' Mr Ridgway was also responsible for producing the Melodramatic spectacle Armstrong or the Scottish Outlaw….'double and treble sword combats by Mssrs Ridgway , Mr…'. Mrs Ridgway was an attendant. [BNA]

[244] Liverpool Mercury, 7 January 1814 , p.8 and 8 January 1813 p.1, the latter states, 'This present Friday 8th January and tomorrow Saturday an entire new Burletta produced by Mr Ridgway, 'Little Aaron'. A Tom is Mr Woolf, and Polly Mrs Ridgway. After this is Timour the Tartar and Mrs Ridgway is Liska (Daughter of Oglou)'. [BNA]

[245] Victoria and Albert Museum Archive Theatre collection, playbill dated 20th November 1816. The V&A archived collection for Covent Garden for 1813 to 1816 do not appear to show appearances by Mr Ridgway, he may have appeared occasionally there, and the playbills are not preserved.

[246] Source V&A playbills.

[247] Wednesday 8 July 1818, Times Digital Archive. [Hooper]

[248] **Thomas Edmund Ridgway's 'will' or letters of administration.** He left £100. 'Thomas Edmund RIDGWAY PROB 6/205 folio 109 July 1829 Surrey.RIDGWAY -Thomas Edmund d.c.1829 - actor, dancer, author. On 29 July 1829 admon [administration] of the goods, chattels and credits of Thomas Edmund Ridgway formerly of Harper House, Harper St., New Kent Rd., and late of Peckham in the county of Surrey, Dancing Master, deceased was granted to Thomas Frederick Ridgway, one of the natural and lawful children of the said deceased, having been first sworn duly to administer, Ann Matilda Distin (wife of John Distin heretofore Ridgway, widow) the lawful relict having first renounced the letters of admon of the goods of the said deceased.' (From National Archives Kew, first researched by R & B Kearin).

To compare the value of a £100 0s 0d Income or Wealth, in 1829 there are three choices. In 2010 the relative: historic standard of living value of that income or wealth is £6,860.00, economic status value of that income or wealth is £119,000.00, economic power value of that income or wealth is £316,000.00.
http://www.measuringworth.com/ukcompare/relativevalue.php [accessed 28th october 2012]. Another website calculator gives the value of £100 in 1829 as £7675.73 in 2013 terms. http://www.moneysorter.co.uk/calculator_inflation2.html#calculator [accessed 10 March 2013].

[249]Tomalin, Claire, 1994 'Mrs Jordan's Profession', p.7. Penguin London.

[250] Burial of Mary Ridgway 2 April 1815. St George the Martyr, Southwark. AncestryLibrary.com and Cowan.

[251] 'The Comical History of the King and the Cobbler' describes a folk tale on which a play might have been developed. The cobbler's wife is Joan. http://www.paganage.com/01/Comical-History-of-the-King-and-the-Cobbler.htm [accessed 1st nov 2012].

[252] Thomas' daughter, Marian indicates that his occupation was a 'gentleman' on her marriage certificate in 1861, 11 August, AncestryLibrary.com.

[253] John David Loder, marriage 10th September, 1808. Walcot, Bath by Licence. Cowan.

[254] Cowan, quoting the following references: Joseph Knight, rev. Nilanjana Banerji Sources: The thespian dictionary, or, Dramatic biography of the eighteenth century (1802); The thespian dictionary, or, Dramatic biography of the present age, 2nd edn (1805). T. Gilliland, The dramatic mirror, containing the history of the stage from the earliest period, to the present time, 2 (1808). Oxberry's Dramatic Biography, 2/19 (1825), 37- 47 The biography of the British stage, being correct narratives of the lives of all the principal actors and actresses (1824). D. E. Baker, Biographia dramatica, or, A companion to the playhouse, rev. I. Reed,

new edn, rev. S. Jones, 3 vols. in 4 (1812). Hall, Dramatic ports. Genest, Eng. Stage. T. Wilkinson, The wandering patentee, or, A history of the Yorkshire theatres from 1770 to the present time, 4 vols. (1795). Adams, Drama; GM, 1st ser., 63 (1793), 962; GM, 2nd ser., 7 (1837), 550– 52; DNB Archives   BL, (British Library) letters to George Colman, Add. MSS 42866– 42895.

[255] Oxford Dictionary of National Biography 2004 p.274.

[256] Clarke p.34.

[257] Clarke p.34. Clarke notes that his cousin Andrew, (son of Andrew Loder and John David's Uncle) also regularly sang with the Harmonic Society at the White Hart and accompanied the glees on the piano.

[258] John David Loder is a witness at Marian's marriage in 1829 in Bath, he is the only family member witness. (marriage records, Somerset Heritage Centre, Taunton).

[259] V&A Theatre archives for the Astleys amphitheatre.

[260] Bill Bryson, 2011 'At Home' Transworld London 2011, p.465 'Until1857….in law a wife had no rights at all – no right to property, no right to expression, no freedoms of any kind beyond those her husband chose to grant her. According to the great legal theorist William Blackstone, upon marriage, a woman relinquished her 'very being or legal existence'. A wife had no legal personage at all'.

[261] Steinbach, S., 2005 'Women in England 1760 – 1914 A Social History' Phoenix, London. p.267.

[262] Steinbach p.269.

[263] http://www.umass.edu/AdelphiTheatreCalendar/m18d.htm (Adelphi Theatre website)[accessed 1st nov 2012].

[264] Adelphi Theatre website Adelphi Calendar. 'In its early years, the theatre was known for melodrama, called Adelphi Screamers. Many stories by Charles Dickens were also adapted for the stage here, including John Baldwin Buckstone's The Christening, a comic burletta, which opened on 13 October 1834, based on the story The Bloomsbury Christening. This is notable for being thought the first Dickens adaption performed. This was the first of many of Dickens's early works adapted for the stage of the Adelphi, including The Pickwick Papers'.

[265] Rose, Algernon, S., Circa 1890. 'Talks with Bandsmen' Republished by Tony Bingham London. pp.209-10

[266] Three pieces of evidence would suggest she wanted to be known as Matilda for at least some of her life. (a) the baptismal record for Theodore, (b) the music she composed at Windsor was written by Mrs M.A.Distin, (c) records of her daughter Louisa's death in Australia give her name as Matilda.

[267] Steinbach p.38.

[268] According to the 1841 census and George's age on his death certificate April 1848. He could have been born as early as May 1817 (conceived around September 1816). Until evidence of his birthdate and birthplace is discovered it is probable he was conceived in the year September 1816 to September 1817. It is also likely that Ann Matilda went away from London, where she was well known, to give birth to George – settling with his family in Plympton St Mary. George's birthplace is given on the 1841 census as Plymouth. AncestryLibrary.com.

There is a query, **who was the mother of the first three Distin sons?** To date the baptism records for George, Henry, and William have not been discovered. The baptism for Theodore states his mother as 'Matilda'. There remains a possibility that there was another Mrs Distin as a wife to John before the birth of Theodore. Considering the close proximity of the birth dates and the later family band activities, another Mrs Distin seems unlikely and this thread has been dismissed unless and until new evidence emerges.

[269] Her name is given as 'Matilda' for the record of the birth of her fourth Distin son, Theodore in Brighton, June 1823. Her grandchildren in Australia, on the death of her daughter Louisa, in 1908, record their grandmother's name as Matilda [nee Loder], presumably her daughter Louisa knew and described to her children her mother as Matilda. Louisa died on 7th January 1908 in Melbourne. Some relatives have researched the records and visited her grave. Hooper, Smith.

[270] Henry Distin New York Times. Extract from New York Times, 7th august 1881, interview with Henry Distin, entitled 'Career of the Great Saxhorn Quintet'. It should be noted that some of the content of this article should be taken with a pinch of salt. In some parts it is possible that either the journalist misreported or Henry misremembered – or didn't know – all the facts. The article gives 1798 as John's date of birth – which has been confirmed by baptism records in Plympton St Mary as 1794. [Cowan].A copy of this article is available online but also was transcribed by Mrs Joan Varley McMaster, Melbourne, Australia. Joan marrried one of Louisa Distin's family and has access to a copy of this article, torn with some parts missing. This would indicate that Henry was in contact with his younger sister in 1881 and sent her a copy of this article. Many of the 20th century accounts of John Distin and his band use this article as their prime source of evidence. On census records Henry's place of birth is given as Westminster London.

[271] William Distin's place of birth is Middlesex from census records.

[272] Ray Farr has noted the appearance of a Jane Distin. Jane published some music, a copy of which is located in the British Library. This Jane is probably the musician wife of Henry Distin. There is a possibility it was another daughter of John and Matilda. Other young Distin children could have been born between 1823 and the arrival of Louisa Distin; there are no records.

[273] Wilson, Ben, 2007 'Decency and Disorder 1789 – 1837' Faber and Faber London.p159.

[274] Information on John Distin, up to 1829, is based on the Henry Distin New York Times article, information from Ray Farr, by email, 3rd December 2012 and from the archivist from the Grenadier Guards.

[275] John Henry Distin born 14 January 1794 in Plympton St Mary, Devon christened, 24 January 1794 in Plympton St Mary, Devon. Cowan – based on research carried out at the Devon Archives, Exeter. Anthony Baines in 'Brass Instruments, Their History and Development',1976 Faber and Faber states that John was born in 1798. The records for Plympton St Mary have confirmed John Distin's birth and baptism in 1794. Cowan.

[276] John's father was probably Thomas Distin, from Paignton. Cowan.

[277] There are 22 Tuckers listed in the 1841 census for Plympton St Mary these are of a range of ages and from different addresses, the main occupation is given as 'agricultural labourer', one is a clay miner, another 'pauper'. http://genuki.cs.ncl.ac.uk/DEV/PlymptonStMary/PlymptonStMary1841.html [accessed 24 nov 12].

[278] Marriage 12 Dec 1790 in Plympton St Mary, Devon, p.24. after banns, John signed and his new wife made a cross. Elizabeth Distin was one of the witnesses. Cowan.

[279] Thomas Distin c: 19 Oct 1791 in Plympton St Mary, Devon. Cowan.

[280] Henry Distin New York Times.

[281] Henry Distin New York Times.

[282] Farr, email information 3rd Dec 12.

[283] Farr, email information 3rd dec 12.

[284] http://www.army.mod.uk/music/24530.aspx [accessed 27 nov 12] extract.

[285] Grenadier Guards archive information, 23rd January 2013.

[286] Grenadier Guards archives, 14 Jan 2013.

[287] Richard Schartz, copyright © 2000, 2001 by Richard I. Schwartz, as below:- CHAPTER 6, MANUFACTURERS, D-G Distin & Sons (London 1846-1850), quoted by Cowan and similar to New Grove Dictionary of Music.

[288] Farr, email information 3 dec 2012.

[289] Grenadier Guards archives, 14 Jan 2013.

[290] Morning Chronicle, London, 1st September 1815, information from Grenadiaer Guards archive.

[291] Diary extracts from Anna Colquhoun Colquitt, from 2nd October 1815 From archive of Grenadier Guards.

[292] Dudgeon, Ralph T. 2004 The Keyed Bugle, describes the situation in 1815, extract and information from the archives of the Grenadier Guards.

[293] Diary of Anna Colquhoun Colquitt, 22nd September 1815, Paris, from the archive of the Grenadier Guards. 'To-day we were much gratified by attending a review of all the British Forces, which including German and Hanovarians, amounted to nearly six thousand men. It was a farewell compliment to the emperor Alexander previous to his quitting Paris. They were drawn up on the plains between St. Denis and the village of La Chapelle. It was a grand sight and particularly so when they first began to move. They were supposed to fight over again the Battle of Salamanca. It really gave a lively image of an engagement, the clouds of dust gave no bad representation of the smoke of cannon. The day was all we could wish, remarkably fine and clear yet very cool. The Duke of Wellington and the Emperor of Russia passed quite close to us several times. There were scarcely any French people of either class present, this showed how deeply they feel, as a spectacle of any kind is generally considered quite irresistible to Frenchmen. The cavalry, especially the Life Guards and Blues, looked very well. I hope, however, never to be so situated as to see another such sight. It is said that the Russians and Prusssians are to leave this immediately and that the English alone are to remain. We have daily, different reports. Now it is said Louis is to abdicate in favour of the Duc d'Angouleme. Nothing can be more distracted than the country seems to be at present '.

[294] Dudgeon 2004, quoted by Grenadier Guards archives, similar to New York Times article. 'My father could not speak French and the Duke spoke the French language and very little English. He was at a loss to know what to do. Then my father was aware that one of the black men that used to be at the head of the band. One used to beat the cymbals and the other beat the triangle. They were dressed in oriental fashion with large Turbans on and they made a great show at the head of the band and they were both Frenchmen and were born in the south of France and were both good scholars then my father got the bandmaster to tell one of the black men to go and interpret for my father. - The Duke said he would like to have one made to send to Russia and after the marching past was over, the Black men went with my father to a band instrument maker by the name of Halery and in two weeks the bugle was finished. My father went with the black man to interpret the particulars to the Duke and gave a bill of the list which was five hundred francs (in English money £20) The Duke then told his attendant to pay the amount and ordered the attendant to give one thousand Francs to my father and said good bye in Russian and then he turned to the black man and said good bye- the attendant who was some noble man said to the Grand Duke "what would you shake hands with a black man?" The Grand Duke turned around and in a very scolding way said "who made him black?" and again shook hands with the black man.

Now my friend Enderly, I think you can make some notice of the above and say how the first bugle was sent to Russia.' (Henry Distin, quoted by Dudgeon). Henry Distin letter to Enderley Jackson 2 April 1896.

[295] Allan Shellard, from Grenadier Guards archives accounts, 1819 – 1844. 'From a band accounts book covering the period 1819-1844 in which John Distin appears until 1821 we

know that there were 35 band members who were paid £1 12s 6d for the months Jan, April, July, September and £1 6s the remaining months, their Bandmaster was Sgt James Blaney. The cost of a new Keyed Bugle was £10 10s – an expensive instrument. The document also tells us that there were Black Percussionist in the band up until 1841 as the turbans which they wore cost 6s 3d per month to have washed.'

[296] Cowan quoting http://home.c2i.net/marianne.kristiansen/huk/brassband.htm [accessed 12 nov 11].

[297] **Lucy Anderson.** Several references are given for Lucy Anderson, including, An Oxford Companion to the Romantic Age. Deborah Rohr, The Careers of British Musicians 1750–1850. Grove's Dictionary of Music, 5th ed. 1954. Temperley, Nicholas (2001). "George Loder jr (b. Bath 1816 d. Adelaide 15 July 1868)". In Sadie, Stanley. New Grove Dictionary of Music and Musicians London: Macmillan. p. 58. ISBN 0-333-60800-3. "Lawleys of Bath Tree". Ancestry.co.uk. Information from Wikipedia http://en.wikipedia.org/wiki/Lucy_Anderson [accessed 24 January 2013].
'Lucy Anderson (12 December 1797 – 24 December 1878) was the most eminent of the English pianists of the early Victorian era. She is mentioned in the same breath as English pianists of the calibre of William Sterndale Bennett. She was born Lucy Philpot in Bath, Somerset in 1797, the daughter of John Philpot, a music seller, who is also described as "a professor of music" or "an obscure double bass player". Grove has it that her sister Fanny, a piano teacher, married into the Loder family, which was prominent in Bath's musical community. However, genealogical research suggests that this was in fact Frances Elizabeth Mary Kirkham, step-daughter of Lucy's sister, Jane Harriet Philpot who became the [second] wife of flautist George Loder, the brother of violinist John David Loder. Lucy had lessons from her cousin, a Mr. Windsor of Bath, and from William Crotch. She first achieved recognition as a pianist in Bath, moving to London in 1818. In July 1820 she married a well-known violinist, George Frederick Anderson.

Lucy Anderson was the first woman pianist to play at the Philharmonic Society concerts. She appeared 19 times between 1822 and 1862, and was the first pianist to play Beethoven's "Emperor" Concerto with the society. She championed Beethoven's concertos and played them more often than any other English pianist up to 1850. In 1843, she was piano soloist in Beethoven's Choral Fantasy, conducted by Ignaz Moscheles. In 1869 she became an honorary member of the Royal Philharmonic Society, a rarely awarded honour.…

In 1837 the publisher Alfred Novello gave Lucy Anderson exclusive rights for six months to play Felix Mendelssohn's Piano Concerto No. 2 in England. This was a condition of an interest-free loan of £30 from her husband, the money being needed by Novello to publish the concerto. She is described as "formidable" and "a manipulator of wide patronage". Two queens appointed her as their pianist, Queen Adelaide in 1832 and Queen Victoria in 1837, Anderson having been Victoria's piano teacher from 1834 or earlier.[13] She taught the piano to Victoria's children, as well as to other high-born ladies.[1] She was a teacher of Arabella Goddard. In 1848 her husband George Frederick Anderson was appointed Master of the Queen's Music. Lucy Anderson retired in 1862, and died in London on 24 December 1878.'

[298] Rohr p 135-6.

[299] Venning, Annabel, 2006 'Following the Drum, the lives of Army Wives and Daughters' Headline Book Publishing London. p.72.

[300] Henry Distin's birth place is registered on some census records, for example recorded on AncestryLibrary.com and Cowan. The HQ of the present Guards is on Birdcage Walk, Wellington Barracks, London.

[301] Jenkins, R. pp.187 -191. Steinbach p.248-9.

[302] Farr, email information, 3 December 2012.

[303] Farr, email information 3 December 2012.

[304] Rohr, p.56.

[305] Farr quoting from Carse, (Carse, Adam, 1946 'The Prince Regents Band in Oxford Journal Music and Letters XXV11' (3) pp 147 -155. p.151.)

[306] Farr information 3 December 2012 – no sources given.

[307] Information of the Royal Band Masters from Groves Dictionary of Music and Musicians, p.756. Information about the Royal household records from Julie Crocker, Assistant Archivist, Winsor Castle, 8th January 2013. The records of the Kings Household 1823 and 1830 (both page 118) list the Band of Music Members by name – 24 of them, and Household Trumpeters (eight named people in 1823, seven in 1830).

[308] Carse pp. 147-155.

[309] Carse. p.149.

[310] Carse p.150.

[311] Carse p.152.

[312] Carse p.154.

[313] Carse p.154.

[314] Scott, Derek B., Professor of Critical Musicology, University of Leeds, Chapter 2, 'The growth of the market for domestic music,' http://www.victorianweb.org/mt/dbscott/2.html#gender [accessed 12 mar 2013] . Additional background information from http://en.wikipedia.org/wiki/Piano [accessed 13 march 2013].

[315] Windsor quadrilles / composed for the piano forte or harp ...Mrs. M. A. Distin of Windsor by Distin, M. A. London: Goulding & D'Almaine,
MUS SNELL mb 786.2 D614
Copy: MUS Snell Petherick Reading Room (Music Collection)
These melodies were published by Goulding & D'Almaine and are to be found in the National archives of Australia in Canberra. There is no date on the publication, nor is the publication available from the British Library, indicating it was a privately published booklet. It appears that the noted publishers were disbanded in 1834. This was a second edition, suggesting demand for the publication. As the inscription states that Mrs Distin was 'of Windsor' it would seem likely that the music was printed after the court of George IV had moved to Windsor in 1826, suggesting the publication was between 1826 – 1830. The booklet has the name 'Louisa' hand written in the top right hand corner of the cover, and was likely to have been given to Louisa Distin around the time of Matilda's death. It is the only artefact known to have survived and taken to Australia with Louisa when she emigrated there in 1851, after the death of her mother. After Louisa's death it would appear that one of her offspring donated the music to the Australian government as part of the 'Snell' collection.

[316] Ambrose, Tom, 2005. 'The King and Vice Queen: George IV's last Scandalous Affair' Sutton Publishing Stroud.

Lady Coyningham was the last of George IV's mistresses. She became the King's mistress in 1819, when she was 49, married with children. She brought her family, including her lawful husband, with her into the royal household. George showered her with jewellery, spending £1m at one London Jeweller alone. In the decade of her time with George she was overweight and depicted with mirth by cartoonists of the time. It was to Lady Coyningham that Matilda decided to dedicate her only known musical compositions. It was presumably good to keep in with the power brokers in court. Patronage was critical to securing small and big favours in the musical world, and it may be that Matilda was trying to create some long term opportunities for herself and her family. It could be that this kind of dedication would help the Distins in the next stage of their professional development to gain the offers and concert opportunities they did in the later 1830s.

[317] **George IV.**Ambrose.(throughout, including pp1, 52, 125, 167-8, 170-2, 175, 209) At George IV's coronation, 19th July, 1821, it was the hottest day of the year and he arrived at Westminster Abbey 30 minutes late, a female witness said, ' anyone seeing this disgusting figure, with a wig the curls of which hung down his back, and quite bending beneath the weight of his roles and his sixty years would have been quite sick.' In the early 1820s, after dinner, the company would retire to the music room where the King would often sing to his guests accompanied by his resident orchestra, the Kings Band. 'With over seventy musicians this was as large as any modern symphony orchestra.' There was a Royal visit to Scotland, to Dalkeith Castle, where the host was the 16 year old Duke of Buccleuch.

Over time the Kings ill health was exacerbated by his increasing weight. But he continued most evenings after dinner to entertain guests in the music room. As late as 1828 his voice remained strong.

George had some paranoia about the dangers of the London crowds, and found a mysterious prophecy had been written on a downstairs window in Brighton and from then he decided to move from Brighton to Windsor, this move took place in 1826. Here he liked to make excursions to an Island in Virginia Water, he and his mistress would be rowed, and alongside them was a larger boat with the King's musicians on board to entertain the guests.
Later, (around 1826-9) he continued to enjoy these trips and as the royal party arrived at the landing stage the band would strike up 'God save the King.'

[318] Ambrose, p.1.

[319] Ambrose p.52.

[320] Ambrose pp.52, 167-8, 170-2, 175.

[321] East Sussex records office, baptism of Theodore Distin 6 Jun 1823 St Nicholas Of Myra, Brighton, Sussex.

[322] Ambrose pp. 167-8, 170-2, 175.

[323] McConnell Stott p.289, quoting the Percival collection vol.5,f.83. This performance is likely to be Grimaldi's Benefit performance in June, reported in the Morning Chronicle, p.4 of 27 June 1828.

[324] Speaight, Charles Dibdin. Speaight, George, Editor (1956) 'Memoirs of Charles Dibdin the Younger' The Society for Theatre Research, London. 1956 (1830) p.107.

[325] Wed 16 Oct 1822 - Davis's Royal Amphiteatre, Westminster-bridge – The Times digital archive. [Hooper]

[326] Speaight/Charles Dibdin p.134.

[327] Speaight/Charles Dibdin p.136.

[328] Cowan.

[329] Speaight/Charles Dibdin p.142.

[330] Speaight/Charles Dibdin p.144.

[331] Speaight/Charles Dibdin p.146.

[332] Speaight/Charles Dibdin p.147.

[333] Speaight/Charles Dibdin p.150.

[334] Beedell, illustration 12, p.147. Playbill for the New Surrey Theatre, 12 September 1825. All three appear in 'Old Commodore; or Cross Purposes'. Mr Ridgway is 'Doctor' and also 'Clod'. Mr.T.Ridgway is 'Nilemps', Mr G.Ridgway 'Second Stump'. Mr Ridgway is recorded as putting on 'A Highland Medley and Fling' with a Mrs Searle. Ref LAD.3/951. London Borough of Lambeth Archives.

[335] Speaight/Charles Dibdin p.152.

[336] Speaight/Charles Dibdin p.155.

[337] http://archive.org/stream/s4theatre01londuoft/s4theatre01londuoft_djvu.txt.
Thomas Ridgway, career in the 1820s. The Theatre, a monthly review, 1883, p.7. [accessed 13th January 2013]. 'Another Pantomime family were the Ridgways. Tom Ridgway was Clown under Madame Vestris's management at Covent Garden.' Chapter XVIII, 'History of the Pantomine,' 1901 R.J.Broadbent.

As well as performing with Dibdin Thomas also worked with Joseph Grimaldi. In 1807, when Grimaldi was playing clown at Sadler's Wells in a pantomime called 'Jan Ben Jan; or, Harlequin and the Forty Virgins,' Mr. Ridgway made his first appearance as Harlequin. Grimaldi, for the benefit of Mr. T. Dibdin, at the Surrey Theatre, March 26, 1822, played his old part of Squire Bugle, in 'Mother Goose,' Ridgway again being the Harlequin.

Broadbent noted that in 1828, on the occasion of Grimaldi's farewell Benefit, Mr. Ridgway and his two sons lent their assistance. The Ridgways were an 'esteemed pantomimic family'. 'Tom Ridgway was a most excellent clown in the days of Madame Vestris's direction of Covent Garden, and he survived to help Mr. Phelps at Sadler's Wells during a season or two. There have been pantomimic Bradburys, since Grimaldi's great rival, the tumbling contortionist clown Bradbury, who wore nine strong 'pads' upon his person one on his head, one round the shoulders, one round the hips, one on each elbow, two on the knees, and two on the heels of his shoes, and thus equipped was wont to hurl and knock himself about in a most alarming manner. He was, from all accounts, an original and surprising clown, but not especially comical.'
In addition Broadbent, R.J., 1901 London. Two aspirins and a comedy.] On line at: http://archive.twoaspirinsandacomedy.com/index.php?post=s1160238015 [accessed 13 January 2013].S

[338] Adelphi records as below show the name Ridgway for two further seasons 1827/8 and 1828/9. The Adelphi researcher inserts a large number of question marks as to whether the Ridgway in question was John Ridgway or Thomas Frederick Ridgway. There appear to be a small number of places in which 'J' is given. The first season was particularly busy with possibly John Ridgway performing in October in La Fille Mal Garde as Simpkin, a comic lover, and in the following March in Thomas Dibdin's version of Don Giovanni. The second season, 28/9 was less busy for the Ridgway family members. John was born in 1811 and would have been about 16/7, and a possible performer, his older brother Thomas Frederick would have been 20/21. It is possible they both appeared at separate times, George Norman may also have appeared.
Adelphi 1808 -9 http://www.umass.edu/AdelphiTheatreCalendar/m08d.htm#Label003 [accessed 1 nov 2012].

[339] Speaight/Charles Dibdin p.90.

[340] Elizabeth Mihill was born in 1812 in Newport, Essex, died on 28 Jan 1871 and was buried in Nunhead Cemetery. Cowan.

[341] A marriage has been found for Thomas Ridgway dated 20 Sept 1828, to Elizabeth Mihill, at St Mary Newington. He was buried, aged 42 years, 15 February the following year, 1829 at St Giles Camberwell. AncestryLibrary.com.

[342] As the date of birth for William has not been discovered, it is not certain whether he was born when John Distin was a Guardsman or after November 1821 when John joined the Royal band.

[343] Thomas appeared to have died intestate and the record of the letters of administration state, Thomas Edmund RIDGWAY PROB 6/205 folio 109 July 1829 Surrey. 'On 29 July 1829 admon of the goods, chattels and credits of Thomas Edmund Ridgway formerly of Harper House, Harper St., New Kent Rd., and late of Peckham in the county of Surrey, Dancing Master, deceased was granted to Thomas Frederick Ridgway, one of the natural and lawful children of the said deceased, having been first sworn duly to administer, Ann Matilda Distin (wife of John Distin heretofore Ridgway, widow) the lawful relict having first renounced the letters of adm[inistrat]on of the goods of the said deceased.'microfiche record National Archives, Kew UK.

[344] Marriage record from Boyds-in-conjunction-with Origins index, recorded by Cowan. The marriage was at St Georges, Hanover Square, Westminster on 17 March 1829. She was named as Ann Ridgway.

[345] http://www.bbc.co.uk/history/british/timeline/empireseapower_timeline_noflash.shtml [accessed 1 April 2013].

[346] Part of Marian's life story is described in her divorce document of 1858. Records in the National Archives, Kew.

[347] Thomas Elliott was from Bristol, but was resident in Bath at the time of the wedding, 1829. Four years older than Marian his mother helped him and Marian out over the next decade by providing pubs and a shop for him to manage. Marian's mother in law, Deborah, was widowed at some time and remarried David Llewelyn, 5 March 1835 in Bristol. David for a wealthy man and known in Bristol. [National Archives, Kew, Kearin researches and Cowan]. Marian and Thomas had three children who survived childhood, Frederick, born in Edinburgh in 1833, George born in Bristol 10 May 1835 and Rose Harriet born in Bristol 1837 baptised 28 May 1837.

[348] Marriage, by banns, to Thomas Elliott, Bath St James, December 1829, witnesses include J. D. Loder, both parties were resident of the parish. Record in Taunton, Somerset Heritage Centre. Original research by B & R Kearin.

[349] Frederick Bruce Elliott was born in Edinburgh, 4 June 1833. Cowan.

[350] Charles Ridgway appears in the 1841, 1851 and 1861 as a tailor/tailor of plain and theatrical clothing. The 1871 census lists him as a disabled pantomimist. He spent out most of his life, according to census material, near to where he was born - in Lambeth. There are some reports of his appearance as a Pantaloon. He fathered many children – the only one of the Ridgway brothers known to have had children. Charles died in 1893. ncestryLibrary.com. Cowan.

[351] Debra Smith, family historian and researcher, has noted that a Hull newspaper described the death of George Ridgway [circa 1831] in this is he described as the son of Ridgway and (whose mother) was the sister of the eminent violinist.

[352] George Ridgway died on 29th February, 1832 in Glasgow, Lanarkshire. Cowan. He died of consumption. He appears to have had a successful performing career to then. It may have been a coincidence that he was in Scotland, the Distins were based at Taymouth some 80 miles from Glasgow.

[353] George Loder was buried on 29 January 1829, his address at that time was Pultney Bridge Bath. (Cowan with information from Anne Buchanan). Two of George's children, George and his half sister Kate were to become well known musicians.

[354] Clarke p.59 quoting the Bath Journal in 1827.

[355] Clarke p.59. Clarke quotes private indenture records, Private Apprenticeship Indentures. BATH DD\S\WI/30 1804-1842. He was apprenticed to the wife of his father's first cousin, Andrew Loder, George Patrick Henry Loder, Birth: 1816 in Kingsmead Terrace, Bath, Somerset. Christening: 14 Nov 1816 St Mary's Chapel, Walcot, Bath, Somerset. Cowan

A note on Andrew Loder, junior - he was the son of Andrew and Jenetta Loder. Cowan. He was christened on 27 Nov 1785 St James Church, Bath, Somerset. Death, 20 Mar 1838 in Ashbourne, Derbyshire. His occupation was a Musician in 1814 at Green Street, Bath, Somerset. Later, in 1822, a music seller of Orange Grove, Bath, Somerset.

In Jan 1799 on the resignation of Mrs. Oakes, organist for St James's Church his services were offered to the Rev Dr Phillott by his father. Bath Chronicle 1149/1785 Bath Chronicle 1172/1785 article:1d From 1820 to 1826 he was a music seller in Bath and then was bankrupted (1827-8).

'16 March 1827 WHEREAS a Commission of Bankrupt, is awarded and issued forth against Andrew Loder, of Orange-Grove, in the City of Bath, Music-Seller, Dealer and Chapman, and he being declared Bankrupt is hereby required to surrender himself to the Commissioners in the said Commission named, or the major part of them, on the 19th and 31st of March instant, and on the 27th days of April next, at Eleven in the Forenoon on each day, at the White Lion Inn, in the said City of Bath, and make a full discovery and disclosure of his estate and effects, when and where the Creditors are to come prepared to prove their debts, and at the second sitting to choose Assignees, and at the last sitting the said Bankrupt is required to finish his examination, and the Creditors are to assent to or dissent from the allowance of his certificate. All persons indebted to the said Bankrupt, or that have any of his effects, are not to pay or deliver the same but to whom the Commissioner shall appoint, but give notice to Mr. Thomas Turner, Solicitor, 6, Harrington-Place, Queen-Square, Bath, or Mr. William Price, Solicitor, 1, New-Square Lincoln's-Inn, London.'

Derby and Bath newspapers mention on September 17, 1834 a reference to: A new organist at the Octagon Chapel in this city (Bath) as successor to Mr. A. Loder, who after 30 years leaves Bath for Ashbourn[e], Derbyshire. Derby Mercury March 28, 1838 - DEATHS - On the 20 inst. at Ashbourne after a short illness, aged 52, Mr. Andrew Loder, professor of music & singing; for many years organist at the Octagon Church, Bath and for the last 3[?] years organist at the Ashbourne Church. As a general musician & teacher he ranked very high, his urbanity and amiable disposition gained him much respect and his loss is deeply lamented by his family & friends.'

Andrew married 3 Feb 1808 in St Mary's Chapel, Walcot, Bath, Somerset a Francis Mary Lee at St Mary's Chapel Walcot Somerset, although some of the information is not clear. Cowan.
[356] George IV died at Windsor on 26 June, 1830.
[357] Carse p.155, Carse quotes The British Bandsman March 1889 p. 132.This information is also given in Henry Distin's interview in the New York Times.
[358] Henry Distin, New York Times article says John played at the coronations for Victoria and William IV. There were only three coronations John Distin could have played at during his lifetime, for George IV, [19th July 1821] William IV [8th September 1831] and Victoria [28th June 1838]. There was a rumour, passed down to Australian descendants of Louisa Distin, probably through one of her children, that John played for four royal coronations. There were other Royal events in which John might have played, including the marriage of Victoria and Albert [10th February 1840].
[359] Louisa Rose Distin was born on the 12th December 1831 and baptised on 11th January 1832 in St Georges, Hanover Square. John Distin's profession was noted as a Professor of Music. (Folio 533, information from Better Kearin). She was long lived, and died in

Melbourne Australia on 7th January 1908. She had nine children. It was noted on her death certificate that her parents were – 'John Distin Musician and Matilda Distin'.

[360] Clarke p.34. Clarke quotes Myles Birket Foster, 1912 The History of the Philharmonic Society of London 1813 -1912 London. Clarke notes that presumably John David would be away from the pressure of work in Bath and elsewhere. In a few months he was playing in London so perhaps he either suffered exhaustion or could not cope with the Philharmonics Society's demands.

[361] Clarke p.38-39. John David Loder had suffered a mental breakdown in 1822 and after various career setbacks moved with his family to London in 1840. He fathered 12 children, he and some of his family are buried in the plot next to the burial place for Ann Matilda in Kensal Green cemetery London.

[362] Cowan.

[363] Clarke p.50 quoting the Bath Journal for 23 April, 1832.

[364] http://www.umass.edu/AdelphiTheatreCalendar/m31d.htm. [accessed 5 January 2013]. The author of this section, Alicia Kae Koger, suggests that one of the 'Masters' was Theodore. Theodore became well known as a musician later and there appears to be no specific evidence of the two 'masters'. As George was initially apprenticed as a jeweller (as suggested in New York Times article, 1881) it may be that these two were Henry and William. Theodore would have only been 9 years old at this time, so it is likely that his elder brothers were involved at the Adelphi with their father. 'Concerto: (andante introduction, recitative, slow air of Mozart's Cavatina) [John?] Distin (trumpet) (07 Aug 1832) duet: Master [Theodore?] Distin (French horn); Master Distin (French horn) (07 Aug 1832).' 'Theatre Royal, Adelphi. Doors open 6:00, curtain 6:45, half price 8:30. Ticket prices: box 4/, pit 2/-, gallery 1/-. 3 October 1831 - 7 August 1832, 212 evening performances.

[365] Farr, email correspondence Dec 2012. Farr notes that John Distin was seven years with Breadalbine.

[366] 1st **Marquis of Breadalbane.** References include: thepeerage.com Lt.-Gen. Sir John Campbell, 1st Marquess of Breadalbane; leighrayment.com Representative Peers – Scotland; The London Gazette: no. 15971. p.1438. 1 November 1806; The London Gazette: no. 18846. p.1833. 9 September 1831. Information from: http://en.wikipedia.org/wiki/John_Campbell,_1st_Marquess_of_Breadalbane [accessed 9th January 2013]. The second marquis, his son, was well connected. The two were both Fellows of the Royal Society, and the younger was very active in national politics. 'Breadalbane sat as Member of Parliament for Okehampton from 1820 to 1826 and for Perthshire from 1832 to 1834. The latter year he succeeded his father as second Marquess of Breadalbane and entered the House of Lords. In 1848 he was sworn of the Privy Council and appointed Lord Chamberlain of the Household by Lord John Russell, a post he held until the government fell in 1852. He held the same office under Lord Aberdeen between 1853 and 1855 and under Lord Palmerston between 1855 and 1858. A freemason, Breadalbane was Grand Master of the Grand Lodge of Scotland between 1824 and 1826. He was elected a Fellow of the Royal Society in 1834 and made a Knight of the Thistle in 1838.' References include, thepeerage.com Sir John Campbell, 2nd Marquess of Breadalbane; leighrayment.com House of Commons: Ochil to Oxford University; and leighrayment.com House of Commons: Paddington to Platting. Information from: http://en.wikipedia.org/wiki/John_Campbell,_2nd_Marquess_of_Breadalbane . [accessed 9th January 2013]. **Taymouth Castle** 'It stands on the site of the much older Balloch Castle (built in 1550), which was demolished to be rebuilt on a much larger scale in the early 19th century by the Campbells of Breadalbane. It was visited by Queen Victoria in 1842.' References include, "Taymouth Castle". Historic Scotland; "Taymouth Castle". An Inventory

of Gardens and Designed Landscapes in Scotland. Historic Scotland; "Taymouth Castle, Kenmore". Buildings at Risk Register for Scotland; "Taymouth Castle". RCAHMS. From, http://cn.wikipedia.org/wiki/Taymouth_Castle. [accessed 9th January 2013].

[367] AA route planner estimates that the 80 mile journey would take two hours using 2013 transport, http://www.theaa.com/route-planner/classic/planner_main.jsp [accessed 9th January 2013].

[368] Henry Distin, New York Times.

[369] Information from Deborah Rohr, 13 September 2012, citing raw data from Brown and Stratton. 'My records show that they were both horn players, both attended the RAM in 1834, both performed at "the public and private concerts in London". ...   and in the 1855 Musical Directory there is an entry for the "Messrs. Distin," who had studied at the Royal Academy of Music, and who lived at 31 Cranbourne Street.'

[370]Newspaper announcement. Caledonian Mercury October 6 1834. Cowan.

[371] Farr states that John Distin served the Breadalbane estate for seven years, from around 1830 to 1837, email information 8 January 2013.

[372] Royal Academy Music Archive: Letter from John Distin to Sir Andrew Barnard, St James's Palace, London. 16th August 1835. From Taymouth Castle. 3pp and envelope. Regarding the Royal Academy of Music and payment. Royal Academy of Music. http://apollo.ram.ac.uk/emuweb/pages/ram/display.php?irn=20829 [accessed 22 jan 2013]. 'With all Submission and respect, I have humbly to beg you will condescend to pardon this liberty of addressing you. Knowing Sir that you are one of the patrons and principals of the Royal Academy of Music, I take the liberty of Soliciting your kind interference in my behalf for more time to be granted me in reference to the Debt I owe the institution for the Six months my two Sons were there - believe me Sir when I assure you my principles are and ever will be just and honest; and had I been so fortunate as my predecessors to receive / what we all expected / - a pension for my Services to his late Majesty, I need never have incur'd a debt at all, but with my large family I have found it impossible to avoid it - I had during my Stay in London a Complication of difficulties to contend with, more than I could struggle thro' - which induced me to leave it and accept the offer of this Situation from the Marquis of of Breadalbane, of one hundred pounds per annum ....but I have been much deceiv'd finding the Highlands the most expensive part of Scotland, so that instead of being (as I Sincerely hoped and intended, ready and prepared to meet the few debts I unavoidably left unsettled, I found myself gone still farther behind by many Pounds more than my income amounted to, and no means of Extricating myself - I therefore told the Marquis of the inadequacy of the terms to Support and clothe so many, who has made it better [underlined] worth my while to remain, by allowing me leave of absence to take a few engagements a few months in the year while he is away - and to make a trial of what we cou'd do, I have within these three or four weeks been to Edinburgh, where we have performed with the greatest Eclat ever known before, ... could have now been Enabled to have the means of Satisfying the Academy and all to whom I was indebted, as our fame has so spread that I have offers the most tempting from all parts of Ireland at my own terms, but am obliged to defer untill my next leave of Absence which will be from next Feby till June, when Please God I live I shall have ample means to shew my wish to be honorable to all - and if you Sir will kindly condescend to use your great interest in my behalf for the extention of time until then. I shall ever feel bound in the most heartfelt gratitude .... with the greatest Submission and respect - most humbly your very Obt. Servt. J. Distin, late Trumpet and Key Bugle Player in the private band of His Majesty George 4[th.]'

Henry Distin, New York Times, states that he and William were supported in the RAM by 'Lord Westmoreland'. This was probably Henry Brougham, 1778 – 1868, the Lord

Chancellor and son of Brougham of Brougham Hall, Westmoreland. He was a lawyer and supporter of Queen Caroline. Brougham oversaw the passing of the 1832 Reform Bill and the Abolition of Slavery Act. He was a colourful character, and according to 'wikipedia' holds the House of Commons record for non stop speaking (6 hours). He doesn't appear to be known for musical matters but may have been the type of individual who RAM members approached for sponsorship.

http://en.wikipedia.org/wiki/Henry_Brougham,_1st_Baron_Brougham_and_Vaux [accessed 6 April 2013].

[373] Cowan notes the newspaper references. Henry Distin, New York Times mentions the Adelphi (Edinburgh) theatre launch of the band.

[374] Scotsman 20 April 1836 p.2. [Hooper] Also Scotsman for 2, 13, 16 April 1836.

[375] Mitroulia & Myers p.1.

[376] Bate, Philip, 1972 'The Trumpet and the Trombone' Ernest Benn Limited London. p.183.

[377] Mitroulia and Myers p.1.

[378] Henry Distin New York Times.

[379] Extract from 'The Illustrated London News', December 14th 1844, p.384. The article states, ' THE DISTN FAMILY' The first appearance of these highly gifted gentlemen at M.Julien's Concerts, was noticed in our journal of last week. They have repeated their performances, with increased effect, during the past week. Mr Distin and his four sons have been for several years before the public. Mr. Distin sen., for more than nine years, was principal trumpet in the private band of King George IV.
The Distin Family have visited various parts of Scotland, Ireland and England, and have given upwards of seven hundred concerts. In December 1843, they proceeded to the continent, and were invited to make a trial of some newly-invented instruments, manufactured by M. Adolphe Sax in Paris. Upon the introduction of the Distin's improved Sax Horns in Paris, they at once ensured success.
Invariably receiving the most enthusiastic applause, Mr Distin was requested by M. Habeneck, the Director of the "Conservatoire Royale de Musique," to perform some of Sebastian Bach's and Handel's compositions – (the former in particular, having very difficult passages for the trumpet) - which he did, and also the obligato to Handel's "Let the Bright Seraphim." – This composition had not been played in Paris for many years, as no French trumpet-player would attempt it.
Mr. Distin's reception was a most brilliant one, the audience and the orchestra manifesting their delight by the most enthusiastic plaudits accompanied with a very flattering letter and address (an honour unprecedented for an English artist in Paris). Mr. Distin and his four sons were also presented with a splendid silver medal by the Committee of the "Societe libre des Beaux Arts," with a very complimentary address, for their performance at their great concert at the Hotel de Ville.
The Distins are at present the only performers on the Sax Horn, which unites the powers of the French horn and those of the cornet-a-piston, but is infinitely superior to both, for it combines the mellowness and sweetness of the former, with all the brilliancy and power of the latter. The pieces which the Distins perform are of their own arrangement, and do credit to their musical skills.'

[380] Rohr, p.53.

[381] Mitroulia & Myers appendix 1 database.

[382] Parish of St George Hanover Square, Westminster records office.

[383] Cowan. Address 16 Apr 1836, 30, St James Square, London. Advertisement for a concert gave this address for buying tickets.

[384] Oberlin Conservatory Library Special Collections. Selch no: FRS-684, has a letter from John Distin, details as follows: John Distin (1793-1863) ms. letter, re. playbills.
Collection Name/Credit: Frederick R. Selch Collection of American Music History, gift of Patricia Bakwin Selch.
Oberlin Conservatory Library Special Link to this Page: http://hdl.handle.net/2374.OBE/8758
Letter, ink ms. From John Distin, Manchester Square. 'Sir… We shall feel pleasure in performing a couple of pieces for you ….. We have just returned from a most extensive tour thro' Germany & have played at nearly all the courts of Europe & should your bills not be out--and we can be properly announced in advertisements Bills …. You will find us very attractive, ….. I am Sir yours truly John Distin.' 'Mr Distin and His Four Sons the original Performers on the Sax Horns….. their Inimitable performances have created an Extraordinary sensation, and have performed at nearly all the Courts of Europe, and called forth the Enthusiastic admiration…. of Meyerbeer and other great composers, will make their first appearance in England this Season.'

'In the Concert: I) Fantasia on themes by Donizetti, arranged and performed on the Sax Horns by Messieurs Distin. After two or three things by the other artists, Fantasia on themes from Meyerbeer. Sax Horns. Messieurs Distin (as performed by them in Berlin before the composer with universal success. These two pieces will only take six minutes each please let me know if this can be arranged our address is No 3 Duke Street Manchester square.'

From the content of the letter it would appear to have been written after mid 1844.
SLibrary.Webmaster@oberlin.edu [accessed 24th nov 12].
[385] Cranbourne Street (the "e" was not used in the 1840s) is the road at the corner of the present Leicester Square underground station.
[386] The Westminster Records Office, London.
[387] Plans for 25 June 1840 can be seen in the Westminster Records Office, but rate records for September 1847, December 1847 and March 1848 show no rate payer for number 31. It is possible that rates were re-assessed on a new banding (possibly related to the industrial use of the building).
[388] Journal:17th January 1846. 31 Cranbourn Street is the address given for both the death certificates for George and Ann Matilda Distin in 1848.[In George's case it was New Cranbourn Street].
[389] Byrne, Paula. 2013'The Real Jane Austen' Harper Collins London. p.111. Byrne describes the carriages, private and public, and the coaching inns. She also describes the importance for a young woman not to be travelling alone, p.113-4.
[390] Jenkins, Simon 2012 'A Short History of England' Profile Books London, 2012 pp.197 - 200.
[391] Road transport. Fares and services varied from year to year and place to place. For instance the Bath Herald of November, 1837, includes typical adverts around the time of the Distins concerts on 4th November 1837.
'THE CHEAPEST TRAVELLING TO LONDON AND NO FEES. Is by the NEW STAGE COACH COMPANY'S BRISTOL, BATH AND LONDON elegant light Post Day Coach, carrying four Inside, leaves the CASTLE AND BALL, every morning at a ¼ before 8 o'clock and arrives at Hatchett's Hotel, Piccadilly, in the evening at ½ past Eight o'clock and Gerard's Hall, Basing Lane, and the Blossoms Inn, Lawrence Lane, Cheapside, as a ¼ past Nine. Route – Chippenham, Calne, Marlborough, & Reading. FARES – Inside……£1.16s. Outside ….18s. Allowance of LUGGAGE to each passenger, Inside 50lbs, Outside 30lbs. Dine at the King's Head, Thatcham, at 2s.6d per Head. ALSO THE NEW COMPANY'S

NIGHT COACH TO LONDON. Route – the same as Day coach – every afternoon at 3 o'Clock, from the CASTLE AND BALL ,BATH, and arrives at Hatchett's Hotel, Piccadilly the next morning at seven and Gerard's Hall, Basing Lane, Bread Street, Cheapside, at a quarter before 8 o'Clock.' Another advertisement at a similar time [Keenes Bath Journal 6th November 1837] shows regular routes to places like Nottingham, Southampton, Bright and Birmingham. It also shows trips to Liverpool and Manchester 'in one day, leaving at a quarter before eight.' The Keenes Bath Journal of 6th November 1837 has an article giving notice of the Bristol and Exeter Railway.

[392] Clarke p.43 quoting both Trewman's Exeter Flying Post, of 30 Dec 1813, 'following an accident Mr and Mrs Loder received severe bruising while travelling between Bath and Bristol' and the Bath Journal of 22nd February 1841.

[393] Christopoulos, Margaret, 2013. Unpublished. 'Chronology of events, Ann Matilda Distin.' For the years 1836-1848 this is a detailed data base of Distin performances during these years, the data has been taken from several sources (a) Mitroulia and Myers 2011, (b) private research records of Dr C. Hooper, (c) information from the British Newspaper Archives-February 2013, (d) information from a contemporary print of Tony Bingham, (e) other sources. The information in this biography of Ann Matilda Distin is summarised from this data base.

[394] Musical World 16 June 1837, p.14, part of this quotes the Review in the Aberdeen Herald. [Hooper]

[395] Musical World 28 July 1837, pp.106-7. [Hooper]

[396] Norma is an opera by Bellini. First produced at La Scala on 26 December 1831, it is generally regarded as an example from the height of the bel canto tradition. 'Casta diva' was one of the most familiar arias of the 19th century. References related to Norma include, Holden, Amanda (Ed.), The New Penguin Opera Guide, New York: Penguin Putnam, 2001; Orrey, Leslie, Bellini (The Master Musicians Series), London: J. M. Dent, Ltd., 1973 ISBN. Information from http://en.wikipedia.org/wiki/Norma_(opera) [accessed25 February 2013].

[397] Henry Distin New York Times.

[398] The Bath Journal 6 November advertises, 'ASSEMBLY ROOMS BATH. MR. DISTIN AND FAMILY having been honoured with the most enthusiastic applause at their performance on Monday evening, by a numerous and elegant audience, amongst whom several distinguished professors who testified their unqualified approbation and delight, beg leave to announce a SECOND AND LAST CONCERT, WHICH WILL TAKE PLACE On SATURDAY MORNING next, November 4th, 1837. The PERFORMERS who will have the honour of appearing are MR. DISTIN, the Celebrated PERFORMER on the TRUMPET And his FOUR TALENTED SONS. Forming a Band of a most Novel and Pleasing Description. THE INSTRUMENTS CONSIST OF A Trumpet, French Horns, Key Bugles, Trombone, &zc. Mrs. Distin will preside at the Piano-Forte. Family tickets, to admit Three, 10s. Single Admission, 3s. 6d To commence at 2 o'Clock precisely'.
An article says in the same Journal [Keenes Bath Journal,Monday 6th November, 1837] 'A MUSICAL FAMILY (by our correspondent Sam Sly). We often hear of one son in a family remarkable as a lawyer, poet, painter or screw driver, but very rarely of the whole circle, standing high as music geniuses, and also with a similar instrument. Mr Distin and his four talented sons, are a striking exception to this rule. Never perhaps has Bath had a greater treat, or been caught more intently by the ear, than at the sounds of their trumpets, at the Assembly Rooms on Monday and Saturday last. To speak in the language of others, it was a performance calculated "to, dazzle the imagination, to enlighten the mind, to soften the to tickle the liver, heart to rouse the soul, to shake the side, to dim the eye, to agitate the spleen, to rouse into tumult, or to sooth into repose, every joint and sinew of body, and every organ

and function of the mind," a concert in a word, deserving of eternal fame, and destined to last, if not for every, at least till they play again, - Every boy can take his fife, and every blind beggar his fiddle; but trombones, trumpets, and key bugles, are instruments most horrible and discordant, at the lips of an ignoramus, but with the Messrs. Distin, the common 'too-too-too' strain, is changed into a melody the most soft and bewitching; every note has power to captivate and enchant. We can sit with perfect ease and confidence, during their performances, knowing there will be no breakings down and the piano. Success to their efforts and "God save the Queen."'

[399] 1841 census, AncestryLibrary.com. Louisa Distin lived in Westgate Street Bath with William and Jane Noble. The street numbering system is unclear, but apparently next door lived a Susanna Richards aged 25, she may have been a relative of Louisa's grandmother. Bathsheba, 'Berthsheba Richards,' her grandmother was at the same time living in Walcot Bath, in Kingsmead Street.

[400] Musical World, V7, No XCI, 8 December 1837, p. 200. From the Bath Herald [Hooper] 'Pleased to find it was Mr Loder's intention to continue such amusement.'

[401] 'Concert' The Bristol Mercury 2496 (December 23, 1847). [Mitroulia & Myers appendix database information].

[402] The British Library Newspaper archive, [BNA] www.britishnewspaperarchives.co.uk [accessed 11 February 2013], shows some 79 records of a Mrs. Distin from 1817 to December 1848, of these two are probably not Matilda. The remaining 77 mention Mrs Distin and her connections with the Distin band.

[403] The Rainers: http://www.stillenacht.at/en/spreading_song.asp http://books.google.com/books?id=pJvzEzjahkQC&pg=PA123&lpg=PA123&dq=rainer+family+singers&source=bl&ots=e8a6lXNSN6&sig=WMqZVL5Z23wOZ9FLK6qYPnBJSHU&hl=en&sa=X&ei=oQQ9Ucn_CajM0AHKqIDICQ&ved=0CDsQ6AEwAQ#v=onepage&q=rainer%20family%20singers&f=false [accessed 12 March 2013]. The Rainers were a group of five Tyrolean singers. They first went to the US in 1834 and toured there from 1839 -1843, where they performed the first version of 'Silent Night' for an American audience. There speciality was harmonic singing and music. Information from Lynne Farringdon, University of Pennsylvania.

[404] The references to places and performance by the Distins are listed in the Ann Matilda Chronological Database. Christopoulos. See note on sources.

[405] 'Theatricals' The Age (October 28, 1838), p. 341. [Mitroulia & Myers appendix database information]

[406] Musical World, V8, No, 47, 22 Nov. 1838, p.182. From the Halifax Guardian. [Hooper]

[407] Mitroulia and Myers appendix database information.

[408] Mitroulia and Myers record, 'The performances would start with a comic piece. On March 4 the comic piece was "Peter the Great", and the Grand Concert would consist of the following: PART I: Strauss Waltzes by the orchestra, and "Homage à la reine de la grand Bretagne". "Mira o Norma a tuoi Ginnochi" from Bellini's Norma arranged for the Distin quintet. Duet "What's a' the steer" by Misses A. and J. Hyland. Air on the French Horn "Lullaby" by Storace by Henry Distin. A Madrigal sung by several singers. Air on the trumpet "O, no, we never mention her" by Bishop played by John Distin. "The Tear" sung by Mr. Hudson. "Echo Hunting Duet" played on the French Horns by W. and H. Distin composed by Distin. The "Highland Fling" by Miss Raine and Mr. Bologna. PART II: Dr. Arne's Fantasia on the trumpet "The Soldier Tired" by John Distin. "We'll go no more a roving" by Miss A. Hyland. Balfe's air on the French Horn "The light of other days" by a member of the Distin family. A selection from Macbeath by the entire musical strength of the

company. "Introduction and Medley" introducing various irish melodies by the Distin quintet. Grand concerted pieces from the opera Torquatto Tasso of Donizetti by the Distin family. "The Minstrel Boy" by Miss A. Hyland. Finale "God save the King" by the Distin family. The entertainment would close with the pantomime of the "Goblin Dwarf" or "Harlequin's Vision", and the "Genii of the moon", also with the "Pas de deux" from the pantomime of Mother Goose, and the laughable "School-boy scene" from Harlequin and the Ocean Queen.' "The Theatre Royal, Dublin, from 1830 to 1851", Dublin University Magazine 73:433 (January 1869), p. 93, and "Theatre Royal, Dublin" Freeman's Journal and Daily Commercial Advertiser (March 4, 1839). [Mitroulia & Myers appendix database information]

[409] **Was Matilda the only pianist for the Distin band, 1837 – 43?** Many newspaper reports specifically mention Mrs Distin as the pianist.[There are c70 newspaper reports mentioning 'Mrs Distin' as the pianist for the Distin band, BNA, April 2013] Occasionally she is described as the sister of the musician Mr Loder of Bath. Most press reports do not name the pianist, but only the phrase, 'the Distin Family'. The contemporary newspapers only appear to record the names of other pianists towards the end of 1844. The final mention of Mrs Distin by name is in Preston, October 1843[BNA]. The first specific mention of a 'new' pianist is December 1844, for a performance at Arundel when a member of the Smith family plays the piano. For a performance in Brighton in November 1844 there is no named pianist [Christopoulos chronology]. For the first seven, or possibly eight, years of its existence the touring Distin band Matilda appears to have been the primary and probable only pianist.

[410] George Loder….. RECOLLECTIONS OF CALIFORNIA & AUSTRALIA. (By a Musician.)Transcription ©Andrew Cunningham Clarke. Unpublished materials, based on The Musical World, 1858. p.39.
EPISODE 12. 'and through his good offices found my teamster, who, after great demur, and considerable diplomatic tact upon my part, consented to convey a square pianoforte to a mountain top, three miles from Downieville, from thence I was to use my own ingenuity in conveying it down a nearly perpendicular pass into the town below. I had to provide him with ropes and blocks, had the piano securely packed I an iron bound case, with rope-beckets or handles at the sides and ends, and sent two men with him to assist. We then started in a large open carriage or rather wagon, accompanied to Park's Bar, the first mining camp upon our route.'

[411] Saturday 16 May 1840, Hereford Times Article p. 3. [BNA]
[412] Falmouth Packet News 27 November 1840, Royal Cornwall Gazette, p.2,3. [BNA]
[413] Thursday 24 December 1840 , Exeter Flying Post , Devon Article Page: 2, 3. [BNA]
[414] 1841 Census High St. Portsmouth HO 107/412/1
Jno Distin 45 Professor of Music Not born in county
Ann Distin, aged 45
Henry Distin, aged 20
William Distin, aged 20
Eliza Smythe, aged 15
In 1841 George Distin was lodging in the High Street, Portsmouth with Theodore. His parents and Henry and William were living a little further on in the High Street whilst his sister was at school in Bath. In 1841 Louisa was aged 9 yrs and living in Westgate Road, Bath with a school master and his wife: William Noble 35 yrs and Sara Noble 35 yrs School Mistress. Cowan, AncestryLibrary.com. Theatrical families often sent their children away at a young age to be educated.
[415] Mitroulia & Myers p.1.

[416] Mitroulia and Myers note, 'J. Distin played on the keyed bugle, George on the trombone, Henry on the cornet-a-pistons, and William and Theodor on the French horns. Henry performed Balfe's air The light of other days' on the new instrument (Distin's walking stick cornetto).' "Provincial" The Musical World New Series CLXXXIII (July 1), p. 14. [Mitroulia & Myers appendix database information]. General press reports from BNA indicate that the names of George, William and Theodore Distin are mentioned infrequently in their performances.

[417] Hampshire Advertiser, p.2. 12 June 1841. [BNA]

[418] Reading Mercury p.3 7 August 1841. [BNA]

[419] Letter written from Maidstone, Kent to Lord Breadalbane; Distins would be at 89 Western Road Brighton from 8th September. Travelling with the family was Miss Josephine Davis – vocalist, performer on the concertina and piano (with Mrs Distin). National Archives of Scotland. [Hooper]

[420] Essex Record Office, Essex Court of Quarter Sessions, Michaelmas Session, Q/SBb 545/21. [Hooper]

[421] Playbill for a Distin family Benefit concert, 31st May 1843 at the Waterloo Rooms, Regent Bridge. (Positively their Last Appearance but One) Scotsman p.1.[Hooper]

[422] Guardian 14th October 1843, p. 4. [Hooper]

[423] National Archives, Kew Information from Marian Elliott's divorce documents 1858. The couple separated in the mid 1840s. Marian kept care of the three children and made her living initially by acting and piano playing. The divorce documents suggest that domestic violence was the cause of the separation. Matilda would have known about this situation in the 1840s, whether she gave support or whether Marian wanted the involvement of her mother is unknown.

[424] Barker p.243 lists various performances of the Distin Family (sax horn players and vocalists), dates listed – 30 October 1840, 12 August 1845, 26 August 1846, 10 June 1847, 14 August 1848 and once in 1850 and 1851.

[425] Baker, Kenneth 1995 The Prime Ministers Thames and Hudson pp92-99.

[426] Gwynedd Archives, XD2/20653 and Gwynedd Archives, XD2/20653. [Hooper]
427http://kimballtrombone.com/2010/03/29/trombone-history-distin-family-brass-quintet/ [accessed 27 jan 13]. This website notes, ' an ensemble known for adopting Adolph Sax's valve instruments, includes a member holding a slide trombone, indicating the instrument was probably used at least during the early days of the ensemble (see above image; public domain) (Baines, Brass plate XI). According to Dudgeon, "The early quintet performances of the Distin family used various combinations of keyed bugle, cornopean, slide trumpet, natural horns, and trombone; all made by the firm of Pace. By 1844, the Distins met Adolph Sax and made the switch to valved saxhorns" (Dudgeon, Keyed Bugle 28)'.
NB The date on this print, 1834, is not correct, as Theodore would have only been 11 years old, it is more likely to be around 1843

[428] Carse, 1945, pp.195-196 quoted by Mitroulia & Myers p.2.

[429] http://www.harmoniousmusic.com/blog/?tag=john-distin [accessed 24th November 2012]. It is not certain how reliable the information on this website is as the page continues, 'Sax was eager to present the Distin's with his creations, according to Henry Distin's recollections. Success for the Distins followed with the receipt of their new instruments. Although the new found friendship between Sax and the Distins was mutually beneficial, it almost certainly did more for the promotion of Sax's instruments. The instruments were taken back to England where they earned a great deal more notoriety. In 1846 the family took saxhorns across the Atlantic Ocean to the United States of America where many heard the instrument for the first

time' [this latter date is incorrect. The remnants of the Distin band first went to North America in the second half of 1848.]

[430] Cowan.

[431] Mitroulia & Myers p.2.

[432] Information from a contemporary Print owned by Tony Bingham, the event was 27 May 1844.

[433] Mitroulia & Myers "Miscellaneous" The Musical World 19:27 (July 1844), p. 223, quoting Galignani. [Mitroula & Myers appendix database information]

[434] Mitroulia & Myers "The Distin Family", The Theatrical Observer and Daily Bills of the Play 7080 (September 2, 1844), pp. 703-704. [Mitroula & Myers appendix database information]

[435] Mitroulia & Myers "Provincial" The Musical World,19:45 (November 7), p. 367, quoting Brighton Guardian, "Provincial" The Musical World,19:49 (December 5), p. 398, quoting Brighton Herald. [Mitroula & Myers appendix database information]

[436] "Provincial" The Musical World, 19:51 (December 19), p. 414 [Mitroula & Myers appendix database information]

[437] 16 December 1844 Times p.4 [C.Hooper]. Also recorded on contemporary print – Tony Bingham and "The Distin Family", Age and Argus (December 21, 1844), p. 11. [Mitroula & Myers appendix database information]

[438] Illustrated London News p.384 [Hooper].

[439] Musical World p.414 [Hooper]. Other references for these pre Christmas concerts –Musical World p.415, 'Miscellaneous', Musical Examiner 3:112 (December 1844), p. 92, and 'Advertisements' The Era 325 (December 15, 1844). [Mitroula & Myers appendix database information] and the Times p.4 [Hooper]. The Boxing Day performance for Windsor Castle is recorded on Tony Bingham's contemporary print.

[440] Recorded on Tony Bingham's contemporary print, also may be linked to the Queen's visit to Stowe [Hooper]. Stowe is moderately near Windsor.

[441] Mitroulia & Myers p.2.

[442] Mitroulia & Myers quoting the Musical World. [appendix database information]

[443] 'Chit-Chat' Theatrical Journal 6:264 (January 1845), p. 8. [Mitroulia & Myers appendix database information], 'Norfolk' is mentioned but it is unclear if the band played in that county in January 1845.

[444] Letter from John Distin dated 4 February re Sax horns – address No 6 F Place, Great Portland Street, London, Musical World Vol XX No.7 p.76 [Hooper].

[445] Information on Hanover concert from contemporary print, Tony Bingham, Queen Performance, 22 May 1845 Musical World, Vol. XX, No. 21, p. 249. [Mitroulia & Myers appendix database information]

[446] Musical World, Vol. XX, No. 21, p. 250. [Mitroulia & Myers appendix database information]

[447] Mitroulia & Myers, p.3.

[448] "Advertisements" The Examiner 1946 (May 17, 1845). [Mitroulia & Myers appendix database information]

[449] 26 June 1845. Musical World, Vol. XX, No. 26, p. 302 [Mitroulia & Myers appendix database information]

[450] 26 June 1845 Musical World, Vol. XX, No. 26, p. 308. [Hooper]

[451] August 1845 Gwynedd Council Archives XD2/21347. [Hooper]

[452] 6 September 1845 'Miscellaneous' The Musical World 20:38 (September 18,1845), p.454, and 'Local intelligence' Liverpool Mercury 1791 (September 5, 1845). [Mitroulia & Myers]

[453] 'Provincial Intelligence' The Musical World 20:34 (August 21, 1845), pp. 403-404. [Mitroulia & Myers]

[454] Cowan: The Scotsman, ran an advertisement for a performance in Edinburgh 'First appearance in Edinburgh since their return from the continent, Music Hall George Street,' 12th November 1845. This shows that A. T . Loder was playing the pianoforte.

Abraham Taylor Loder was Matilda's nephew - a son of her brother John David Loder and his wife Rose. Abraham. He was born in Milsom Street, Sion Hill, Bath, Somerset and christened 12 Jun 1822 St Michael, Bath. He is found living with his parents and siblings in Chelsea, London in the 1841 census, he is listed as a Barber's apprentice aged 15. John David's occupation is given as a Musick Seller. 1851 UK census Abraham is at 29, Bridge Street, North Bishop, Bishopwearmouth, Durham: Abraham Loder, 28 yrs, professor of music, born Bath, Somerset. His death is recorded in 1866, March Q, Sunderland, Durham.

[455] "Miscellaneous" The Musical World, 20:50 (December 11, 1845), p. 596. [Mitroulia & Myers appendix database information]

[456] 6 February 1846. "Chit-Chat" Theatrical Journal 7:323 (February 1846), p. 63. [Mitroulia & Myers appendix database information]

[457] 22 March 1846, possibly at Charlottenberg. "Foreign Intelligence" The Musical World 21:15 (April 1846), pp. 168-169. [Mitroulia & Myers appendix database information]

[458] Times, p.5 [Hooper], performance 3rd December 1846. The Musical World report that Miss Kate 'Anderson' plays the piano. "Arundel Castle" The Musical World 21:49 (December 1846), p. 626. [Mitroulia & Myers appendix database information]

[459] Mitroulia & Myers p.4.

[460] Mitroulia & Myers p.4.

[461] Cowan. Death of John David Loder 13 Feb 1846 in 156, Albany Street, St Marylebone, Regents Park, London of Dropsy and ossification of the Heart. Burial: 19 Feb 1846 All Souls, Kensal Green Cemetery, Kensal Green, Willesden, London. Confirmation of his age recorded at his burial verbal information from Kensal Green Cemetery, November 2012. 'John Loder, the eminent violinist, who published an excellent class book for his instrument, and was for many years the leader of orchestras at the great provincial festivals of the Philharmonic Society, and of the Ancient Concerts, expired on Friday evening at his house in Albany Street, Regents Park, London, from dropsy and ossification of the heart.'
The Scotsman Sat. February 21st 1846. Lloyd's Weekly London Newspaper. Cowan.
Bristol Mirror, 21.2.1846 'Obituary of John Loder, the eminent violinist, on Friday evening 13 February, at his house in Albany Street, London, from dropsy and ossification of the heart. Mr Loder was born in this city,[John was baptised in Bath] where he was Leader at the Theatre and Concerts for many years. He was in his 58th year. He has left five sons and two daughters, amongst the former are Edward Loder, the composer; John Loder, the leader of the Lyceum band; and Wm. Loder, first violon cello at Drury Lane Theatre.'

On Feb 17 1846 plot 5956 in Kensal Cemetery was bought by John Fawcett Loder of 79, Stanhope Street, Regent's Park, Middlesex. In this plot are buried John D. Loder, William S. Loder, John F. Loder, Rose Loder, Dominick Hervey and Mary Loder. Originally George F. Distin was buried here in 1848 but he was moved to the adjacent grave, after a few months when his mother was buried.

John David left a will. A footnote to the will gave his place of death as Duke St., Portland Place, Middlesex.
'Will of John David Loder

This is the last Will and Testament of me John David Loder of Duke Street Portland Place in the County of Middlesex Professor of Music First I direct that all my just debts funeral and testamentary expenses be fully paid and satisfied by my executrix hereinafter named with all convenient speed after my decease I give and bequeath all my household goods furniture plate[?] china books music musical instruments money securities for money and all and singular other the Personal estate and offices that I may die possessed of. Of what nature or kind soever the same may be unto my dear wife Rosamond Charles Loder for her absolute use and benefit and I hereby appoint my said wife executrix of this my will in virtue whereof I have hereunto set my hand on this twenty fifth day of November one thousand eight hundred and forty three - John David Loder signed and declared by the above named Testator as and for this last will and Testament in the presence of us present at the same time who in his presence and in the presence of each other have hereunto set our names as witnesses thereto. John Abbott solicitor 40 Charlotte Street Bedford Square John Abbott solicitor Bexley Heath Kent'.

'Proved at London the 23rd Feb 1846 before the worshipful / Thomas Pratt Dr of Laws and Surrogate by the oath of Rosamond in the will written Rosamond Charles Loder Widow the Relict the sole executrices to whom admin was granted having been first sworn duly to administer.' Cowan.

[462] Clarke p.45. Clarke gives the following notes: Theatrical Journal, February (1846), 71. The burial was attended by three sons, John, Edward and William.
Freemason's Quarterly Review, Second Series (1846). Clarke, The Bath Messiah, 28. The lessee of the New Assembly Rooms, a Mr Bellamy, 'not only granted the use of the rooms but also provided the lighting (no small matter) at his own expense.'
[463] Rohr, pp124, 126.
[464] Rohr's catalogue, extracts 14th September 2012. These include the following details:
Loder, John David 1788 - 1846
(Brown and Stratton) violinist, writer wrote the Modern Art of Bowing, and other violin instruction books. Sons: Edward James and John Fawcett
(Grove 1879) he was the leader at the 3 Choirs Festival; prof. at the RAM
(Doane directory) in 1794 was a member of the New Musical Fund, performed violin and viola, and lived in Bath
(NMF records) member of the New Musical Fund in 1815 (when living in Bath), and in 1825.
(Philharmonic Society account books): he performed as leader in the orchestra from 1819 to at least 1843. His wages were (in pounds): 1819 - 31.10; 1820 - 31.10; 1822 - 21; 1823 - 21; 1830 - 21; 1840 - 52.10; 1843 - 27.
[465] Clarke pp.35 – 44, there are several notes, including Richard Doyle, A Journal, in the Year 1840 (n.p., 1886), 127. Bristol Mercury, 20 March, 1841 (Bankrupcy). Myles Birket Foster, The History of the Philharmonic Society of London, 1813-1912 (London, 1912). Presumably the view was that he would be away from the pressure of work in Bath and elsewhere. Clarke states that John David, within a few months, was playing in London and the presumption has to be that he either suffered exhaustion or could not cope with the demands of the Philharmonic Society.
GB-Lbl RPS MS 351.230. Frederick Corder, A History of the Royal Academy of Music, from 1822 to 1922 (London, 1922).
Andrew Loder [junior] had been declared bankrupt soon after a fire at his property in 1825.
[466] Personal relationships are difficult to verify without diaries and similar personal evidence. One indicative piece of evidence is the fact that the two siblings have adjacent burial plots

and George Distin was initially buried alongside his uncle in that family grave. Another piece of circumstantial evidence is the employment of A.T.Loder, Ann Matilda's nephew as a pianist for the Distins.

[467] Identical articles appear in two publications, the London Morning Post, 26 July 1847, p.7 and the Manchester Courier and Lancashire General Advertiser 28 July 1847, p.6. [BNA]

[468] Matilda chose a doctor who had recently published on the subject of cataracts, as described in the Bucks Herald, 6 March 1847 – under 'Literary Novelties' , p.6. His publication is noted as '8vo, 2s6d' The Liverpool Mercury published an article , 30 November 1847, p.4 [BNA] which noted, 'The Use of Chloroform …several important and most painful operations were performed at the workhouse Hospital by D F.H.Brett…a new agent for producing insensitivity' It describes various operations… 'the fourth operation was for cataract, which being of soft nature, the drilling method through the cornea by means of a delicate needle was selected. The fluid portion of the soft lenticular body being freely exposed to solution in the acqueos humour'. Dr Brett may have been a dodgy character as a few years later, in 1855 several papers report similar stories to the one in the Morning Chronicle, 3 October 1855, p.4, under the title, 'Military Imposter' 'We are requested by the authority of the War Department to warn the public and more especially our Continental readers, against the impositions of a person calling himself Dr F. H. Brett who has raised money at Aix=la-Chapelle, Frankfurt, Cologne and Strasburg, by falsely representing himself to be a retired surgeon of the Bengal Army, and a staff surgeon of the British army in the East. The Commission of Dr Frederick Harrington Brett who is supposed to be personated by the person in question was cancelled on the 6th of July, and that gentleman does not belong to her Majesty's medical services.'

[469] Mitroulia and Myers p.4.

[470] Guardian, Saturday November 17th 1847, Page 7.[Hooper]

[471] Jenkins, S. p.197 – 200.

[472] Banbury Scrapbooks: Case F, folder 2 (1846-48, folios 15-29).[Hooper]

[473] He was initially buried in the grave at Kensal Green cemetery London of his Uncle, John David Loder. His remains were reinterred later in 1848 to a new adjacent grave, where his mother Ann Matilda was buried. Records of Kensal Green Cemetery. Elizabeth Hope, inmate present at death, certified his body, at 31, Cranbourn Street. He had suffered from this illness for a year and a half, before an abcess formed.1848 Q Jun St. Martin vol 1 107. Death certificate stated chronic perforation of the tympanic membrane. Symptoms & signs : small perforations cause minimal hearing loss. Complications : cholesteatoma mastoiditis'. George Frederick died 4 Apr 1848 in 31, New Cranbourn Street, Long Acre, St Martin in the Fields, Westminster, London of Inflammation of Tympanum. Caries of hardened bone. Abscess on cerebellum. Mastoiditis. Cowan.

[474] Mitroulia & Myers p.4.

[475] Mitroulia & Myers p.4.

[476] Banbury Scrapbooks Case F, folder 2, folios 15 to 29, Arts and Humanities Research Council. http://www.concertprogrammes.org.uk/html/search/verb/GetRecord/4252 [accessed 9th February 2013].

[477] UK records of Births, marriages and deaths. 1848 Quarter June St. Martin vol 1 113. . The informant, Ann Latham lived at 21, Great Windmill Street, Haymarket The Times article is from the 24th June, 1848 (Times Digital Archive). There are also notices in the Westmoreland Gazette 1 July 1848 p.3, and the Morning Post 26 June 1848, p.8 states, 'On the 23rd instant, after a severe illness, aged 57, Mrs Distin, wife of the celebrated performer on the Sax-horn, who survived her eldest son a few weeks.' [BNA]

[478] Information from Kensal Green cemetery records, February 2010. Cowan. Those buried in plot 7639 were John Distin, Ann Matilda, George Frederick (who was re interred from the adjoining Loder plot 5956) in 1848, Mary Ruddock Distin (1853), Henry John Distin (1855), Louisa Distin (1857), Sarah Distin (1863), Emily Distin (1868), James F. Distin (1877) and William Alfred Distin (1880).

[479] http://www.thepeerage.com/p52957.htm [Accessed 18 November 2012]. Henry and Jane married 9th September 1848, Ancestry.com

[480] British Library on line, http://explore.bl.uk/primo_library/libweb/action/search.do?ct=facet&fctN=facet_creator&fct V=Distin%2c+Jane.&fctN=facet_domain&dscnt=0&vl(174399379UI0)=any&scp.scps=scop e%3A(BLCONTENT)&fctV=bll01music&frbg=&tab=local_tab&dstmp=1365705233417&sr t=rank&ct=facet&mode=Basic&dum=true&indx=1&tb=t&vl(freeText0)=distin&fn=search& vid=BLVU1 [accessed 10 April 2013].

[481] 'Music at Bristol' The Musical World 23:36 (September 2, 1848), p. 572. [Mitroulia & Myers appendix database information]

[482] Times, p. 4 [Hooper] 2 October 1848. A similar note appears in the Times 7 October 1848 p.5. [Hooper]

[483] "Messers. Distin Concert" The Musical World 23:42 (October 14, 1848), p. 663. [Mitroulia & Myers appendix database information]

[484] 'Miscellaneous' The Musical World 23:52 (December 23, 1848), pp. 822-23. [Mitroulia & Myers appendix database information] The name Harriett also appears as Morriatt, this may be a printing error.

[485] Henry Distin New York Times.

[486] Two reports, one mentions Miss Moriat O'Connor – 16 February, Dramatic and Musical Review, Vol. 8 (NS 2), No. 316, pp. 60-1[Hooper], the second -27 February mentions Louise (H Earle Johnson, p. 83 [cited by Hooper]). The latter publication shows some confusion as a 'Henry senior' and 'Henry junior' are noted, it may have been that the author mistakenly thought John Distin's name was also Henry. It is also unclear what Miss O'Connor's name is, it is given as both Moriat and Harriet, and may have been a stage name. It is presumed that her name was Harriet.

[487] 1,2 November 1849 'Provincial' Theatrical Journal 10:519 (November 1849), p. 371. [Mitroulia & Myers Appendix database information]

[488] Letter to Lord Breadalbane, 26 June 1850 National Archives of Scotland. [Hooper]

[489] Letter to Lord Newborough from Liverpool 10 November 1851, Gwynedd Council Archives. XD2/23586 .[Hooper]

[490] 27 June 1857 National Archives of Scotland. [Hooper]

[491] Cowan. The names of the four surviving men were given.

[492] Rose p.210.

[493] Information from Kensal Green Cemetery, February 2010. Information of Publications from British Library website, http://catalogue.bl.uk/primo_library/libweb/action/search.do?vid=BLVU1 [accessed 10 March 2013]. Census information confirmed by Cowan 1861 RG 9/430.

[494] Mitroulia & Myers p.5.

[495] Rose pp.210 -11.

[496] Several sources including Scholes, Percy, 'The Mirror of Music' vol. 1 opp p.97, reprinted from the Graphic, 27 June 1874, 'Tuning up the big Kettledrum', the Distin drum is a vertical standing drum rather like a giant gong. [Hooper]

[497] The New Grove Dictionary of Music and Musicians, second edition ed Sadie, S., vol 7 p381-2. Musical Instrument Makers of New York, a Directory of Eighteenth and Nineteenth

Century Urban Craftsmen, Grove, N., Pendragon Press NY, 1991. 13 October 1903, Death Notice, New York Times. [Hooper]

[498] Rose p.210.
[499] Cowan quoting Woodcroft 1984, p. 231. This is found on the website, http://www.angelfire.com/music2/thecornetcompendium/manufacturers_d_g.html [accessed 11 November 2012] and this contains information on the Distin band by Richard Schartz. Copyright © 2000, 2001 by Richard I. Schwartz.
[500] Possibility raised by Australian researcher, (D.Smith).
[501] Quotation provided by Ray Farr 28 sept 2012. Burial information from Kensal Green Cemetery.
[502] The Era (London) Saturday April 22, 1893, p12, p.15, [BNA]. Cowan.

DEATH OF THEODORE DISTIN

'We have to record the death on Wednesday, 12th inst., in his seventieth year, of the veteran vocalist and composer, Mr Theodore Distin. The deceased was a son of the once famous trumpet player, John Distin, who is credited with the invention of the keyed bugle, and who was trumpeter to George IV, and bandmaster to the Marquis of Breadalbane. As a boy he studied the French horn, and when only thirteen he, with his father and three brothers, formed the Distin quintet band which played at Windsor Castle and at several of the German Courts, and also later on at Jullien's concerts. In 1844 Distin learned singing under Tom Cooke, one of the teachers of Mr Sims Reeves, and he was for a considerable time a baritone in the Pyne and Harrison company. Theodore was to become better known as a vocalist than as an instrumentalist in the latter years of his life he was bass at Lincoln's-Inn Chapel. He had a fine resonant voice and a clear enunciation, and he sang with great expression. His fame as a composer was, however, greater than his fame as a vocalist, and he in his long life gave us glees which deserve to live. He was latterly a successful teacher. Mr Theodore Distin was a prolific composer of songs and part songs, and he wrote a full service in C, and for St Paul's Cathedral a service in G. his glee, "Sing, let us sing," carried off the prize offered by the Abbey Glee Choir in 1865, while his "Bacchus on thee we call," won the City Glee Club prize in 1867, and "Jack Horner," the Huddersfield prize in 1879. Among the best known of his compositions are his part-songs, "When some sweet flower I see," full of beautiful melody, and his madrigals, "Break of day" and "Damon and Phyllis." He was undoubtedly one of the finest glee writers of his generation. As a musical lecturer he was also popular. He used to tell some most amusing and interesting stories of his travels with the Distin family. He earned the great esteem and respect of all who knew him, and died, beloved by all. A loss indeed! He leaves several unfinished compositions.'

'On Saturday last he went to his last resting place. The funeral service was conducted by the Rev. Flood Jones. Dr. Bridge officiated at the organ, and the Westminster Abbey choir (boys and men) sang one or two hymns and Bridge's setting of Tennyson's "Crossing the Bar." The coffin was covered with wreaths from the many friend and admirers of deceased. Mr Distin whose mother, Miss Loder, was an aunt of that charming Kate Loder, who became Lady Thompson was a link which bound this musical generation to a greater generation, in which his father was not one of the least distinguished figures. A fellow of infinite jest, he was full of anecdote. One of his best stories may bear repetition here. During one of his visits to Glasgow he observed a tall gaunt Scotchman gazing intently at one of the family's announcement bills; after a while, he turned to a friend and said, "Sandy, my mon, I dinna see hoo they'll dee it." "Do what?" "Why, it says, 'Muster Distin and his four sons will play upon sax horns.' I'll gang the nicht and see." Playing one night in Brighton to a wretchedly poor house he sadly remarked, "Tis Distins lend enchantment to the few."'

[503] Cowan.

[504] Cowan. The "Nottinghamshire Guardian dated Nov 7, 1850 shows Nugent Varley to be the Manager of the Corn Exchange where the Distin Family performed on Nov 18, 1850". [Cowan and BNA]

[505] Newspaper - An advertisement placed in Mount Alexander Mail" on 17th & 20th July, 1857 initial source Bette Kearin, confirmed by Cowan, other sources: Cowan and Barbi [Varley] Solnordal, much of this information researched by Debra Smith.

[506] Transcription of New York Times made by Mrs Joan Varley McMaster, copy given to B. & R. Kearin.

[507] Details of Louisa and Violet researched by many members of Louisa's family including Mrs McMaster, and Debra Smith, also www.emelbourne.net.au/biogs/EM01486b.htm [accessed 7 February 2013]. Other information from Cowan.

[508] Information about Births, marriages and deaths from both Ancestry.com and Cowan.

[509] McConnell Stott p.245.

[510] McConnell Stott p.307. Stott refers to 'Tom' Ridgway, and his death in c1832, at an age of 28. Tom (Frederick) Ridgway lived on for a few more decades, still performing as a dancing teacher. Stott gives a reference of the Caledonian Mercury for 13 December 1834, neither Tom nor George were 28 years old in c1832.

[511] AncestryLibrary.com.

[512] Cowan.

[513] Temperley, N.,ed. The Romantic Age 1800 – 1914 Blackwell History of Music Athlone Press, 1981 p.272, Rohr research catalogue (unpublished) – based on Stratton and Brown directory, Cowan, and Temperley, N. 1966 'Raymond and Agnes' in Musical Times vol. 107 no.1478, April 1966.

[514] Biddlecombe, George, 1994 'English Opera from 1834 to 1864'. Garland Publishing Inc New York and London p.97.

[515] Apprenticeship records researched by Clarke, ref GB-Tro Private Apprenticeship Indentures. BATH DD\S\WI/30 1804-1842. Obituary record, http://oa.anu.edu.au/obituary/loder-george-14275 [accessed 11 March 2013].

[516] Times 1846 praises Kate Loder as a talented pianist (3 November 1846 p. 5). 1851 census information shows Kate aged 25 staying with Rose Loder in 36 Manchester Street, Marylebone, London.

[517] Rohr biosketch, included in article on the Royal Society of Female Musicians (J. of Musicological Research 1999). Information from Rohr September 2012.

[518] Details of Matilda's grandchildren can be traced on the Cowan Rootsweb facility.

[519] Venning p.96.

[520] Marian's son George was 12 years old at his Grandmother's death and his older brother 15. His younger sister and mother were in London at that time. He married in 1862 in St Martin in the Fields, Westminster, just a few minutes' walk from Great Newport Street where John Distin died a year later, in the Distin factory building. Some of these relatives were living 'cheek by joule', to each other. George Elliott married Ellen Fletcher, 3 Aug 1862 in St Martin in the Fields, Westminster, London (National records of Births, marriages and deaths and AncestryLibrary.com). George's son, Frederick, wrote his own and some family history in c 1940. He wrote about another great grandmother, in Bristol, and about his grandmother Marian. There was no mention of Ann Matilda. Unpublished personal memoire.

[521] Rose pp.226-7.

[522] Henry Distin New York Times, 1881.

[523] **Frances Abington.** Perry, Gill with Roach, J., and West, S., 2012 'The First Actresses', National Portrait Gallery, London pp.44-5. Other references found in http://en.wikipedia.org/wiki/Frances_Abington {accessed 18th nov 12].

'She was born Frances Barton, the daughter of a private soldier, and began her career as a flower girl and a street singer. As a servant to a French milliner, she learned about costume and acquired a knowledge of French which afterwards stood her in good stead. Her first appearance on the stage was at Haymarket in 1755 as Miranda in Mrs Centlivre's play, Busybody.

In 1756, on the recommendation of Samuel Foote, she became a member of the Drury Lane company, where she was overshadowed by Mrs Pritchard and Kitty Clive. In 1759, after an unhappy marriage to her music teacher James Abington, a royal trumpeter, she is mentioned in the bills as "Mrs Abington". Her first success was in Ireland as Lady Townley (in The Provok'd Husband by Vanbrugh and Cibber), and it was only after five years, on the pressing invitation of David Garrick, that she returned to Drury Lane. There she remained for eighteen years, being the first to play more than thirty important characters, notably Lady Teazle (1777). In April 1772, when James Northcote saw her Miss Notable in Cibber's The Lady's Last Stake, he remarked to his brother "I never saw a part done so excellent in all my life, for in her acting she has all the simplicity of nature and not the least tincture of the theatrical". Her Shakespearean heroines -Beatrice, Portia, Desdemona and Ophelia – were no less successful than her comic characters – Miss Hoyden, Biddy Tipkin, Lucy Lockit and Miss Prue. It was as the last character in Love for Love that Sir Joshua Reynolds painted his best portrait of her. In 1782 she left Drury Lane for Covent Garden. After an absence from the stage from 1790 until 1797, she reappeared, quitting it finally in 1799. Her ambition, personal wit and cleverness won her a distinguished position in society, in spite of her humble origin. Women of fashion copied her clothing, and a headdress she wore was widely adopted and known as the Abington cap' .

[524] http://www.pickeringchatto.com/major_works/the_diaries_of_elizabeth_inchbald [accessed 4th December 2012].
[525] **Inchbald , Elizabeth (1753–1821),** Perry, Gill pp46-7. Also Spencer, Jane. Oxford Dictionary of National Biography, Oxford University Press, 2004, [quoted by Wikipedia, 4th December 2012].
[526] **Elizabeth Linley.** Perry, G., pp50-51. Bor, M. and Clelland, L. 1962 'Still the Lark, a biography of Elizabeth Linley' Merlin Press London. Additional information from Toogood 2010 and from http://en.wikipedia.org/wiki/Thomas_Linley_the_elder [accessed 4th December 2012].
[527] There is a plaque on a house in Pierrepoint Street, Bath, marking the house where the Linleys lived in the early 1770s in Bath. Margaret Christopoulos, March 2012.
[528] **Sarah Siddons** Information from Toogood, pp 57 – 68, Perry pp 52-3 with additional information from: http://en.wikipedia.org/wiki/Sarah_Siddons [accessed November 2012]. Sarah was born in Wales, the eldest daughter of Roger Kemble, the manager of the touring theatre company, the Warwickshire Company of Comedians which included other members of his talented family. Initially her parents weren't keen on her career choice because it was not regarded as respectable. She said in the 1770s: 'banished from Drury Lane as a worthless candidate for fame and fortune'. However, she built her reputation in Bath and elsewhere and returned to great acclaim to Drury Lane in 1782. Her most famous role was that of Lady Macbeth; she held her audiences spellbound by the murderous passions. She was tall and striking, with powerfully expressive eyes. For two decades she was the undisputed queen of Drury Lane. In 1802 she left Drury Lane and subsequently appeared from time to time on the stage of the rival establishment, Covent Garden. It was there, on 29 June 1812, that she gave perhaps the most extraordinary farewell performance in theatre history. She was playing her most famous role, Lady Macbeth, and the

audience refused to allow the play to continue after the end of the sleepwalking scene. Eventually, after tumultuous applause from the pit, the curtain reopened and Siddons was discovered sitting in her own clothes and character — whereupon she made an emotional farewell speech to the audience lasting eight minutes. Mrs. Siddons formally retired from the stage in 1812, but occasionally appeared on special occasions. Her last appearance was on 9 June 1819.

[529] **Dora Jordan.** Tomalin, Clare, 1994, Mrs Jordan's Profession, Penguin, London. p.7, 42, 44, 45, 164, 165 and throughout. Also Perry pp.58-9.

[530] **Mary Wells.** Information from her Memoirs, 'Memoirs of the life of Mrs Sumbel, late Wells in three volumes by herself. 1811 [Also known as Mary Davis]. Additional information from: http://en.wikipedia.org/wiki/Mary_Wells_(actress) [accessed 1st December 2012].

[531] **Elizabeth Billington]** Elizabeth Billington, Memoirs of Mrs Billington (1792) www.pickeringchatto.com/major_works/women_s_theatrical_memoirs [accessed 16th Nov 2012]. Perry pp. 60-1. Additional information from-http://en.wikipedia.org/wiki/Elizabeth_Billington [accessed 16 nov 2012].

[532] www.pickeringchatto.com/major_works/women_s_theatrical_memoirs [accessed 16th Nov 2012].

[533] **Marie Therese de Camp [Decamp].** Information from Rebecca Jenkins biography of Fanny Kemble, Marie's daughter. Also references P.H. Highfill et al. (1982) A Biographical Dictionary of Actors, Southern Illinois University Press ISBN 0-8093-0919-X and 'Kemble, Charles'. Dictionary of National Biography. London: Smith, Elder & Co. 1885–1900, additional information from, http://en.wikipedia.org/wiki/Marie_Therese_De_Camp [accessed 4th December, 2012].

[534] **Jane Scott.** References include the Adelphi Theatre Project, The editor is Joseph Donohue, Professor of English, University of Massachusetts, USA , and Bratton, Jacky. "Scott , Jane Margaret (bap. 1779, d. 1839)." Oxford Dictionary of National Biography. Ed. H. C. G. Matthew and Brian Harrison. Oxford: OUP, 2004. Also, http://en.wikipedia.org/wiki/Jane_Scott_(theatre_manager) [accessed 4th December 2012].

[535] **Maria Foote.** A reference - "Foote, Maria". Dictionary of National Biography. London: Smith, Elder & Co. 1885–1900. Also http://en.wikipedia.org/wiki/Maria_Foote [accessed 1st December 2012] 'Foote was born 24 July 1797(?) at Plymouth. Her father, Samuel T. Foote (1761–1840), sold out of the army, became manager of the Plymouth theatre, and married a Miss Hart. In July 1810 Miss Foote appeared as Juliet in Romeo and Juliet at her father's theatre, Foote afterwards took an hotel in Exeter. The business did not succeed, his daughter appeared at Covent Garden Theatre, 26 May 1814, as Amanthis in the Child of Nature by Elizabeth Inchbald. In this part, which suited her, she made a great success. Her second appearance was at the same theatre in the same character in the following season, 14 September 1814. In 1815 appeared in tragedy roles and as Fanny inThe Clandestine Marriage. Her abilities proved to be limited. She had, however, a reputation for beauty sufficient to secure her constant engagements at the patent theatres and in the country. She played with success in both Ireland and Scotland, and accompanied actors to Paris, where they all acted with unsatisfactory results. In 1816 she formed at Cheltenham a relationship with Colonel William Berkeley, by whom she had two children. An alleged promise of marriage made by him was not kept. Joseph 'Pea Green' Hayne then proposed to her and was accepted. He retracted, however, his offer, and as the result of an action for breach of promise of marriage had to pay £3,000 damages. These proceedings gave rise to pamphlet warfare, through which and through some opposition on the stage Miss Foote retained a measure of public sympathy.

At Covent Garden she played every season up to 1824-5 inclusive, frequently in subordinate parts. At Bath on 13 and 14 January 1826 she was the object of hostile demonstrations on the part of a portion of the audience. Her singing and dancing and her way of accompanying herself on the harp, guitar, and pianoforte added to her popularity. She is said to have traversed England, Ireland, and Scotland every year for five years, in course of which she posted twenty-five thousand miles.'

[536] **Madame Vestris.** Madame Vestris' lifespan was similar to and contemporary to Ann Matilda's. Reference includes, Stephen C. Fisher, "Jansen [Janson, Jansson; Bartolozzi], Therese", in The Grove Dictionary of Music and Musicians, online edition, Oxford University Press, 2010. Additional information from: http://en.wikipedia.org/wiki/Lucia_Elizabeth_Vestris [accessed 2nd December 2012] 'She was named Elizabetta Lucia Bartolozzi in London in 1797, the first of two daughters of the highly regarded German pianist Theresa Jansen Bartolozzi and Gaetano Stefano Bartolozzi (1757–1821).[1] He was a musician and son of the immigrant Francesco Bartolozzi, a noted artist and engraver, appointed as Royal Engraver to the king.Gaetano Bartolozzi was a successful art dealer, and the family moved to Europe in 1798 when he sold off his business. They spent time in Paris and Vienna before reaching Venice, where they found that their estate had been looted during the French invasion. They returned to London to start over, where Gaetano taught drawing. They separated there and Therese gave piano lessons to support her daughters.

Lucia studied music and was noted for her voice and dancing ability. She was married at age 16 to the French dancer, Auguste Armand Vestris, a scion of the great family of dancers of Florentine origin, but her husband deserted her four years later. Nervertheless, since she had started singing and acting professionally as "Madame Vestris", she retained such a stage name throughout her career.

Her contralto voice and attractive appearance gained Madame Vestris her first leading role at age 18 in Italian operain the title-role of Peter Winter's Il ratto di Proserpina at the King's Theatre in 1815. She had immediate success in both London and Paris. In the French capital city she appeared at the Théâtre-Italien and various other theatres. Her supposed interpretation - reported by several critics - of Camille at the Théâtre-Français to Talma's Horace, however, has never happened. The mistake derived from a misreading of Talma's Mémoires where the actor recalls an episode in which a Madame Vestris - not Eliza Vestris, as she was born several years later, but Françoise-Marie-Rosette Gourgaud, who married Angiolo Vestris - played Camille to his Horace in 1785.

Her first hit in English was in 1820 at age 23 at the Drury Lane in Stephen Storace's Siege of Belgrade, "and she remained an extraordinary favourite in opera, musical farces and comedies until her retirement in 1854. At the King's Theatre she sang in the English premières of many Rossini operas: She excelled in "breeches parts," and she also performed in Mozart operas, such as The Marriage of Figaro and Don Giovanni. She was credited with popularizing such new songs as "Cherry Ripe", "Meet Me by Moonlight Alone" I've been roaming," etc. She also took part in world premieres, and, above all, that of Fatima in Oberon or The Elf King's Oath, "the Grand Romantic and Fairy Opera" by Carl Maria von Weber, which was given at the Theatre Royal, Covent Garden on 12 April 1826.

In 1830, having accumulated a fortune from her performing, she leased the Olympic Theatre from John Scott. There she began presenting a series of burlesques and extravaganzas—for which she made this house famous. She got married in 1838 for the second time, to the British actor Charles James Mathews and accompanied him on tour to America. She aided him in his subsequent managerial ventures, including the management of the Lyceum Theatre and the theatre in Covent Garden. Mme Vestris and Mathews inaugurated their management of Covent Garden with the first-known production of Love's Labour's Lost since 1605; Vestris played Rosaline. In 1840 she staged one of the first relatively uncut productions of A Midsummer Night's Dream, in which she played Oberon. This began a tradition of female Oberons that lasted for 70 years in the British theatre.

In 1841 Vestris produced the highly successful Victorian farce London Assurance by Dion Boucicault, with possibly the first use of a "box set"] The play has been popular ever since, receiving its most recent revival at the National Theatre in 2010.

About her time in charge at Covent Garden, a note by the actor James Robertson Anderson reported in C.J. Mathews's autobiography, says:

Madame was an admirable manager, and Charles an amiable assistant. The arrangements behind the scenes were perfect, the dressing rooms good, the attendants well-chosen, the wings kept clear of all intruders, no strangers or crutch and toothpick loafers allowed behind to flirt with the ballet-girls, only a very few private friends were allowed the privilege of visiting the green-room, which was as handsomely furnished as any nobleman's drawing-room, and those friends appeared always in evening dress....There was great propriety and decorum observed in every part of the establishment, great harmony, general content prevailed in every department of the theatre, and universal regret was felt when the admirable managers were compelled to resign their government. Another writer George Vanderhoff in Dramatic Reminiscences also bears testimony to the fact that: 'To Vestris's honour, she was not only scrupulously careful not to offend propriety by word or action, but she knew very well how to repress any attempt at double-entendre, or doubtful insinuation, in others. The green-room in Covent Garden was a most agreeable lounging place, from which was banished every word or allusion that would not be tolerated in a drawing-room.

Her last performance (1854) was for Mathews' benefit, in an adaptation of Madame de Girardin's La Joie fait pour, called Sunshine through Clouds. She died in London in 1856. Her musical accomplishments and education were not sufficient to distinguish her in grand opera, and in high comedy she was only moderately successful. But in plays like Loan of a Lover, Paul Pry, Naval Engagements, etc., she was "delightfully arch and bewitching. "However, many an observer (and Chorley among them) "never quite forgave her for not becoming the greatest English operatic contralto of her age:"

"About the same time it was that Madame Vestris made her last appearance on our Italian stage. There, if she had possessed musical patience and energy, she might have queened it; because she possessed (half Italian by birth) one of the most luscious of low voices—found, since Lear's time, excellent in woman great personal beauty, and almost faultless figure, which she knew to adorn with consummate art — and no common stage address. — But a less arduous theatrical career pleased her better; and so she, too, could not— one might perhaps say, because she would not— remain on the Italian stage.'
[537] http://en.wikipedia.org/wiki/Lucia_Elizabeth_Vestris [accessed 2nd December 2012]